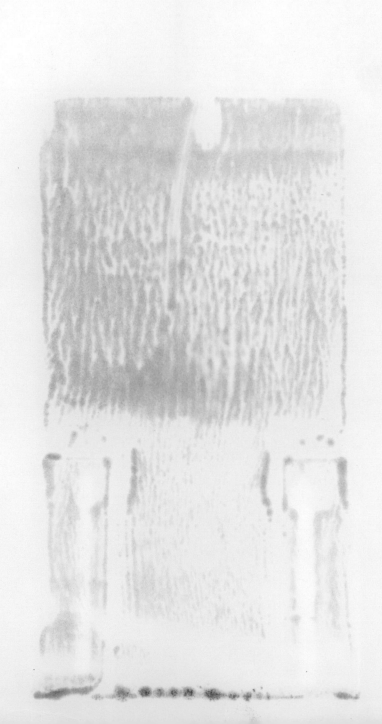

HENRY VIII AND HIS COURT

Right The young King : a
miniature of Henry VIII.
Attributed to the Flemish
artist Lucas Horenbout.

Overleaf Henry at the
Field of Cloth of Gold,
1520; detail from a painting, possibly by Hans
Roest, which is reproduced
in its entirety on pp. 74–5

Endpaper Hampton Court
Palace, as drawn by
Anthony van Wyngaerde
on his visit to England in
about 1555.

HENRY VIII AND HIS COURT

Neville Williams

THE MACMILLAN COMPANY

NEW YORK, NEW YORK

To J.H.K.

Macmillan Company
866 Third Avenue
New York, N.Y. 10022

Collier-Macmillan Canada Ltd.,
Toronto, Ontario

Henry VIII and his Court first published in 1971 by
Weidenfeld and Nicolson, London

Designed by Rodney Josey
Library of Congress Catalog Card number 70-125407

First American edition 1971
Second Printing 1971

Contents

Sources of illustrations

The photographs on pages *4*, 15, *22–3*, 27, *42–3*, *54–5*, 67, *74–5*, 104, 118, *119*, 128/2, *129*, 137, 165, *188*, 192, *199*, *200*, 205/2, 224, 225, *229*, 232, 251, 255/1, 255/2 are reproduced by gracious permission of H.M. the Queen; on page 227 by permission of His Grace, the Duke of Norfolk; and on pages *120* and *130* by courtesy of the Archbishop of Canterbury (Copyright reserved by the Courtauld Institute of Art and the Church Commissioners).

A.C.L.: 260; Archives Photographiques: 72; Ashmolean Museum, Oxford: 20/1, 20/2, 26/1, 113; Barber Surgeons' Company: 145, 204, *217*; Batsford: 114–5, 214/1; Bibliothèque de Méjanes, Aix-en-Provence: 13; Bodleian Library, Oxford: *56/1*, *56/2*; British Museum: 19, *21/1*, *21/2*, 35, 64, 78, 86, 116, 133, 141, 149, *158*, *159*, *169*, 177, 185/1, *187*, 195, 196, *198*, 203/1, 203/2, 207, 226/2, 228, 239, 246, 253; Christie's: 76; A.C. Cooper: *22–3*, *42–3*, *54–5*, 62/2, *74–5*, *119*, *200*, *229*; Country Life: 241; Courtauld Institute of Art: 189, 232; Eton College, Windsor: 38, 81; Fitzwilliam Museum, Cambridge: *3*; John Fleming: *159*; John Freeman: *120*; Frick Collection, New York: *147*; Gabinetto Fotografico: 153; Goldsmiths' Company, London: *76*; Ian Graham: 96, 164; Hardwick Hall (National Trust): 189; Jarrold & Sons: 240; A.F. Kersting: 26/2, 103, 126–7; Kunsthistorisches Museum, Vienna: *18*, *130*; Kunstmuseum, Basle: *247*; Lambeth Palace: *120*, 230; Ronald A. Lee: 203/3; Edward Leigh: 214/2; Hinz Basle: *247*; Q. Lloyd: 25; London Museum (Crown Copyright): 79, 166/1, 166/2, 166/3, 166/4, 185/2, 220, 234/2, 235; Louvre, Paris: *44*, *170*; Magdalen College, Oxford: 39; Magdalene College, Cambridge: 214/2; Mansell Collection: 68, 110, 154, 191; Mauritshuis: 122; Paul Mellon Centre: 68; Ministry of Public Works (Crown Copyright): 51, 62/1, 115, 121, 141, 163, 202/2, 205/1; Lord Montague: 223; National Gallery, London: 171, *197*; National Gallery of Art, Washington: Andrew Mellon Centre: *148*; National Monuments Records: 45/1, 59/1, 98, 117 (Crown Copyright), 132, 242, 245; National Portrait Gallery, London: *17*, *53*, 57, 85, *101*, 128/1, 157, 161, *219*, 226/1, 231, *248*; La Pensée Universitaire: 13; Pitkin Pictorial Ltd; 223; Prado, Madrid: *102*; Public Record Office, London: 59/2, *73*, 89, 151, *160*, 179; Radio Times Hulton Picture Library: 16, 29, 48, 111, 139, 155, 182, 233, 234/1, 249, 256–7, 259; Ramsay & Muspratt: 243; Royal College of Arms: *24/1*, *24/2*; Royal College of Physicians: 83; Lord St Oswald: 84; Schloss Nymphenberg, Munich: 190; Staatliche Museen, Berlin: 126; Walter Steinkopf: 126; Thyssen Collection, Lugano: *218*; Tower of London (Crown Copyright): 51, 183, 202/1, 202/2; Vatican Library: 107; Victoria and Albert Museum, London: 142–3, 211; Walker Art Gallery, Liverpool: *157*; Warburg Institute: 12, 30, 45/2, 60/1, 60/2, 61, 99; Earl of Yarborough: *41*.

Unpublished material in the Public Record Office in which Crown Copyright is reserved is reproduced by permission of the Controller of Her Majesty's Stationery Office.

Introduction

The figure of Henry VIII still dominates English history, even as he appeared to contemporaries as a colossus, so that everyone interested in the sixteenth century sooner or later becomes drawn to its principal character and the stage on which he acted. Personal monarchy has always implied a court, a setting in which the sovereign lives out his public and private lives, but Henry's is the earliest English court for which there is sufficient, if not always systematic, evidence to enable a study to be written. Certainly his personality and his style of kingship produced a court of unsurpassed brilliance; 'he is a wonderful man and has wonderful people round him', observed a Frenchman, amazed at the splendour of all he saw. Although there is necessarily much about King Henry in these pages, this is not another biography – still less is it a chronicle of an eventful reign even though, for convenience, the book is arranged chronologically. This is instead a personal account of the sovereign, his six wives and his children, his ministers, officials and servants who together formed the court, and this personal history counts for much, even in the realms of high policy.

Everybody who was anybody came to court for at least part of the year, for this was the hub of affairs, the fount of patronage and power, the avenue to profit and promotion. The ambitious youth from the provinces may have dreamt that the streets of London were paved with gold, but he soon found on arrival that it was the corridors of the palace that held the glint of a fortune, if in waiting and watching he could catch the King's eye. To adapt a famous phrase of A. F. Pollard's, Tudor despotism consisted largely in the dominance of the court over the rest of the kingdom. As a counterpart to the workaday affairs of government and the perennial quest for position, Henry was to make his court the centre of cultural as well as social life, with dazzling spectacles, great banquets and fine music. It was to be the chief place in the realm where there was always something happening, generally something new and often something of significance, whether it was the steps of a new dance, new fashions in clothes, the debut of a singer, the launching of a new dish, the conversation of acknowledged wits or the debates between scholars of international repute. In effect the palace had become the national theatre, concert hall and art gallery, and people were drawn to the pastimes of the Privy Chamber as in later times they would flock to the drawing-rooms of great hostesses.

The great potentates, who would have troubled the King's peace if left to themselves in distant domains, quarrelled and plotted, were attracted to service at court by Henry, who redirected their energies towards tasks in his administration. To be forbidden to come to court and denied access to the sovereign was the hardest blow a courtier could suffer this side of confinement in the Tower. In feudal times military service had been the overriding obligation for a tenant-in-chief, but now it was to be personal service about his King that counted above all else. An outcast courtier was in the shadows, deprived of news and even of informed gossip, out of touch with the world that mattered and condemned to the tedium of provincial life. Ministers of state, peers and officials both of the household proper and of departments of state all had quarters at court and many of their wives enjoyed posts in the Queen's household. Near to the sovereign were the gentlemen of the Chamber, ushers, grooms, pages and the rest, and the officers of the Guard. Below them came the host of servants of differing degree, devoted to making the establishment run smoothly and to catering for the physical needs of the court. It was, as we shall see, still very much an itinerant court as it had been from early medieval times, with King and courtiers moving with the calendar principally between Westminster, Greenwich, Richmond, Hampton Court and Windsor. But in the late summer, when Henry would go on progress into the shires with a few friends for the hunting, for most courtiers 'term' was over and they would be free to go to their homes until Michaelmas, or later. Yet the firmest arrangements would inevitably be overturned by outbreaks of the plague.

Such are the themes of this book. For the sake of clarity in all quotations from contemporary material both spelling and punctuation have been modernised and the use of capital letters rationalised. Throughout the book's preparation I have derived much benefit from the generous advice of Mr Christopher Falkus and in the later stages of production have leant heavily on Miss Margaret Willes. The illustrations owe much to the skill of Miss Gila Curtis. I am indebted to Mrs Peggy Hill for her sterling work in typing my manuscript and, as always, owe more to my wife and children than they often realise.

Hampstead Garden Suburb   N.W.
21 December 1970

1 Pastime with good company

Above A drawing of Henry as Duke of York.

Left Torrigiano's silver gilt effigy of Henry VII on his tomb in the Henry VII Chapel in Westminster Abbey.

'The wealth and civilisation of the world are here; and those who call the English barbarians appear to me to render themselves such. I here perceive very elegant manners, extreme decorum and great politeness; and amongst other things there is this invincible King, whose acquirements and qualities are so many and excellent, that I consider him to excel all who ever wore a crown.'

Francisco Chieregato, papal nuncio in England

Winter was over. The contrast between crabbed age and youth in the April of 1509, when the trees were coming into blossom at Richmond, was so marked that it seemed scarcely possible that Henry Tudor, the dying King, was only in his fifty-third year. His successor, proclaimed by a herald at the palace gates 'Henry VIII by the grace of God, King of England and France and Lord of Ireland', was nine weeks and four days off his eighteenth birthday. He was too young to follow easily his father's style of government, yet too old to be put under the tutelage of a council of state. Overnight the generation gap between the old sovereign and the new posed far-reaching questions for all at court – the great officers of state, household officials attendant on the King's person and servants of the Crown in every degree. Would he, or she, continue in office under the new régime or lose the preferment to another? How far would this extensive royal patronage of appointments be exercised personally by so inexperienced a monarch? What changes would their young master bring to the staid routine of court? Some feared, others welcomed, the future; perhaps a few recognised that this would be a turning point in their own lives, but none can have guessed that the accession would one day be seen as a watershed in England's development, effectively marking the end of the Middle Ages.

The final years of the old reign had been a period of reaction, when Henry VII had developed stringent policies to ensure the loyalty of his barons and had gone to great lengths to exploit the financial resources of his realm. He was never popular, and courtiers found his household gloomy without a queen and with their master in poor health, as suspicious as ever about pretenders and potential disaffection. Older courtiers remembered the jovial, open-handed Edward IV, who had brought new dignity to the palace by making innovations 'after the manner of Burgundy' where suc-

13

cessive dukes had set examples to all the courts of Europe in ceremonial and pageantry. Since those days, despite Henry VII's alliance with Spain, England had become too insular, effectively cut off from the exciting developments in art and letters that were transforming Italian life. Compared with Florence of the Medici, his court had few intellectual or cultural pretensions and those stemmed, as we shall see, from his mother, Lady Margaret Beaufort.

Since Queen Elizabeth of York's death, the master of the Revels had not been called on to stage any spectacle of note and in his later years Henry Tudor had found little amusement in the simple slapstick of tumblers and fools – the Flemish giantess, the wrestling priest or the man that ate seacoal. He had wanted to pay only for as much splendour as was sufficient to impress observers, especially foreign envoys, and the colourful festivities arranged for the reception of Catherine of Aragon in 1501 were an oasis in a desert of drabness. His reputation as a patron of the arts would rest on his chapel at Westminster Abbey, where his executors were charged with providing a tomb of great splendour, fitting for the founder of a dynasty.

Exceptionally tall and well-proportioned, the young Henry naturally commanded the stage with an easy authority. Looks and stature were not everything in a King, but to tower over all others helped. Short, stocky sovereigns, ugly even, and indifferently dressed, as Louis XI of France had been, could dominate their courts, but a King who had the figure and features of a Greek god and moved gracefully was in an enviable position. The most ignorant of subjects could easily identify him as he rode by. Keeping himself trim with exercise, there was as yet no suspicion of surplus weight, no hint that this handsome youth would swell into a grotesque, gross Goliath. A foreigner thought him 'the handsomest potentate I have ever set eyes on . . . with an extremely fine calf to his leg.' Indeed his youth gave Henry an unfair advantage over the Emperor Maximilian I, with his snub nose and huge jaw, over Ferdinand I of Aragon, whose shifty looks did not belie his nature, and over the old *roué* Louis XII of France, riddled by syphilis. Henry was clean shaven, had a very fair complexion and his auburn hair, 'combed short and straight in the French fashion' set off a rounded face with the features so delicately formed that they 'would become a pretty woman', though his throat and neck were 'rather long and thick'.

Outside England both his character and appearance were unknown; yet a single meeting was enough to give a lasting impression of his personality and potential. 'Hitherto small mention has been made of King Henry, whereas for the future the whole world will talk of him,' predicted a Venetian in London. England, it was soon apparent, was ruled by a colossus who could not be ignored. That shrewd political commentator, Niccolò Machiavelli, who never met Henry, described him by repute as 'rich, ferocious and greedy for glory'.

England was to have a Queen again, who with her own train of attendants would enliven the palace and smooth some of the roughness of manners at court. Since the death of Elizabeth of York in 1503 Henry VII had put out diplomatic feelers for a successor and even made tentative proposals for the hand of the mad Joanna of Castille, but he had remained a widower.

Arthur, Prince of Wales (1486–1502), Henry's elder brother, who married Catherine of Aragon in November 1501.

The new King announced he would in fact marry Catherine of Aragon, to fulfil his father's death-bed wish – the same princess who had been brought from Spain as the bride of his elder brother, the ill-starred Arthur. Since Arthur's death she had lived, almost incarcerated, in Durham House on a meagre allowance amidst quarrelsome servants and intriguing confessors, wondering if she would ever marry Henry, to whom she had been betrothed since his twelfth birthday.

Henry and Catherine were married very quietly six weeks later in the chapel of the Franciscan Observants at Greenwich, to enable the coronation on Midsummer Day to be a double crowning of King and Queen. The coronation was scarcely over when the death of the old Countess of Richmond, Henry VIII's grandmother, and the pillar of English humanist studies, snapped another link with the past.

The coronation set the tone of lavish pageantry for the whole reign, for Henry wanted it talked about in superlatives, and though time for preparations was short, the robes and trappings for the procession were duly described as 'more rich' and 'more curious' than had ever been seen, and the banquet in Westminster Hall considered 'greater than any Caesar had known', even though we lack detailed accounts of these ceremonies.

Henry had inherited eight principal residences, three in the capital, the others in the home counties, which had come to the Crown down the centuries. He was destined to acquire or build another eight, again three of them in the capital. 'Capital' is in a way an inexact term, for London was still in 1509 essentially the medieval city, with its walls intact, a square mile of ninety parishes north of the Thames. Though building had begun along all the roads leading from the gates, there was much open country, except in the west where the Strand, the umbilicus joining London to Westminster, had been developed by bishops and some of the newer nobility for town houses; and most of these properties along the Strand boasted 'water gates' and landing-stages, for the Thames was still the main thoroughfare.

Westminster, the separate political capital of the realm, began at Temple Bar. By the Abbey was the palace first built by Edward the Confessor, given its great hall by William Rufus and lovingly extended by Henry III to cover six acres. This had remained the headquarters of English monarchy and was still at Henry VIII's accession much more than a ceremonial palace to be used for state receptions and banquets, for it was his chief London house. As a palace Westminster had severe limitations. The King could not use the great hall in term time, because the law courts sat there, and he could not use the lesser hall when Parliament was in session, since the House of Lords met in it. Yet Henry still slept in the Painted Chamber (86 ft × 26 ft) in the massive four-poster bed above which was the mural commissioned by Henry III, depicting the coronation of Edward the Confessor, and would awake to the colourful Old Testament battle-pieces painted on the other walls. Tapestry hangings kept out draughts and wood fires and charcoal braziers took the chill off the air, but the palace was too near the river not to feel damp. Behind all the pomp and pageantry at Westminster there was acute discomfort.

Within the precincts of the City of London the King owned two residences on his accession and soon would have a third, all by the Thames – the

The coronation of Henry VIII and of Catherine of Aragon, Midsummer Day, 1509. The artist includes in his symbolic imagery the Tudor rose and the pomegranate of Spain.

Tower, Baynards Castle and Bridewell, which he began building in 1515. The upper floor of the White Tower, William the Conqueror's imposing keep which had become down the years the innermost citadel of a great fortress, was a palace in miniature, with banqueting chamber, privy chamber, bedrooms and council room, but it was cold, cramped and inconvenient. Its royal associations were not of the happiest, for here Henry VI had been imprisoned, Edward V and his brother murdered and here Henry's own mother had died when he was only twelve. Perhaps it was the steep climb up the one hundred and fifty-two steps of the narrow, spiral staircase that proved too much for her when her hour was nigh, for she died in childbed on the top floor. Henry, as of custom, had slept in the White Tower the week before the coronation, but before long, as we shall see, he became forced by circumstances to make greater use of the accommodation here than his immediate predecessors.

Baynards Castle in Thames Street had been transformed by Henry VII into a comfortable house and the new buildings were 'not embattled, or so strongly fortified, castle-like, but far more beautiful and commodious.' The site was, however, constricted and his son embarked on a spacious mansion nearby, the Bridewell, on land between Fleet Street and the Thames, along the bank of the Fleet River. A bridge over the Fleet passed through a gap in the city walls to connect the palace with the Blackfriars Convent, so that the chapter house and other parts of the convent could be used as an annexe for state occasions. By 1522, when Bridewell was at last finished, it had cost the King £14,000.

The most up-to-date of all the palaces in 1509 was Richmond in Surrey, Henry VII's *tour de force*. There had been a series of royal homes on this site, all known by the name of Sheen Manor, but a disastrous fire gutted the palace when Henry was seven years old, while he and his family were

The Renaissance Prince – Henry VIII in 1511, by an unknown artist.

16

staying there for Christmas. His father had replaced it within two years by a great Gothic residence, built like a college round a paved court. The privy lodging containing the royal apartments was decorated with fourteen turrets and boasted an unusual number of windows. Well satisfied with the work of his master masons and glaziers, Henry VII decided to give the new buildings a new name; it would be called, he decreed by proclamation, 'Richmond', to commemorate the earldom of Richmond in Yorkshire, which had been his title before he vanquished Richard III.

Five miles downstream from the Tower lay Greenwich. Originally built by Humphrey Duke of Gloucester, the Maecenas of Renaissance scholarship, as 'Bella Court', it had been much embellished by Margaret of Anjou into her 'Pleasance' and enlarged by Henry VII, who refaced the entire building with red brick and changed its name to Greenwich Palace. Henry VIII had been born here and remained very attached to Greenwich. Most of the significant events of his early life took place within its walls, and in the first half of his reign he was in residence here for longer periods than at any other palace. His interest in the navy may well have stemmed from seeing, as a child, the wooden walls of England at anchor, or on their way to the dockyards.

Nearby was Eltham, also set in a spacious park. Henry Tudor had

Holbein's design for a fireplace at Bridewell Palace. Henry began building this London residence in 1515.

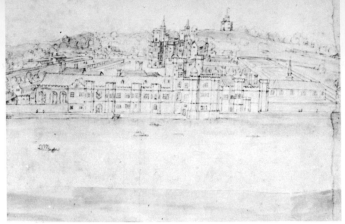

renovated the great hall – with its hammer-beam roof that still stands – but his son found the apartments cramped, and enlargement was hampered by the moat. Eltham provided suitable accommodation for a royal hunting party, but was not designed for the activities of a full-scale court. Henry soon made the place more comfortable, adding a new bedchamber for his Queen and a study for himself, and interested himself in the new chapel, which he ordained must have 'comely windows, most chapel-like, as well at the high altar as on both sides.' Tunnels were dug under the moat so that the kitchen refuse could be removed unseen. One day, looking out from the window, he was suddenly convinced that the view was spoilt by rising ground to the north of the orchard, so workmen were at once instructed 'to take away the hill.'

In the early years of his reign Henry made very little use of Windsor Castle. The first Chapter of the Order of the Garter was in fact held at Greenwich and when the new knights were admitted in May (a ceremony postponed from 23 April which fell in the period of court mourning for the late King) Henry returned to London the same day. He was in Windsor for the day in November and it was not until July 1510 that he stayed at the Castle. In some years, as in 1515, even the Garter ceremonies on St George's Day were held at Greenwich. The new St George's Chapel, begun by Edward IV, was going majestically forward and would be completed in 1519. Later on Henry would rebuild the castle gateway but make few other changes. Compared with his apartments at Greenwich and Richmond the Castle was at this time rather a bleak house, little better than the Tower. Henry's son was to think of it as a gloomy place: 'methinks I am in prison; here be no galleries, nor no gardens to walk in.'

The last residence and by far the furthest from London was Woodstock in Oxfordshire, which was by now little more than a tumbledown hunting-lodge. Henry did not visit it until the autumn of 1511.

These eight houses were the fixed points in Henry's world and, Woodstock apart, the roads joining them were the best in the kingdom. Significantly Henry VII had bequeathed the considerable sum of £2,000 for the repair of the highways and bridges from Windsor to Richmond, and thence from Southwark to Greenwich. But most of these palaces were on the River Thames, or within easy access of it, and Henry used the royal barge frequently for his journeyings. River transport eased the task of moving stores from one residence to the other for, quite apart from provisions,

Above Anthony van Wyngaerde's drawings of the palaces of Henry VIII, made when the artist visited England in about 1555. *Left* Richmond Palace, built by Henry VII out of the ruins of Sheen. *Right* Greenwich Palace as seen from the Thames with its three interconnected quadrangles, Fountain Court, Cellar Court and Tennis Court. To the south of Fountain Court, nearest to the river, is Henry's Banqueting House.

Overleaf The meeting between Henry and his ally, the Emperor Maximilian I, in their war with France, 1513. Henry was adamant that he should be on equal terms with the Holy Roman Emperor, and this painting at Hampton Court records the events of the summer in the manner of a 'strip cartoon'. In the foreground the monarchs first meet; in the centre, once their camps are pitched, they discuss the campaign: in the scene above, the allied cavalry clashes with the French, while in the distance are shown the siege works at Tournai and Thérouanne.

Right Henry walking in procession to Parliament, under a canopy, attended by lords temporal, 1512.

Edward Stafford
Duke of Buckingham

Henry by the Grace of God King of England &c.

The Marquesse of Dorsett Tho: Grey

The Earle of Northumberland Henry Algernons ff Percy

The Earle of Surrey Thomas Howard Treasurer of England

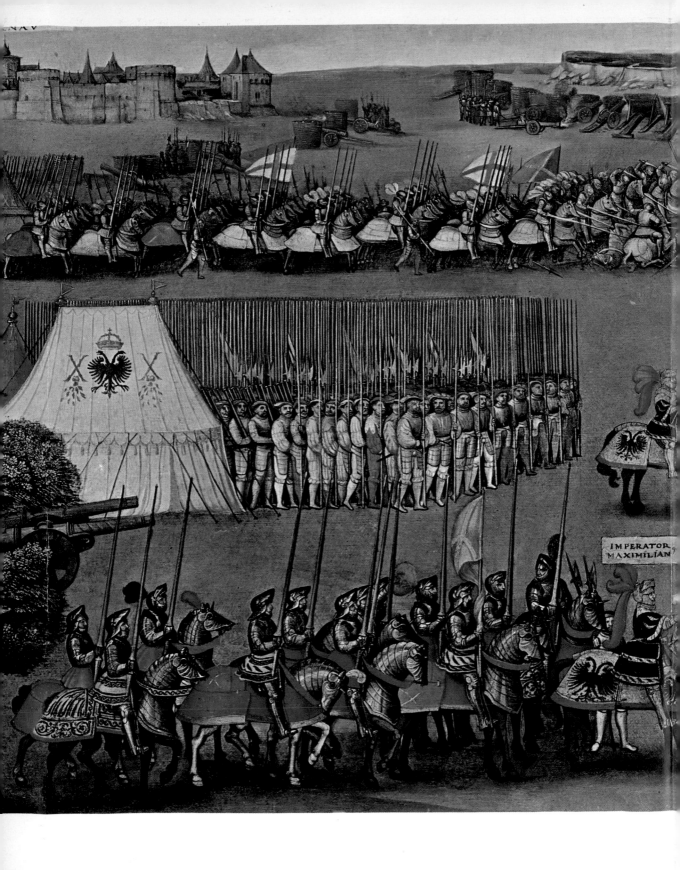

Eltham Palace, Kent; the great hall with its fine hammer-beam roof.

Left Two scenes from the Great Tournament Roll of Westminster. *Above* Henry jousting before Catherine of Aragon at the tournament held 12 February 1511 to celebrate the birth of Henry, Prince of Wales who lived only seven weeks. *Below* Trumpeters on horseback, one of them a Moor, summon the challengers. The banners show the arms of England and France, and are fringed with green and white, the Tudor livery colours.

much furniture and equipment still accompanied the sovereign.

At the end of April 1512 the greater part of Westminster Palace was destroyed by fire, while Henry was residing at Greenwich, making preparations for an invasion of France. Though Westminster Hall and the Painted Chamber miraculously escaped, the rest of the royal apartments, the kitchens and extensive domestic quarters were in ruins. The buildings were never rebuilt for use as a royal residence. The destruction of the old palace, 'edified before the time of mind', was a seminal event in the development of the court, a dividing line between medieval and modern kingship almost as significant as the Reformation itself.

Immediately Henry made use of Baynards Castle and accommodation in the Tower, though in fact the chapel of St John on the floor below the royal apartments was also badly burnt that same year. He put up temporary buildings in front of the White Tower to house court officials who had lost their premises at Westminster and used rooms in the Lanthorn Tower as a privy chamber and bed chamber. Later on he began building the half-timbered King's House within the precincts of the Tower. Desperately short of suitable accommodation in London he also began Bridewell Palace. For sixteen years he was to put up with these makeshift arrangements, while all the time Wolsey's residence at York Place in Whitehall grew in splendour. It would have been too much to bear had Henry not had the compensation of his own Greenwich and the comforts of Richmond, where he spent more and more time, until the Cardinal's fall brought him the rich pickings of both York Place and Hampton Court.

Above left Anthony van Wyngaerde's view of West-minster and Whitehall, from Lambeth, *c.* 1555. This shows old Palace Stairs by the river, St James's and Charing Cross – an area almost entirely redeveloped during Henry's reign.

Thereafter York Place, renamed Whitehall and vastly enlarged, became the setting for the New Monarchy of the Reformation.

For the moment he was content to leave the direction of policy in the hands of those who had served his father so well. Henry had had virtually no training for the Crown, but the old brigade, retained in their posts, soon found he quickly grasped the problems of government and had a mind of his own. In the earliest weeks of the reign his grandmother, Margaret Countess of Richmond, wielded considerable influence and was anxious to bridge the gap by continuing appointments, except for Empson and Dudley, who were hounded out of office amidst public applause. An unexpected assertion of the new King's personality, that warned ministers and officials to be on their guard, came in August 1509. He had approached Louis XII asking him to confirm the existing peace made with his father and an ambassador had come over to renew the treaty, but when the man produced the letter purporting to be Henry's own work, the King scanned it angrily and exclaimed: 'Who wrote this letter? I ask peace of the King of France who dare not look at me, let alone make war!'

Fundamentally the King's household of 1509 was still of supreme importance in the management of the kingdom as a whole and was the normal source from which trained officials could be found for all kinds of administrative tasks; before long there would be manifold changes, but for the present the medieval system persisted at court whereby someone who had entered the King's service, as a yeoman of the buttery, for instance, might find himself as baggage master for an embassy, captain of a fortress or working on any one of a hundred different missions.

Ecclesiastics held three key posts, for William Warham, Archbishop of Canterbury, had been Lord Chancellor since 1504, and Richard Foxe, Bishop of Winchester, had been Lord Privy Seal for twenty-two years. Henry appreciated the worth of this skilled diplomatist and remarked to the Spanish ambassador, 'Here in England they think he is a fox, and such is his name'. Next in importance was Ruthal, Secretary since the turn of the century and appointed Bishop of Durham just before Henry's accession; he was noted for his hard work. A fourth churchman waited in the wings. Thomas Wolsey, aged thirty-six, had been a chaplain to Henry VII though his appointment was not at once renewed. Later in the year he became dean both of Hereford and Lincoln cathedrals and, of much greater significance, in November 1509, royal almoner, a post which brought him into regular

Above Windsor Castle: the Henry VIII gateway.

contact with the King, who became impressed by his great ability. Wolsey was fortunate that Christopher Bainbridge, consecrated Archbishop of York the previous year, died so early on a mission to Rome, and within a few years Secretary Ruthal would be singing treble to Wolsey's bass.

Of the laymen at court the most powerful was the Lord Treasurer, the Earl of Surrey. Thomas, head of the house of Howard, had fought for Richard III at Bosworth, where his father had been slain, but he was too valiant a soldier and too experienced an administrator to be confined indefinitely in the Tower, and in 1501 he had become Treasurer. Five years later, when he had trounced the Scots at Flodden, Henry would restore him to his father's title of Duke of Norfolk; his son was to succeed him as Treasurer and, by a hair's breadth, survive the King. The naval counterpart to Surrey was John de Vere, Earl of Oxford, who had been Lord Admiral since 1485. There was no change in the principal officers of the royal household itself, Charles Somerset, Lord Herbert of Raglan, the Lord Chamberlain, and George Talbot, Earl of Shrewsbury, who was Lord Steward. These three churchmen and four peers formed the quorum of the privy council, a select number of principal officers, who met in the King's presence almost as often as a modern Cabinet meets. There were two other councillors, neither of them peers, who attended whenever they were not away from court on special duties. Sir Thomas Lovel's first post as Chancellor of the Exchequer was at this time much less important than his other

William Warham, Archbishop of Canterbury (1504–32), drawn by Holbein.

appointment as Constable of the Tower. Sir Edward Poynings, the Warden of the Cinque Ports, had made his mark in Irish affairs and been specifically recommended to the new King by Henry VII in his will. Lovel and Poynings, like Foxe and Ruthal, were to fade into the background once Wolsey came to power.

There were, then, no surprises in Henry's first new appointments, for most of the men had proved themselves by service to his father and were now reckoned worthy of promotion. Sir Henry Marney had been made a knight of the Bath for his part in routing the pretender, Perkin Warbeck, and the Cornish rebels in 1497. Now, twelve years on, he became vice-Chamberlain of the Household, Captain of the Yeomen of the Guard and a privy councillor. Henry Bourchier, Earl of Essex, who bore the sword of state at the coronation, became Captain of the Gentlemen Pensioners and Constable of Windsor Castle, to maintain the military reputation of his family established by his grandfather. Though Edward Stafford, Duke of Buckingham, had been both Lord High Constable and Lord High Steward for coronation day, he received no personal office of state, but was in frequent attendance on the King. By his descent from Gloucester, the youngest son of Edward III, Buckingham had himself a claim to the throne, and this was to prove his undoing. The constant companion of the King in his leisure moments was Edward Neville, with a pedigree linking him with Warwick the Kingmaker, who shared Henry's tastes and even resembled him in appearance.

The coffers in the treasury, replenished so successfully by Henry VII's carefulness, were raided to finance the new magnificence at court. Penny-pinching prudence was at an end and the reserves of gold seemed so unlimited that the new King felt no qualms about being regally open-handed, if not downright spendthrift. To carry out his father's will he asked all people with claims on the Crown for debts or injuries to come forward and, as a result, the council was overwhelmed with petitions and complaints of extortion and injustice, for which they sought redress. By a shrewd touch Henry had soon bowed to this popular outcry in bringing to trial as traitors the tyrannical tax-collectors, Empson and Dudley, while he ate greedily of the fruits they had picked. He wanted to give his court a style of its own that would be the envy of foreign princes, and the splendours of Greenwich put to shame the court of the Holy Roman Emperor who was 'frugal and an enemy to pomp'.

'Our time is spent in continuous festival', wrote Catherine of Aragon to her father, for gaiety abounded at court and Henry's enthusiasm for enjoying life to the full was infectious. May Day festivities might last for four whole days; two days a week, said the Spanish ambassador, were devoted to single combats on foot in imitation of the heroes of romance, Amadis and Lancelot. Now there was laughter in the corridors of power. Gone were the long dull evenings, the loneliness, the boredom of an old routine. Here was an athletic King, vigorous enough to tire out horses in the chase and opponents in the tennis court, who danced everyone off their feet, who could drink most men under the table, a King who could shoot a straighter arrow than his own archers, who actually took the lead in tournaments and jousts, a monarch who loved dressing up, music and talking with learned men with equal relish.

Erasmus, by Holbein.

If England was at his feet, he would begin his reign by enjoying himself, so he kicked over the traces like a schoolboy on holiday, free from the tyranny of lessons, regular bed-times and a small allowance. Yet there was a youthful freshness about everything that Henry did, so frank and genuine, that it saved the unbounded revelry of these early months from being vulgar. Regality kept on coming through.

The effect of the change in style of life at court was electrifying. High-born and lowly were hypnotised by the commanding figure of his majesty. The contrast between the young hero of all England, generous and muscular, and the gloomy memories of the old King, reserved, miserly and scheming, was over-powering. Never had a King come to the throne on such a wave of popularity. In Italy Erasmus heard from his friend Lord Mountjoy about the new sovereign, written within five weeks of the accession. If the scholar could only realise how nobly and wisely King Henry behaves he would set out at once for the English court.

If you could see how everyone here rejoices in having so great a prince, how his life is all their desire, you would not contain yourself for sheer joy. Extortion is put down, liberality scatters riches with a bountiful hand, yet our King does not set his heart on gold or jewels, but on virtue, glory and immortality. The other day he told me 'I wish I were more learned'. 'But learning is not what we expect of a King', I answered, 'merely that he should encourage scholars'. 'Most certainly', he rejoined, 'as without them we should scarcely live at all'. Now what more splendid remark could a prince make?

Erasmus smiled as he remembered the dignified boy of eight, acting as host at dinner at Eltham Palace, when he had gone there with Thomas More, and had asked him to write a Latin poem. Truly this friend of scholars would transform his court into a university! So he set out on the difficult journey, hopeful of royal patronage and found on his arrival that his friend Mountjoy had become master of the Mint.

The influence of Henry's grandmother, the devout and scholarly Lady Margaret Beaufort, linked the court with the earlier humanism of the Yorkists. She had patronised that prince of printers, William Caxton, and given financial support to Wynkyn de Worde's imaginative publishing programme, while her magnificent foundations brought the New Learning to Cambridge. She was, moreover, a rich benefactor of three religious houses near London, where learning was the handmaiden of religion – the Franciscan Convent at Greenwich, where her grandson had married, the Carthusians at Sheen, near Richmond Palace, and the Brigettines at Syon House.

Erasmus soon reported that there were 'five or six excellent scholars in London who have not their equal in Italy'. William Roper recalled how the young King, eager for knowledge, would walk off with Thomas More into his private apartment, 'and there some time in matters of astronomy, geometry, divinity and such other faculties, and some time in his worldly affairs, to sit and confer with him, and other whiles would be in the night have him up into the leads, there to consider with him the diversities, courses, motions and operations of the stars and planets.' Catherine shared her husband's friendship with scholars more successfully than she shared

his taste for masques or hunting. She had been educated by leading human-ists in Spain, had delighted the Lady Margaret by her grasp of the classics and kept up her regimen of reading in her isolation as a spurned princess at Durham House. Both Erasmus and his Spanish follower Juan Luis Vives, whom she was to invite to England, thought her a model of feminine learning. Her patronage of Vives enabled him to complete his commentary on the *City of God*, which he dedicated to Henry, while Catherine received the dedication of his tract on feminine education. Vives has left an account of a conversation he enjoyed with his patron as they returned by barge from Syon House, where she had been praying, to Richmond. When the dis-cussions turned to the changes of fortune, the Queen who had known despair as a widowed princess, opted for an even, tranquil life; but if she had to choose, she said, between extreme adversity and great prosperity, as she now enjoyed, she would prefer the former, since 'if the unfortunate lacked consolation, real loss of spiritual integrity usually visited the prosperous'. The choice was to be thrust upon her a dozen years from their conversation.

Six years older than Henry, Catherine was now in her twenty-third year, petite beside her husband, dainty and graceful, with fine eyes and a delicate complexion. He was young enough to be in love with love and easily became captivated by the princess it was his duty to marry. 'If I were still free, I would still choose her for wife before all others', he told her father. For her part she was no less attracted by his magnetism and in these early, honeymoon days she shared as fully as she could in his life, his cares of state and his pleasures. She, too, loved music and the stately dances, delighted in jewels and rich colours. More mature than Henry, her sense of dignity compensated for his flamboyance, and her ladies, too, helped to give the court a more serious tone without in any way putting a damper on the King's high spirits. They were like 'two love birds', with each the centre of the other's universe.

As Princess, in the first days of the reign, Catherine had had assigned to her a total household staff of forty-four, considerably more than when her marriage to the heir to the throne was still very much in doubt. Once she became Queen her household establishment was swollen overnight to one hundred and sixty, but only eight of these were Spaniards.

Her household was directed by her chamberlain, the Earl of Ormonde, an aged Irish peer and a widower, who had spent most of his life in England. He was a veteran of the battles of Towton and Tewkesbury, had been attainted by Parliament long before any other Tudor servant had been born, and was in truth a survival from another world. Henry VII had employed him to oversee alterations to the Palace of Westminster. The brunt of the work fell on Sir Robert Poyntz, an efficient little man who had gone up in the world by marrying the natural daughter of the Earl of Rivers; his elder son became a squire of the Body to the King and his daughter Elizabeth was to be chosen nurse for Catherine's first child.

Catherine's eight ladies-in-waiting, unlike the six ladies of her household as princess, were either dukes' daughters or countesses. They were headed by the Duke of Buckingham's sisters, Elizabeth, who had married Lord Fitzwalter, and Anne, left a widow in her teens, who had recently married Sir George Hastings, later Earl of Huntingdon. These Stafford sisters were

Torrigiano's effigy of Lady Margaret Beaufort, Henry VIII's grandmother, from her tomb in Westminster Abbey.

involved, as we shall see, in a scandal at court in 1510. Next came two other sisters, Margaret de la Pole, the unhappy wife of the Earl of Suffolk who had been in the Tower as a potential claimant to the Crown since 1506, and Elizabeth, second wife of the Earl of Oxford, the Lord Admiral; their father was Sir Richard Scrope. Agnes, the Countess of Surrey, was the Lord Treasurer's second wife, and like his first, came from the Lincolnshire family of Tilney. Anne, Countess of Shrewsbury was the mother of eleven children, one of whom, Lucy, was a maid of honour to Catherine; by contrast Lady Essex, whose husband was Captain of the Gentlemen Pensioners, was childless. The last of the ladies-in-waiting, the Countess of Derby, was the youngest and lived on until 1550; as sister of Sir George Hastings, she had become sister-in-law to Lady Anne Stafford.

The relationships between the ladies-in-waiting made them a close-knit group, an inner circle of peeresses. Serving under them the ladies of the Bedchamber and maids of honour also constituted a formidable cousinage. Tough Lady Dacre and sickly Lady Scrope, Ladies Percy, Ferrers, Burgavenny and Mautravers had left their seats respectively in the North Country, the Welsh Marches and the Midlands to answer the call of service with the Queen, and their husbands in general were in the King's household. There were two exceptions to high rank; one a relic of Catherine's past, the other foreshadowing her future. Doña Maria de Salinas, who had stayed by her mistress throughout the difficult years of near penury at Durham House, was her great favourite whom 'she loves more than any other mortal'. In June 1516 she was lent Greenwich Palace for her marriage to the widowed Lord Willoughby, master of the Royal Hart Hounds, and though she left the Queen's regular service for an English house of her own at Parham, she frequently returned at Catherine's request and was with her when she died at Kimbolton. The other exception was Lady Elizabeth Boleyn. By birth the Earl of Surrey's daughter, she had married Thomas Boleyn of Hever, who was created a knight of the Bath at Henry's coronation and soon became a knight of the Body and Keeper of the Exchange at Calais. It was their daughters, first Mary, then Anne, who were to undermine Catherine's position as wife and Queen.

The most influential man in Catherine's service was not her old Irish chamberlain, but her confessor, half his age, Friar Diego Fernandez, whom she also termed her 'chancellor'. A Franciscan from old Castille, he had become her confessor in 1507 and as such had a considerable hold over her. Haughty, jealous of his special position and an inveterate intriguer, he was the bane of successive Spanish ambassadors, who embroidered all sorts of hearsay yarns about him. They said he changed his habit for layman's clothes and went roistering in the city on stolen money, even that he was Catherine's lover, though we may be sure that had there been anything in such a tale, Henry would have ferreted it out and used it during the divorce proceedings. Diego was certainly devoted to Catherine and was bent on weaning her from being pawn in her father's diplomatic game into an English queen, for there the future lay; she should 'forget Spain and gain the love of the English'. The friar largely succeeded, for though her foreign accent remained, she rarely spoke Spanish at court. She was heartbroken when, in 1515, he was dismissed from her service. At a time of strained Anglo-Spanish relations, Diego was prosecuted in an ecclesiastical court for fornication and sentenced to be deported to Spain. He was succeeded as confessor by Jorge de Atheca, for whom Catherine secured the bishopric of Llandaff, yet he never held in her household, or her heart, the friar's unique position. Among other Spanish servants were her secretary for the Spanish Tongue, John de Scutea, an apothecary and a physician, who were paid far better stipends than their counterparts in the King's household.

Within King Henry's household there was a division of authority between the Lord Chamberlain and the Lord Steward which had originated in early medieval times and would long persist. All the 'above stairs' servants who waited personally on his majesty in the Chamber or other royal apartments came under the rule of the Lord Chamberlain – gentlemen of the Bedchamber, sewers (or servants at table), ushers and grooms, messengers and pages, esquires of the Body who kept watch in turn outside the door of the Bedchamber during the silent watches, and the physicians, surgeons, musicians and entertainers from the master of the Revels to Martin, the King's fool. These servants in regular contact with the King totalled one hundred and seventy. Although the chaplains, gentlemen and choristers of the Chapel were immediately under the Dean of the Chapel, these forty-two men and boys came within the Lord Chamberlain's jurisdiction.

The Lord Steward had a more far-reaching command, for under him came the army of 'below stairs' staff who saw to the provision of the King's creature comforts and the needs of his inner man. Aided by the treasurer, the vice-treasurer and the controller of the Household, the Lord Steward directed the work of some twenty-five separate departments – bakehouse and pantry, cellar and buttery, saucery and spicery, wafery and confectionery, scullery and laundry, boiling-house and scalding-house, and so on, each with a serjeant, clerk and purveyor and junior assistants. The bulk of the food supplies were handled by the Acatary and the Poultry, and the responsibilities of each, though somewhat illogical, had hardened into a rigid division; the Acatary was concerned with meat, including mutton, yet the provision of lamb had always been one of the Poultry's tasks. Purveyors from each of these victualling departments went out to the counties to buy corn and cattle and into the city markets and down to the docks to drive hard bargains for the King's supplies, to supplement what was available from the royal estates. Purveyance had always been unpopular, allowing the King's men to take first pick at their own price, and the commandeering of carts and horses to move supplies was an added grievance, especially for farmers in the Home Counties.

Altogether, in 1509 the Lord Steward had charge over a commissariat two hundred and twenty strong and in peace-time he controlled more expenditure than any other single individual in the realm. He would sometimes preside at the infrequent meetings in the counting-house with the treasurer, controller, cofferer and clerks, sitting round a table covered with a green baize cloth, an august council busily checking accounts, taking stock of supplies and planning menus, that was even then being termed the Board of Green Cloth.

The Lord Chamberlain's men waiting at table might be praised for the sumptuous fare they served at a state banquet, but the credit was due to the Lord Steward's men. Greenwich became, during the King's stay, a grand hotel, where meals would be regularly provided for nearly 1,000 men and women, and on red-letter days, or when an embassy was being entertained, for even greater numbers. The following account of one such banquet by an appreciative Italian, shows the range of expertise of the kitchen staff:

The guests remained at table for seven hours by the clock. All the viands placed before the King were borne by an 'elephant', or by 'lions', or 'panthers' or other 'animals', marvellously designed . . . The removal and replacing of dishes the whole time was incessant, the hall in every direction being full of fresh viands on their way to table. Every imaginable sort of meat known in the Kingdom was served, and fish in like manner, even down to prawn pasties. But the jellies of some twenty sorts perhaps, surpassed everything, being made in the shape of castles and animals of various descriptions, as beautiful and as admirable as can be imagined.

A third great officer of state, the master of the Horse, was responsible for the royal stables, including the provision of fodder for the horses and the maintenance of carriages. His staff, numbering sixty, had quaint-sounding names like yeoman of the chariots, yeoman of the stirrup and groom of the hackneys. In the royal kennels a staff of ten looked after the packs of greyhounds, harthounds and harriers.

The entire domestic staff on the King's payroll was about five hundred, while the Queen's separate establishment numbered one hundred and forty-seven, and the royal guard was three hundred strong. As always at the beginning of a reign the staff had a heightened interest in their daily tasks and Henry had no suspicions that there were supernumeraries about the palace or that men were performing their tasks by proxy. The domestic staff found there was more money about for everyday articles that should long ago have been replaced. The menus were longer, there was less of a fuss about waste. They caught glimpses of the unending series of spectacular entertainments and the music from the hall drifted down to their quarters late into the night. They worked harder, yet their efforts were appreciated; their new master was approachable and joked as he passed by. When Will Wynesbury, the Lord of Misrule for the first Christmas of the reign, asked the King for five pounds on account, he dared to add, 'If it shall like your Grace to give me too much I will give you none again, and if your Grace give me too little I will ask more.' This cheeky note worked, for it amused Henry. Under his father such an episode would have been unthinkable. Despite the departmentalisation of the royal household, still in 1509 'any and every officer might be employed in the ordinary business of government'.

The words of the song Henry wrote at this time for setting to music and singing himself, sum up his youthful ideals, his coming of age from a sheltered childhood. Away with solitude and idleness! Let me enjoy the company of worthy friends and use my leisure as fully as I use my working hours in the business of kingship. Above all let me follow my conscience to do that which is right:

> Pastance with good company
> I love and shall until I die
> Grudge who will, but none deny,
> So God be pleased this life will I
>   For my pastance,

Henry's song, 'Pastance with good company'.

Hunt, sing, and dance,
My heart is set,
All goodly sport
To my comfort
Who shall me let?

Youth will needs have dalliance,
Of good or ill some pastance;
Company me thinketh best
All thought and fancies to digest,
   For idleness
   Is chief mistress
   Of vices all;
   Then who can say
   But pass the day
   Is best of all?

Company with honesty
Is virtue – and vice to flee;
Company is good or ill
But every man hath his free will.
   The best I sue,
   The worst eschew;
   My mind shall be
   Virtue to use;
   Vice to refuse
   I shall use me.

Henry was passionately fond of music of all kinds, from the plainsong tones and four-part anthems of the chapel to the love lyrics sung to the lute in the Privy Chamber and the bawdy drinking songs of the backstairs. He applauded the sheer virtuosity demanded by a difficult keyboard piece and yet revelled in the music for masques and dances from his consort of viols. Besides becoming a skilled performer on the lute, the organ and other keyboard instruments, Henry had a good singing voice and some talent for composition. On progress during the summer of 1510, we are told he amused himself playing the recorders, flute and virginals and also 'in setting of songs, making of ballads and did set two goodly masses, every of them five parts' – a prodigious output considering all the other activities of the progress. Two of Henry's motets, *O Lord, the maker of all things* and *Quam pulchra es*, composed in 1530, are still regularly sung. As with Frederick the Great and Prince Albert, his was much more than a dilettante's interest and his ability as a musician would have ensured a successful professional career. He acquired a fund of rare knowledge about the making of instruments and was fascinated by the technical problems involved in improvements to organ-building.

As Prince of Wales Henry had two minstrels on his staff and when he became King he was determined to increase the modest establishment of musicians that had sufficed for his father's household – fifteen trumpeters, two players on the sackbuts (or trombones), two on the shawms (or oboes), three drummers formerly in the service of Elizabeth of York and a handful of general 'minstrels'. These had done little beyond providing fanfares and a martial beat for state occasions and were augmented for special events. The new King, able to spend money freely on his hobbies, founded 'The King's Musick' as a regular group of instrumentalists and singers attendant on him. As a result, music of a high professional standard became an integral part of court life, a secular counterpart to the singing of the services by the choir of the Chapel Royal. By 1547 Henry had on his payroll some sixty musicians as well as the gentlemen and children of the Chapel Royal.

Because of the stipends Henry could offer, the finest English musicians and some of the most talented from the Continent became attracted to his service. The gentlemen of the Chapel and their colleagues of the Privy Chamber lived like gentlemen, not like servitors, for they were paid three times as much as the average parish priest. Unlike so many professional musicians of the day they had no anxieties about their livelihood and so they could devote themselves to developing their talents. The King's Musick and the Chapel thus combined to hold a position in England that corresponded to a great academy. Under a sovereign who cared deeply about their work and was bent on providing the finest resources for music-making, they found the environment of the court stimulating. The royal musicians led the developments in instrumentation and composition and set standards of performance, certainly for the country as a whole and probably for the courts of the west. Visitors from abroad commented in their letters home in the most favourable terms on the music of Henry's court, the beauty of the choristers' tone, the dexterity of the viol playing and the sheer amount of music-making that went on. At the French court by contrast, the choir failed to sing in time or in tune because the chief singing-master was unable to read music at sight and was frequently drunk; so ill-qualified a fellow would never have found the humblest place in the King's Musick in England.

At this time the most distinguished English musician was Robert Fayrefax. He had been organist of St Alban's Abbey, which boasted a fine, modern instrument, and became a doctor of music at Cambridge in 1504. Henry appointed him a gentleman of his Chapel at his accession and he was soon put in charge of teaching the choristers. Fayrefax wrote motets and five-part masses for use in the chapel and secular songs such as *Somewhat Musing* and *My harte's lust*. It was Dr Fayrefax who first explored the range of the counter-tenor as a solo voice. As a sideline he copied out music, charging about £20 for a beautifully illuminated 'prick-song book'. Though Henry found him a pensioner's place as a poor knight of Windsor, Fayrefax asked to be buried at St Alban's and in 1521 the King paid for a fully choral funeral for him in the Abbey.

Aware of the limitations of native talent Henry set out deliberately to entice musicians from abroad to take permanent posts in his service. From Italy came the first of the prolific Bassano family, which numerically dominated the band of royal musicians for six reigns, and from the Netherlands arrived an ancestor of Frederic Delius. Many of the brass and woodwind players came from Flanders, Milan, Cremona and Germany, and even a French drummer (or tabret player), Marquesse Loreden, was recruited. But the musicians for the stringed instruments – lutes, viols and

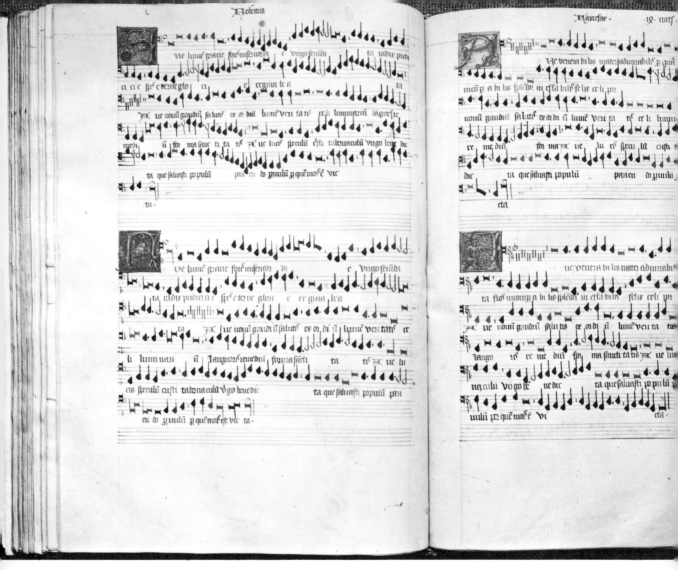

rebecs – were mainly English. The King did not look to Scotland for his bagpiper, nor to Wales for his harpists, though after the Statute of Wales, bringing English law and administration to the Principality, he established the post of 'Welsh Minstrel' at court, first held by Robert Reynoldes.

The most remarkable of the foreign musicians to find service at court was the Venetian Friar Denis Memmo, who resigned his post of organist of St Mark's Venice in 1516 to come to England, bringing with him 'an excellent instrument at great expense'. The first time Henry heard him he was hypnotised by the beauty of his playing and swore he would appoint him his chief musician; he would write to Rome to have the friar unfrocked so he could take a royal chaplaincy as a secular priest. This was soon accomplished and Memmo's virtuosity was acclaimed. Sometimes he kept King and courtiers enthralled for four hours at a time by his playing. The ex-friar sought out musical talent among the Venetian colony in London and found a lad who was such a prodigy as a lutanist that Henry never wearied of listening to him.

Memmo became so indispensable that he could ask for a higher salary

Above Robert Fayrefax's motet in praise of the Virgin Mary, written for four voices; all four parts, from the Eton Choir Book, are shown.

John Colet, Dean of St Paul's (1504–19).

and composed a four-part song, the Latin words hinting broadly at fresh preferment. In August 1517 the King accordingly appointed him rector of the wealthy living of Hanbury in Staffordshire, where a paid curate discharged his duties, for Memmo stayed on at court. When the plague was severe in London, the Venetian was one of the very few companions chosen to stay with the King as he passed the dangerous weeks shut up in Windsor Castle or in his country manors. He became firmly established in the royal family circle. When Princess Mary was only two years old she was brought one day to be presented to the ambassadors who were enjoying an audience with her father. As she came in she caught sight of Memmo and called out 'Priest, priest!' to make him play a tune for her delight. When he had finished King Henry picked up his daughter in his arms and said to the nearest ambassador: 'By God's grace, he is the most honest fellow imaginable and one of the dearest, for no one has ever served me better or more faithfully.'

Others were fired by Memmo's successful career at the English court to try their own luck, such as Zuan da Leze, the natural son of the lord lieutenant of Cyprus. As with Memmo, the organ was his instrument and he built his own. Yet Henry was not much pleased at the man's playing and Zuan was so despondent at not getting the post on which he had set his heart, that he hanged himself, after an abortive attempt at stabbing himself to death. It is in connexion with Zuan's unhappy end in 1525 that we have the final clue about Memmo himself; for by then he had departed from England for fear of his life and was said to be living in Portugal. He had certainly died by 1533 when Hanbury gained a new rector.

The Chapel Royal was not at this time a single building, but a body of chaplains, lay clerks and choristers traditionally attendant on the King, for singing the daily services in the chapel of the royal house at which he happened to be in residence. Men and boys, like a touring company, moved with the sovereign from Greenwich to Richmond and on again. Not until 1533, with the foundation of a royal chapel at the new St James's Palace, did they lead a more settled existence.

If there was a sudden dearth of promising voices when vacancies occurred in the ranks of choristers, the places could be filled by impressing boys from other choirs, though a few favoured foundations, like St Paul's Cathedral and Westminster Abbey, were exempt from this poaching. Henry grew very envious of the musicians employed by Wolsey at Hampton Court and seems to have devised a competition between the two choirs, requiring each to read at sight the same composition, and Hampton, in his very professional view, 'more surely handled' the work. Not long after this Wolsey took the hint and transferred one of his best boys to join the Chapel Royal, and the boy's new choirmaster was full of praise, 'not only for his sure and cleanly singing, but also for his good and crafty descant'. The ten or twelve choristers were boarded with the master of the Chapel, who was to teach them the rudiments of grammar and each boy was expected to take up at least one instrument. It was not quite so small a school as it sounds, for the master was required to teach all boys, and men, about the court who had an inclination towards learning. When a boy's voice broke, he probably stayed on to sing a man's part, and if he showed ability at his schoolbooks, a royal place would automatically be found for him at Oxford or Cambridge, which usually led to ordination and a further claim on royal patronage.

At this time there was no regular organist, for much of the singing was unaccompanied and various of the gentlemen, or lay clerks, took turns at playing the organ. The master of the Chapel, besides teaching the choristers, was in charge of the spectacles and pageants that were becoming a regular part of court entertainment. In these hybrid productions, there was solo and choral singing, ballet, poetry and other spoken dialogue, scenic display and, frequently, mock combat. The choristers left their stalls for the stage, to sing the soprano lines or impersonate the spoken parts of female characters and, because of their light weight, they were often used for peopling the tableaux and other devices in triumphal cars made of somewhat insubstantial material.

Theology already fascinated the young Henry, who was loath to leave the interpretation of dogma or the Scriptures to his clerics, though his orthodoxy was above reproach. If his conscience pricked him when hearing a sermon he would take it up with the preacher afterwards, as when on Good Friday 1513 John Colet pleaded from Greenwich pulpit for the King to abandon his plans for even a just war. He called on Dean Colet; 'I have come to clear my conscience, not to take you away from your studies', he began, and succeeded, in his view, in convincing Colet of the necessity of the French War if the Holy League were to be saved. Over a glass of wine – though it was Good Friday – the King toasted his preacher. 'Let every man have his own doctor; this one is mine.'

Two years earlier Pope Julius II had sent him the symbolic rose, which he had blessed at Passiontide, signifying the flowers that came before the fruits of Our Lord's passion, and so holy a symbol meant much to Henry, who was attracted to the ritual of the Church and faithfully followed its observances. Such religiosity, rather than piety, had its outward effect at court. None could recall a King who 'hears three masses daily when he hunts and sometimes five on other days', who heard vespers and compline every day in his Queen's Chamber. Did not, some asked, this augur a Reformation?

To establish himself as a Renaissance Prince, presiding over a splendid court, Henry set out to attract artists from abroad, no less than musicians. One of the first to leave Italy for his service was the Florentine sculptor Pietro Torrigiano, who had been working for the Borgias at Rome and then campaigning as a soldier of fortune in the Italian Wars. Torrigiano specifically came to design and execute the tomb of Henry VII in Westminster Abbey (1512–17), but he stayed on to make a marble altar, with terracotta angels in the Henry VII Chapel, that was to be destroyed by Puritan iconoclasts in the Civil War, and also to begin work on an even more grandiose tomb for Cardinal Wolsey at Windsor, which was annexed by the King for his own use, but was never completed.

Torrigiano tried to persuade Benvenuto Cellini to help him with his work at Westminster, but the latter could not abide his violent temper, for he vividly remembered that ugly scene some years before in Florence when the young Pietro had permanently disfigured Michaelangelo by a boxer's blow on the nose; 'I felt bone and cartilege go down like biscuit under my knuckles', Torrigiano said later. Moreover, Cellini had no desire, as he put it, to spend even a year's exile among 'such beasts as the English'. This was

Right Wedding portrait of Henry's younger sister, Mary Tudor, Dowager Queen of France, and her second husband, Charles Brandon, Duke of Suffolk, 1515.

Overleaf The Battle of the Spurs, August 1513, when the English and Imperial cavalry routed the French; this picture is a counterpart to the illustration on pp. 22–3.

The Bataile of Spvrs. anno.

the reputation for uncouth philistinism that the new sovereign was determined to bury.

Apparently, Torrigiano's swaggering hot-headedness made it advisable to flee from England to Florence in 1519, though he made a brief return before ending his days in Spain, where he was pursued by the Inquisition and took his own life. On his last visit to Florence, however, he succeeded in persuading Antonio Toto, an artist who had studied under Ghirlandaio, to settle in England and Antonio, after humble service in painting scenery for court revels, at length became the King's Serjeant Painter.

Among other Italian artists who came to England in these years was Vincent Volpe of Naples who was first heraldic painter to the King's navy and as such was responsible for the magnificent embellishment of the great ship *Harry Grace à Dieu*. Giovanni da Maiano had preferred to enter Wolsey's service and was busy sculpting at Hampton Court. Yet Henry also engaged a number of artists from the Netherlands, like the Flemish Galian Hone, who was royal glazier from 1517 and designed much stained glass in royal houses before undertaking the windows in the chapel at King's College, Cambridge, and the painters John Corvus of Bruges and Lucas Horenbout of Ghent, who was enticed from the household of Margaret of Austria. The greatest of them all, Hans Holbein the Younger, was finally to settle in England in 1532.

In the formal entertainments arranged for the red letter days of the year by the master of the Revels, the court became a domain of brilliant allegory, where all men were chivalrous knights and all ladies damsels in distress. These spectacles had been introduced to England from the

Burgundian court and the lavish displays that are still staged in Brussels, Bruges and Ghent today, though shorn of political significance, are a reminder of the tradition that was adopted by the Tudors. An outstanding event in this genre was the New Year's Eve production at Greenwich in 1512. Into the hall was borne a castle, with gates, towers, artillery and a dungeon. This bore the name *le Fortresse dangerus* and inside were six ladies, dressed in russet satin overlaid with gold and wearing coifs and caps of gold. Then in came Henry with five of his favoured courtiers in parti-coloured coats, half of russet satin, spangled all over, half of cloth gold. 'These six assaulted the castle; the ladies seeing them so lusty and courageous were content to solace with them and, upon further communication, to yield the castle; and so they came down and danced a long space'. The ladies led off the knights into the castle, which suddenly vanished.

Six days later, on Twelfth Night, always the climax of the court's Christmas festivities, the King and eleven courtiers

were disguised after the manner of Italy, called a mask, a thing not seen afore in England. They were apparelled in garments long and broad, wrought all with gold, with vizers and caps of gold; and after the banquet done, the maskers came in with six gentlemen disguised in silk, bearing staff torches, and desired the ladies to dance. Some were content, and some that knew the fashion of it refused, because it was not a thing commonly seen. And after they danced and communed together, as the fashion of the mask is, they took their leave and departed, and so did the Queen and all her ladies.

These proceedings were not quite such a novelty as was once supposed, for a 'disguising' pageant had first been produced at court in 1501 by William Cornish before he became master of the children of the Chapel, and these disguisings, combining music, poetry, mock combat, scenic effects and dancing, were his speciality, though there had been no scope for his talents in the last years of Henry VII. Cornish was himself responsible for the 1511 Twelfth Night entertainment and established 'the masque' as an art form in England. The novelty which surprised the ladies present, and the chronicler who wrote about it, was the fact that disguised persons actually danced with members of the audience.

Gambling was popular at court, especially with the servants of foreign ambassadors. Traditionally the Knight Marshal of the Household was the man who organised these games of chance and even acted as a bookmaker at tournaments. Henry had a spell of heavy wagering at dice in 1511, when he was egged on by a group of Italian bankers, so that he lost considerable sums to them and, feeling he had been cheated, kept them out of the palace. But banquets often ended with the English game of mumchance, where the stakes would be high.

The legend of Bluff King Hal was fostered by the unexpected 'happenings' – as they would be called today – in which he always cast himself in the principal role. He appeared *incognito* in the lists at Little Park, Richmond in January 1510 and was much applauded for his jousting before he 'discovered himself', to the amazement of all but the few who were in the secret. A week or so later he made a carefully prepared invasion of Queen Catherine's chamber one morning, with a dozen companions, all in short coats of Kentish Kendal with hoods on their heads, each with his bow and arrows, sword and buckler, 'like outlaws, or Robin Hood's men, whereof the Queen, the ladies and all other there were abashed'. Only after dancing did the men reveal their identity.

Unlike Henry VII, he showed himself to his people everywhere. He had, it is true, a boyish desire to be popular, but he already knew the importance of being seen in all kinds of activities, formal and informal, by as large an audience as possible, for to be a showman was a branch of statesmanship. Let ordinary folk be admitted to the palace grounds to see tournaments, let them watch as a great procession formed, let them see him on his way to the tennis court or to chapel, let some of them even be found seats in the gallery at banquets, for it was laudable that they should want to see their anointed King and doing so was a form of paying homage. On progress, as Henry went about the realm, he took himself and his court to country people, so that though Londoners had the lion's share of the pageantry they did not have a complete monopoly of it. And as he journeyed for hunting and hawking he would bestow his customary largesse. Royalty shared many of its pleasures. The May Day festivities in the woods near Greenwich in 1515, where the royal revellers were served at banquet by Robin Hood and his Merry Men and on the way home were entertained by Lady May and Dame Flora, all this was watched by a considerable crowd, even if an eye-witness's estimate of '25,000' people is wishful thinking.

In the early hours of New Year's Day 1511 Catherine was delivered of a son at Richmond and Henry was beside himself with joy. He had cossetted Catherine in this pregnancy most cautiously, painfully mindful of her earlier miscarriages, and now he was a father. Bonfires were lit and free pipes of wine set in London streets to mark the birth of Henry, Prince of Wales. Everyone thought it marvellous good fortune for England to be provided with a male heir so early in the reign, to have the succession settled at a stroke; for Henry to have so soon the prize for which every husband longed and for the sake of which other kings would readily divorce their barren queens, it seemed truly as if providence smiled on him. Before January was out he rode to Walsingham on a pilgrimage of thanksgiving to make his offering at the shrine of Our Lady. He gave the midwife ten pounds and the nurse, Elizabeth Poyntz, thirty pounds and persuaded the King of France and the Duchess of Savoy to stand as godparents by proxy at the christening held when the baby was four days old.

The arrival of a Prince of Wales meant the enlargement of the court. He was soon assigned an establishment of forty persons as the skeleton staff of a separate household, including a clerk of the signet, a serjeant of arms and three chaplains, and a special room at Westminster was set aside as the Prince's council chamber. Incredible as it may seem, though he was a breast-fed baby, his staff boasted a carver, a cellarman and a baker.

The high-point of the festivities was a tournament at Westminster on 12 and 13 February, in which King Henry took a prominent part as 'Coure loyall', one of the four knights to deliver the allegorical challenge, who entered the tilt-yard in a pageant car decorated as a forest, 'with rocks, hills and dales'. In the middle of the forest stood a castle of gold and outside its gate sat 'a gentleman, freshly apparelled, making a garland of roses for the prince'. The pageant car, drawn by a pantomime lion and antelope, stopped in front of the Queen and when the foresters blew their horns, out

rode the four knights on horseback, ready-armed, who dismounted to present their shields to Catherine. At the end of the combat she awarded prizes of two hundred crowns to the challenger and defender with most marks for each of the days; Henry's skill secured him the challenger's prize on the second day, to everyone's intense relief. The whole proceedings were lavishly set down for posterity, with sundry illustrations, in the Great Tournament Roll of Westminster, where Henry is described as the Tenth Worthy.

Later on the second day, after Evensong and a banquet, all at court foregathered for entertainment in the White Hall of the palace, fitted out with scaffolding and rails to take many spectators. An interlude was performed, praising the infant Prince, there were songs and dancing and then a pageant. It was a sophisticated set-piece, with six ladies sitting in a bower, their white and green satin clothes embroidered all over with the letters 'H' and 'K' in gold. Henry himself appeared as 'Coure loyall', with five knight companions, and their 'hose, caps and coats were full of posies and H. and K. of fine gold in bullion'. The six couples led a dance and then the King in a fit of generosity invited the ambassadors and courtiers present to come and take the golden letters from his and his companions' clothes. 'The common people . . . ran to the King and stripped him into his hosen and doublet, and all his companions likewise. Sir Thomas Knyvett stood on a stage, and for all his defence, he lost his apparel. The ladies likewise were spoiled, wherefore the King's guard came suddenly and put the people back'; however all ended happily with a further feast in the King's Chamber.

Nine days later the hope of England was dead. His father gave the baby prince a most lavish funeral at Westminster Abbey, with 974 lb. of wax provided for candles on the hearse alone. To comfort the Queen, who was overburdened with sorrow, he tried to conceal his own feelings at this, the cruellest blow he had ever been dealt. Henry soon busied himself with preparations for an expedition to Spain to aid his father-in-law against the Moors and, though his intervention was a fiasco, he was determined to rescue England's military reputation in a grandiose manner.

Naturally the galaxy of beauty at court was a constant delight for men with roving eyes. When Venetian greybeards praised Henry for being 'free from every vice', they did not mean that he refrained from having casual affairs. By the standards of the age the young Henry was reckoned a faithful husband, for by all accounts he kept his infidelities to the times when Catherine was pregnant, or recovering from childbirth, and intimacy was not possible. Like queens in other European courts she accepted such passing sexual adventures as one of the facts of life in a man's world; had not her own father kept a succession of mistresses? Better by far for Catherine to wink at a series of fleeting affairs than endure the presence of an acknowledged mistress, a permanent power behind her own throne.

The traditional ground plan of English palaces, going back to early medieval times and faithfully reproduced in Henry VII's new building at Richmond, included a Queen's suite of rooms as well as a King's, just as the organisation of the royal household had always provided a consort with her own separate staff of attendants. Catherine, now married to a King, found she had a bedchamber of her own, as well as an audience chamber and withdrawing room, in every royal residence, whereas as Prince Arthur's bride she had shared his quarters at Ludlow. This duplication of the royal marriage bed down the centuries had increased the temptations for kings and queens with an inclination for unfaithfulness. It was to make it far easier for Henry to take a mistress, like Elizabeth Blount, and was to provide Catherine Howard with her death warrant.

Henry's withdrawn upbringing had made him shy with women, but marriage to Catherine gave him confidence. At masked dances he was now happy to be surrounded by young women; he found himself at ease with them and was not slow to flirt and romp in a teasing, harmless way. The first hint that her husband was being attracted by other women occurred in May 1510, when Catherine was pregnant.

It was merely women's gossip, passed on by Francesco Grimaldi to the Spanish ambassador, but there may well have been some truth in the rumours. The Duke of Buckingham's elder sister Elizabeth, who was married to Robert Radcliffe, Lord Fitzwalter, had been one of the Queen's ladies-in-waiting from the first days of the reign and was a great favourite with Catherine. The younger sister, Anne, had remarried George Hastings, later Earl of Huntingdon, and when he became an esquire of the Body she herself came to court as one of the Queen's ladies. Her apartment was

Henry escorted to the tournament in honour of the birth of the short-lived Henry, Prince of Wales, 1511, from the Westminster Tournament Roll.

watched, for Sir William Compton, a groom of the Bedchamber and one of Henry's boon companions, came to flirt with her and the King, too, was eager to pay his respects to Anne. Lady Fitzwalter grew alarmed that her sister should be having an affair with her sovereign and alerted her brother, so one evening Buckingham came to Anne's chamber to find her closeted with Compton and there was a violent quarrel. The Duke straightway told Hastings, who carried his wife off during the same night to a convent sixty miles away. Meanwhile Compton had informed the King, who ordered Buckingham to his presence and rated him for meddling in other people's affairs. The Duke bowed himself out in a fury, declaring he would not pass another night in the palace. Next morning Henry required the Queen to dismiss Lady Fitzwalter, who left the court with her husband. Believing there were other women working for Lady Fitzwalter, 'such as go about the palace insidiously spying out every unwatched movement in order to tell the Queen stories, the King would have liked to have turned them all out, only it appeared to him too great a scandal. Afterwards almost all the court knew the Queen had been vexed with the King, and the King with her, and thus the storm continued.' The honeymoon period proper of Henry and Catherine was over.

Mars was supplanting Venus among the royal household's gods. Was it possible that Henry would be able to confine his displays of personal courage and military prowess to the tiltyard indefinitely or remain satisfied with the glory to be won by overcoming an opponent merely for the chivalric love of a lady? Ambition to cut a figure in European politics, concern to break a lance for a righteous cause as well as to extend England's Continental power beyond the marches of Calais could not be suppressed for ever. To lead an army into battle was in a different category from playing at soldiers in Greenwich Park.

Three weeks after his accession the French had won a great victory over the Venetians at Agnadello to become the masters of northern Italy; but the next year Pope Julius II had detached himself from the League of Cambrai, made his own terms with Venice and then turned against France. Before long Louis XII was besieging the Pope in Bologna and assembling a schismatic council of the Church at Pisa, to undermine papal authority. In October 1511 Julius formed the Holy League with Spain and Venice 'to defend the unity of the Church', but more especially to expel the French from Italy as the essential preliminary to attaining this unity. A month later Henry VIII joined the League and abandoned England's isolation.

Undoubtedly Queen Catherine played her part, as a dutiful daughter of Ferdinand of Aragon and a devout upholder of papal primacy, in bringing Henry into the Holy League. Yet the chief instrument in weaning him away from peace was his almoner, Wolsey, who had recently entered the privy council at the instigation of Bishop Foxe, himself anxious for support against Lord Treasurer Surrey, the leader of the war party. Wolsey was able to persuade Henry that Rome was the fountain of power and honour, for a King as well as for an ecclesiastic, though he found he was largely preaching to the converted. Henry soon inveighed against the King of France and others 'who would lacerate the seamless garment of Christ', and as a loyal son of the Church felt impelled to join the Holy League. 'I was dreaming of an age that was really golden', wrote Erasmus from London, 'and isles that were really happy . . . when that Julian trumpet summoned all the world to arms.'

The last days of 1511 were a watershed, for they marked the revival of the Hundred Years War with France, that would outlast Henry's own death. The first phase of this struggle, extending to the summer of 1514 shaped Henry's destiny. His four months in the field in France gave him a taste for campaigning and much was made of his presence at the battle of the Spurs. The sieges of Thérouanne and Tournai suggested tournaments on a grand scale. The war, one way and another, affected the fortunes of most people at court. Wolsey commanded two hundred men, Ruthal and Foxe one hundred apiece. There were three hundred of the King's household retainers serving under the trinity banner, while with Henry and his guard were priests and choristers from the chapel, his secretaries, sewers, grooms and pages of the Chamber. It was like a summer progress in southern England, but with the ladies left behind. The King's boon companions of the lists and the chase took the field with their master; Charles Brandon, now Marshal of the army of invasion, was promoted to become Lord Lisle and Edward Neville was knighted at Tournai. In the North Country the Earl of Surrey inflicted a crushing defeat on France's ally at Flodden, where James IV was slain, leaving Henry's sister Margaret as regent of Scotland for her baby son. Howard was in consequence of this victory restored to the dukedom of Norfolk. The war indeed altered the lives and re-orientated the duties of many others; for instance the clerk of the larder was hiring wagons for the expedition to Tournai and the clerk of accounts to the Lord Steward was buying stores for Surrey's Northern army. Of the notabilities, the only ones to remain behind at Greenwich were the Queen's personal servants and the Archbishop of Canterbury. The Queen and her ladies were 'horribly busy with making standards, banners and badges', wrote Catherine to Wolsey in that hectic summer of 1513.

The smoothness of the preparations owed most to Wolsey, and it was the successive declaration of war, its waging and the advantageous peace which he secured from Louis XII that accounted for the lord almoner's rapid rise to become Henry's chief minister.

Foot combat armour of Henry VIII, showing his slim athletic figure as a young man.

2 Proud prelate

Why come ye not to court?
To which court?
To the King's court,
Or to Hampton Court?
Nay, to the King's court.
The King's court
Should have the excellence;
But Hampton Court
Hath the pre-eminence.

John Skelton

The campaigning season over, Henry and his chief courtiers in arms returned home in triumph in October 1513. He was overjoyed that his ally, the Emperor Maximilian, had yielded him the place of honour when they entered Thérouanne together and had deferred making his entry into Tournai 'that he might not detract from the King of England's glory'. The men who had achieved the victories in France and Scotland received their rewards at Candlemas, when Lord Treasurer Surrey regained the family dukedom of Norfolk, his son, the Lord Admiral, became created Earl of Surrey, Charles Brandon, Marshal of the army in France, was created Duke of Suffolk and Lord Herbert, the Lord Chamberlain, was advanced to the earldom of Worcester. This ceremony took place at Archbishop Warham's palace at Lambeth, with many crowding into the hall to watch, even though the doors were strictly manned. Among the spectators was the Duc de Longueville, 'captain of the 100 gentlemen of the French King's house', who had been taken prisoner of war, and the almoner, Wolsey, whose reward was yet to come, for in March he was appointed Bishop of Lincoln. The struggle for power at court in capturing the King's confidence during the next fifteen years was to be fought out among three of the men elevated that spring – Wolsey, Norfolk and Suffolk.

The butcher's son from Ipswich who had risen by sheer ability in the King's service to be almoner, a canon of Windsor and registrar of the Order of the Bath, was able to quicken the pace of promotion to high office to a rate quite without precedent. England had seen royal favourites before, but never a minister so highly favoured. In February 1513 he acquired the

Right Queen Catherine of Aragon in middle age, by an unknown artist.

Overleaf The scene at Dover as Henry embarks for Boulogne, 1520. The royal flagship in the foreground is probably the *Henry Grace à Dieu*, separately illustrated on p. 198.

the Iudges that poynt Counsell please how that
moovcawe in to the Chamre e sitteng there vntill a toven of the clok Ha
spitt e determining of other matters. And from thence he wolde dy
was got into the Starr chambre, as occasion should seve. or there he noth
carrid highe nor lowe, but iudged ther estate, according to his moviti

outgar the counsell chambre, wythin wer sett vpp to broad e long tables vpon t
we vppon was sett, suche a noumber of plate of all sortes, as was all most incrediblee
gylt Chambre were sett out vpon the table nothing but gylto plate, And vppo

deanery of York and in the September he added the precentorship of St Paul's and the deanery of St Stephen's Westminster. After a mere five months as Bishop of Lincoln, the archbishopric of York fell into his grasp in August 1514, while the next month as a personal spoil of the war he was assigned the rich bishopric of Tournai. His master had written to Rome urging the Pope to bestow a cardinal's hat on Wolsey, since 'his merits are such that the King can do nothing of the least importance without him and esteems him among the dearest friends', so eventually, in September 1515, while the Archbishop waited with ill-concealed impatience the appointment was secured. In November the red hat arrived at Dover and, given a symbolic welcome by the gentlemen of Kent, was brought to London 'with

Right Cardinal Wolsey, portrait by an unknown artist.

such triumph as though the greatest prince of Christendom had come into the realm'. As England's only cardinal, Wolsey outshone Warham, Archbishop of Canterbury, and it was a natural step for Wolsey to succeed him as Lord High Chancellor on Christmas Eve, 1515.

Wolsey's preferment did not stop at the cardinalate and the Woolsack, for in May 1518 he became legate and with papal permission held in succession the bishoprics of Bath and Wells, Durham and Winchester until his death, leaving one see as a richer became vacant. From December 1521 he was in addition Abbot of St Alban's, England's wealthiest abbey. Never before had one man amassed so many important offices in church and state, and his wealth, like his power, was regal in scale. 'A good philosopher, very eloquent and full of wit, but for pride, covetous[ness] and ambition he excelled all other.'

Everyone remarked on the Cardinal's 'great mental activity and diligence'. He accumulated offices, yet he was a born administrator with an appetite for patient, ministerial paperwork, the stamina for working excessively long hours and a genius for recruiting talented staff to whom he could delegate routine matters. He transacted unaided, we are told, the same amount of business as that which occupied 'all the magistracies, offices and courts of Venice, both civil and criminal'. Of necessity he neglected his archiepiscopal duties in the North, yet the Cardinal never shunned even the most disagreeable tasks of secular affairs and proved himself an outstanding Lord Chancellor. Above all he took the burden of governance off the King's shoulders and Henry was encouraged to shed even more of the load. Already in 1516 one acute observer styled the Cardinal 'another King', a second remarked that he was 'constantly occupied by all the affairs of the Kingdom' and a third noted that Henry 'devotes himself to accomplishments and amusements day and night, and is intent on nothing else, leaving business to the Cardinal of York, who rules everything sagely and prudently'. By 1517 Francisco Chieregato was writing 'The Cardinal does everything. The King occupies himself with nothing but scientific amusements. All negotiations pass through the Cardinal, who manages everything with consummate ability, integrity and prudence. The King pays the Cardinal such respect that he speaks only through his mouth.'

At the height of Wolsey's influence Sebastian Giustinian looked back to his first days in England in 1515 when the Cardinal would generally say to him 'His Majesty will do so and so'. By degrees he found himself saying 'We shall do so and so', until by 1519 he had reached such a pitch that he used to say 'I shall do so and so'. Theirs had ceased to be a partnership. The Venetian even thought it would be less harmful to diplomatic relations to slight Henry rather than to upset Wolsey, while in France, Francis I scoffed at the responsibilities the churchman had acquired for it 'showed he held the honour of his King in small account'. Foreign envoys were convinced they were negotiating 'not with a cardinal, but with another King'. *Alter rex* was indeed the common phrase, and it implied *altera curia*.

Within five months of becoming Archbishop of York Wolsey had acquired from the Knights Hospitallers a ninety-nine year lease of the manor of Hampton Court and began building his great house for a court to rival the King's. There is a tale that he engaged a physician to visit possible sites for a suburban residence and that at the end of his tour the man pronounced

Wolsey's closet at Hampton Court.

Accounts for Henry's alterations to the Cardinal's palace at Hampton Court.

Hampton to be highly salubrious. It was, at any rate, away from the smoke
and the plague of London, yet within easy reach of Westminster by barge.
Ellis Smith drew up plans and soon an army of workmen was putting
them into effect. During the spring of 1515 a moat was dug, the herb garden
was laid out with parsley and thyme, carroway and colleander, and building materials converged on Hampton – timber from Weybridge and
Reading, Reigate and Barnet stone, lime from Ruislip and red bricks baked
in nearby kilns by Richard Reculver, costing three shillings the thousand.
To speed the operations Wolsey had a crane on the site and the building
went forward so rapidly that already in May 1515 there was work for a
glazier putting in the sixty-five foot run of windows on both sides of 'my
lord's gallery'. With an almost unhealthy obsession about hygiene, Wolsey
ordered the construction of brick sewers three feet thick and five feet high
to run from the palace to the Thames, and to safeguard his water supply
had leaden pipes brought some distance. Such niceties were unknown at
Westminster; soon in every respect the Cardinal's home outshone neighbouring Richmond Palace and became acknowledged the finest in the realm.

Above The ceiling of Wolsey's closet at Hampton Court, which is decorated by the symbols of the Tudor rose, the Prince of Wales' feathers and the sun-burst, in red and blue, picked out with gold.

Detail of the frieze to the closet, showing the decorative motifs in Renaissance style.

It was Wolsey rather than the King who was the patron of artists and sculptors, and led the way in introducing distinguished Italians to England. The Florentine Giovanni da Maiano, for example, came to work at Hampton in 1521 to make a series of terracotta roundels with the heads of Roman emperors, which embellish the gatehouses of Base Court and Clock Court. These medallions, for which de Maiano was paid £2 6s. 8d. each, are of exceptional beauty; the heads themselves are indeed imperial in execution, while the emblems, like the crouching griffon surmounting Otto's bust, and the decorative borders display intricate workmanship of the highest order. The same sculptor made panels of the 'Histories of Hercules' for the oriel windows of the great gateway at Hampton, which were replaced by the King's beasts when the palace became Henry's. Another fine example of Italian terracotta work commissioned by Wolsey, but in a very different style, was the panel with his arms over the gateway of Clock Tower, complete with cardinal's hat, archiepiscopal cross and thunderbolts (symbolising, perhaps, his supreme authority as papal legate). The shield's supporters are two nude *putti* of exquisite beauty.

York Place, Westminster, London home of the archbishops for two centuries, had not had much money spent on it in the years during which Wolsey's predecessor, Cardinal Bainbridge, was living as ambassador at Rome, but when James Bettes, the surveyor, suggested the new incumbent might put in hand modest repairs he found to his pleasure that Wolsey was bent on extensive rebuilding. Red bricks made in Battersea were brought by barge to Westminster for the new hall, kitchens and cellars; (we can now see something of the grandeur of Wolsey's design from the remnant of the old York Place cellars brought to light during the renovation of the Treasury Building in the early 1960s). Neighbouring properties were acquired, including Scotland Yard, and in his first year as archbishop Wolsey spent £1250 on York Place, rather more than he spent on Hampton. It was at York Place that he did most of his entertaining. Here, said the Venetian Giustinian, 'one traversed eight rooms before reaching his

audience chamber. They were all hung with tapestry which was changed once a week. Wherever Wolsey was, he always had a sideboard of plate worth 25,000 ducats.' He could indeed afford to build with such magnificence and live in such style, thanks to his fees as Lord Chancellor and his revenue from all his ecclesiastical preferments; his unique position brought in countless gifts, solicited and unsolicited. He knew the businesslike Signory of Venice would count it a sensible investment to send him a hundred Damascene carpets, and in certain years his New Year's gifts exceeded the King's in value.

Like the King, the Cardinal sought to add to his residences. When he became Abbot of St Alban's he managed to acquire two of the monastery's most attractive manor houses for himself and planned extensive renovations. Tittenhanger in Bedfordshire was too far from London to see very much of Wolsey, but the More, near Rickmansworth in Hertfordshire, was to become the Cardinal's favourite country retreat once Hampton Court became too institutionalised.

In contrast to Wolsey's many mansions, Henry's lack of accommodation in the capital after the great fire at Westminster in 1512 is forcibly brought home by royal itineraries of these years. He did not spend a single night at Westminster in 1514, but stayed for part of February in Archbishop Warham's palace at Lambeth and a day in May with the Bishop of London. He had begun the year at Richmond and, after his Lambeth visit, went on to Greenwich where he stayed until the beginning of May; then he transferred to Eltham for three months, broken only by his visit to St Paul's. For most of August he was at Greenwich again, but at the end of the month went on progress through Surrey and Kent, visiting Guildford, Farnham, Croydon, Otford, Canterbury and Dover; at the last he stayed in the Castle, but for the other halts in his progress he was entertained by the Bishop of Winchester and the Archbishop of Canterbury, who was still Lord Chancellor. Henry returned to Eltham early in October and then spent the last two months of the year at Greenwich. Windsor Castle saw nothing of its monarch that year.

Henry's court was about to lose its fairest jewel, Princess Mary, his younger sister. She was nearing her eighteenth birthday when Charles Brandon, the man with whom she had fallen in love, was created Duke of Suffolk, but princesses, as pawns in the dynastic game of chess, could not marry where their affections led them, and from early days Mary had been betrothed to Charles of Castille, heir to the Hapsburg dominions. Mary Tudor was like a fairy-tale princess, 'a nymph from heaven', whose appearance brought out the superlatives in everyone's descriptions; men had never set eyes on 'a more beautiful creature, or one possessed of so much grace and sweetness', she was without doubt 'the most attractive woman ever seen'. Above average height, very fair and with a wonderful complexion, Mary moved with a natural grace. 'Her deportment in dancing and conversation is as pleasing as you would desire. There is nothing gloomy or melancholy about her.' Peter Martyr, who was hard to convince in these matters, noted that her beauty was achieved 'without the aid of cosmetics'.

In March 1514 Ferdinand and Maximilian deserted England and the Holy League by making a separate peace with France and Henry, already incensed that the long-arranged Spanish marriage had so often been post-

Giovanni da Maiano's terracotta roundel of Julius Caesar, on the gatehouse at Hampton Court.

Wolsey's arms over the gateway of the Clock Tower at Hampton Court – a fine example of Italian terracotta work.

poned without reason, now announced that Mary's betrothal to Charles must be dissolved. That summer Wolsey's negotiations for peace with France led to a marriage treaty between Mary and the widowed Louis XII. At the royal manor of Wanstead on 30 July, in the presence of Wolsey and of the dukes of Norfolk and Suffolk, the Princess formally renounced her marriage contract with Charles of Castille, requiring the lords present to communicate her decision to her royal brother, and within a few days there was proclaimed 'a treaty of peace by way of marriage' between England and France. Henry was anxious to proceed with the wedding as soon as possible and, indeed, the bridegroom, weaker and less active than his fifty-two years would suggest, was no less anxious for Mary to travel to France. At Greenwich on 13 August there took place the proxy marriage in an upper room, where the vows were exchanged and a gold ring was placed on the fourth finger of Mary's <u>right</u> hand. The ceremony was followed by high mass and that, in turn, by a banquet and a ball that lasted for two hours; Henry became so animated that he threw formality to the winds by removing his gown and dancing in his doublet. Later that day took place the proxy consummation of the marriage when the Queen of France, changed into a robe representing a nightgown, was led by Catherine and her ladies to a bed of state to be bedded down in the presence of many witnesses. De Longueville 'with one leg naked from the middle of the thigh downwards, went into bed and touched the Princess with his bared foot'.

If all eyes were on the vivacious Mary for her state entry into Abbeville, her train of attendants impressed all spectators. Henry had spent freely to ensure that the English contingent, 'well and sumptuously attired', made a great show, so that 'in truth the pomp of the English was as great and costly as words can express'; the grandeur of the occasion was unprecedented, and Henry must surely have felt relieved as well as proud, when the reports reached him, that his own honour and reputation had been upheld so majestically. Among the aspects of English court etiquette that aroused interest were the ways in which the Queen's cupbearer and her food-taster remained kneeling and bare-headed throughout banquets. But soon Louis XII had most of Mary's English ladies dismissed, on the grounds that they came between husband and wife, and this widened the rift between the young Queen and her decrepit husband. There was nothing now of the romantic about Louis, son of the poet Charles of Orléans who had endured a long captivity in England after Agincourt. Calculating in war, diplomacy and love, he had on his accession cast aside his first wife, Joan the Lame, to marry his predecessor's widow, Anne of Brittany, to preserve her duchy as part of the kingdom; and now 'the Father of his People' still clutched at the idea of a son. In November Peter Martyr wrote: 'If he lives to smell the flowers of Spring you may promise yourself 500 autumns' and on New Year's Day he died, being succeeded by his nephew, Francis, Duc d'Angoulême, a dashing fellow of twenty, who had married Louis' elder daughter Claude, an imperious beauty of seventeen. The Queen Dowager retired to Cluny for royal mourning. Francis I, who would have been handsome but for his awkwardly long nose, was determined to shine as a Renaissance prince. He easily assumed the parts of connoisseur of the arts, master builder, patron of scholars and gallant professional soldier, so that Henry was quick to identify him as a dangerous contender to the place he had

chosen for himself in the leadership of the new Europe.

Later that month Henry sent Suffolk to France, ostensibly to carry his condolences for the demise of the Crown, but in reality to prevent the widowed Mary from being married off to the Duke of Savoy. In February Mary shamed Suffolk into making a runaway match and risking the consequences of her brother's displeasure. After a painful correspondence with Henry and Wolsey they were allowed to return to England in May.

Henry had long known of the love affair and had the previous year grudgingly agreed to Mary's one condition for going through with a marriage to Louis – that when he died she should be free to take a husband of her own choosing; but before Suffolk had left on his embassy the King and Wolsey had extracted from him an oath that he would not propose marriage to Mary. Faced with the *fait accompli*, and well aware that it was his sister's impulsiveness that had overcome Suffolk's loyalty, Henry merely insisted on a public re-marriage at Greenwich. Their union was unpopular in England, for men reckoned the King had lost to a subject a Queen Dowager who might yet have become Queen of Spain, but Henry inwardly rejoiced to have Mary and Suffolk home again and could not conceal his delight at the tournament to celebrate their English wedding. The couple soon left court for their estates in East Anglia, and in their absence Wolsey convinced Henry of the need to take his pound of flesh to balance the account of the expenses of the French wedding: they were to make over to Henry Mary's dowry from France and pay a fine of £24,000 by instalments – a crippling sum that was never fully paid. Nevertheless, Suffolk's marriage had weakened him politically, rather than financially. Until then men had thought he had authority 'scarcely inferior to the King himself', but now the Duke spent more and more time away from the centre. 'He has ceased to reside at the court', it was noted in 1517, 'secluding himself on account of the accusations prevalent in great courts, where favour does not always remain stable'. And the Cardinal, while always claiming to be the Duke's friend, was the gainer.

Catherine had been delivered of a still-born son in September 1513 while Henry was with the army in France and at the end of November 1514 she gave birth to a premature child – 'a prince who lived not long after' – and this further loss of a potential heir was a bitter cup for both parents. A series of pregnancies was leaving a mark on Catherine's once delicate figure and, indeed, the six years' difference in age between wife and husband was beginning to be remarked upon. Young Francis I of France had even dared to say that the Queen of England 'is old and deformed'.

While Catherine was carrying the child Henry's roving eye took in Bessie Blount, daughter of a Shropshire knight and a cousin of Lord Mountjoy, who had found her a place at court as a maid of honour in 1513. By the end of the next year she had suddenly blossomed into womanhood. A sober dean described Elizabeth as 'eloquent, gracious and beautiful', but she had, too, a natural vivacity that swiftly assured her entrée to the inner group of Henry's companions; the flippant postscript of a letter of that great womaniser, Charles Brandon, Duke of Suffolk, written from France to his sovereign in October 1514, asks him to tell 'Mistress Blount and Mistress Carew the next time I write unto them or send them tokens', they must definitely send a reply, and the bantering tone of Suffolk's remarks to the King about a

The marriage of Louis XII of France to Mary Tudor, Henry's younger sister, at Abbeville in 1514. This forms one of a series of drawings made by an eye-witness, Pierre Gringoire.

65

maid of honour still in her first year at court speaks volumes for her personality. At court masquings and mummings this nubile girl of fifteen was soon
playing leading roles. At the Christmas entertainment at Greenwich,
Elizabeth was joining Lady Carew, Lady Margaret Guildford and the wife
of the Imperial diplomat, Lady Fellinger, to play the four ladies from
Savoy, dressed up in blue velvet, with bonnets of burnished gold, opposite
the four knights from Portugal, played by King Henry, Suffolk, Sir Nicholas
Carew and Fellinger. Their 'strange apparell' especially pleased Queen
Catherine, who invited the four couples to her bedchamber for masked
dancing by torchlight, and Henry partnered Mistress Blount. There were
the usual shrieks of laughter when they 'put up their visers', yet Catherine
warmly thanked her husband for 'her goodly pastime and kissed him', for
she had been happily distracted by the fun from her own sorrows. Perhaps
it was to ward off any suspicions his wife had about his affection for her
maid of honour that in the Twelfth Night masque at Eltham a few days
later Henry had Elizabeth replaced; while the three other ladies who had
acted Savoyards at Greenwich now played Dutch damsels in distress opposite the same four knights, the fourth damsel was Jane Popyngcort.

The Flemish born Jane Popyngcort had been a maid of honour to Queen
Catherine since 1509 and when the Duc de Longueville came to the English
court as a prisoner of war, she became his mistress. When Henry's sister,
Mary, was affianced to Louis XII she practised French conversation with
Jane and de Longueville, who was to accompany Mary to France, secured
Jane's appointment as one of Mary's ladies-in-waiting. Yet the English amb-
assador in Paris told King Louis all about Mistress Jane's 'evil life' and he
struck her off the list, saying he wished the lady burnt, so she remained behind in England. There are reasons for thinking that with de Longueville
back in France, Henry himself now enjoyed a fleeting affair with Jane
Popyngcort. When, on Louis' death, she left for a post at the court of
Francis I, Henry gave her £100. She was soon installed in the Louvre as de
Longueville's mistress and for some years kept up a lively correspondence
with Mary, now Duchess of Suffolk, reporting details about Parisian fashions
and sending her head-dresses. Henry had soon forgotten about Jane, but
Elizabeth Blount remained at court to remind him of her charms and when
Queen Catherine again became pregnant their liaison was becoming an
open secret, so that she held the position, unknown to the English constitution,
of *maîtresse en titre*.

Catherine had taken to her childbed at Greenwich on 18 February 1516
and there was much rejoicing that the baby lived, even though she was a
girl. She was christened Mary at the friary church outside the palace gates
where Henry and Catherine had been married; the Cardinal was her godfather, the Duchess of Norfolk her godmother, while Sir Thomas Boleyn
was among the select group of courtiers holding the canopy. 'The Queen
and I are both young', Henry told the Venetian ambassador, 'and if it is a
girl this time, by God's grace boys will follow.' At any rate Henry was proud
of his baby daughter and boasted that she never cried. He took no immediate
steps to assign a separate establishment for her, as he had done for Henry,
Prince of Wales, but a few more servants were added to the Queen's household – such as the four rockers of the cradle. When later on Lady Bryan was
appointed governess, she favoured a separate 'Princess's household' in name,

Margaret Tudor, Henry's
elder sister, Queen of
Scotland (1504-41).

if not in fact, and during Mary's third year this little establishment was costing £1,400.

These rejoicings were soon followed by another family occasion, for Henry's elder sister, Margaret, Queen of Scotland, had been forced by the twist of politics to take refuge in England, and in May 1516 journeyed to London. Henry had not seen Margaret for thirteen years, when she had set out for Edinburgh as a girl of fourteen. Since then she had lost her husband, James IV, at Flodden and married Archibald Douglas, Earl of Angus. Angus, no less than the infant James V, was conspicuously absent when Henry met his sister at Tottenham, but she had with her their three-month-old baby, Margaret. Their visit was to last for a year. After a state entry to London the Scottish Queen was lodged in the newly finished Baynards Castle; later in the year, through Wolsey's graciousness, she was allowed to transfer to Scotland Yard, once the London residence of Scottish sovereigns.

Henry was in high spirits and in his sister's honour held jousts on 19 and 20 May in which he rode against Sir William Kingston. Margaret, who had come south 'with much poverty', marvelled at the luxury of her brother's court and gladly accepted any gift he proferred. In December she became anxious about buying the New Year presents she was expected to bestow at court and persuaded Wolsey into lending her £200. A family Christmas was kept in style at Greenwich and her younger sister Mary of Suffolk, Dowager Queen of France, already carrying her second child, had obeyed Henry's summons and so for a few weeks Greenwich became the court of the Three Queens. Old animosities were forgotten and Catherine of Aragon delighted in having her sisters-in-law and their babies around her. For the children of Henry VII this family reunion was a calm before the various storms that lay ahead. Margaret was the first to experience matrimonial troubles, for the confused course of Scottish politics, centring round the custody of her son, intensified her estrangement from Angus. Their violent quarrels led to rival factions, little removed from permanent civil war, and if there was some doubt about Queen Margaret's 'over tenderness' to the pro-French Duke of Albany, no one seriously disputed that Henry Stewart, Lord Methven, her treasurer and lord chancellor, became her lover. To her brother's horror she was to divorce Angus in 1527 and marry Stewart, yet within eight years she would be attempting to repudiate him. Mary remained faithful to Suffolk, though their relations were badly scarred by Henry's own divorce proceedings, for while Mary was to stay steadfast beside Catherine, her husband was to prove himself the King's invaluable ally. Neither sister in 1516 could have predicted that Henry would marry another five times, particularly with so beautiful and undemanding a mistress as Elizabeth Blount.

As Hall, the chronicler, happily put it, Mistress Blount exceeded all other damsels 'in singing, dancing and in all goodly pastimes', so that she soon won her sovereign's heart and showed him such favour that in 1519 she bore him a son. Before then she had been married off to Gilbert Tailboys, son of the mad Lord Kyme, who had been in Wolsey's service. Henry had purchased for them Blackmore Manor, later nicknamed Jericho, in Essex, in which Henry Fitzroy was born. The royal father proudly showed off his illegitimate son at court and Catherine must have shed her tears of bitter-

Henry Fitzroy, Duke of Richmond, Henry VIII's natural son by Elizabeth Blount, (1519–36)

ness and shame, reproaching herself anew for failing to provide England with a prince.

The cuckolded husband became Sir Gilbert, served as sheriff and MP for Lincolnshire, received grants of many lands and acquired a peerage before his death in 1530. His widow, who had long since passed out of Henry's life, now married a Lincolnshire neighbour, young Lord Clinton, and survived her royal son by some four years.

The year 1518 saw Wolsey as the architect of the Peace of London, intended as a general settlement of the disputes between the nations of Western Europe which would enable a united crusade to be undertaken against the Turk. Pope Leo X sent Cardinal Campeggio to England as his legate to further European peace as a preliminary to a holy war against the Infidel, but Wolsey kept him kicking his heels in Calais for two months until he, too, was granted equal authority as a legate. He did this on the grounds that it was unusual for a foreign cardinal to exercise legatine responsibility in England, and never in an England where the King's chief minister was himself a Cardinal Archbishop. Having gained his appointment, Wolsey saw to it that his colleague Campeggio was put in the shade; 'less respect for the papal see could scarcely have been shown', it was noted. Concurrently with the peace-making Wolsey was conducting negotiations with the Bishop of Paris and Admiral Bonnivet for the betrothal of the two-year-old Princess Mary to the Dauphin, born to Francis I that February; and he was therefore playing a complex game. As Thomas More declared, the Cardinal of York alone dealt with the French ambassadors and only told the Council when everything had been decided, 'so that the King himself scarcely knew the state of affairs'. The Peace between England, France, the Empire, Spain and the Papacy was sworn to at the high altar of St Paul's Cathedral on Sunday 3 October, when Wolsey celebrated mass with a splendour that defied exaggeration. Nobody had much to say about the meal provided after the service by Henry in the Bishop of London's palace, but the state banquet which Wolsey gave that night was more sumptuous than any feast 'given by Cleopatra or Caligula'. After dinner there was masqued dancing led by Henry and his sister, the Dowager Queen of France, and countless dishes of confections and other delicacies were served, while large bowls full of ducats were brought in for those wanting to play mumchance.

The proxy marriage celebrations between Dauphin and Princess took place at Greenwich two days later, when Wolsey lifted Mary into his arms and placed a minute ring with a diamond on her finger, leaving Admiral Bonnivet to pass it 'over the second joint'. Afterwards Mary said to the Admiral, 'Are you the Dauphin of France? If you are, I want to kiss you!' The rest of the week was spent in jousts, 'with the King shivering eight spears', and entertainments and 'pageants of such a sort as one rarely sees in England'. At the banquet at Greenwich on the Thursday guests were seated at a table in the shape of a great horseshoe, with ladies sitting alternately with men, which must have been an unusual arrangement for it was remarked upon. 'On the buffet were 82 vases of pure gold of various sorts, the smallest being the size of a tall glass, one foot high, and drinking cups 4 foot high.' The Queen, who was pregnant, retired to bed after dinner (which was just as well, because the entertainment lasted until 2 a.m.) but the rest of the party went to a hall on the ground floor for a disguising devised by Master Cornish around the topical themes of the Anglo-French marriage, peace in Christendom and a crusade. After further refreshments when Henry, in his gold brocade with the silver lining, was walking in the gallery with the chief guests, Monsieur de St Meme for a jest said to him, 'Sire, I never saw a robe more to my liking than that which your Majesty is now wearing.' The King immediately took the robe off and gave it to him. Next day it was arranged by Wolsey that Henry and Francis should meet each other the following summer near Calais, and though the meeting had to be postponed because of the Imperial election, the great encounter between the rival sovereigns took place in 1520 at the Field of Cloth of Gold.

Henry's quest for glory had been heightened by the Emperor Maximilian's extraordinary suggestion in 1513 that he might resign the Empire to him, and later he had talked of adopting him as a son and granting him the Duchy of Milan, preparatory to arranging for his election. Only once in the long history of the Holy Roman Empire had there been an English 'King of the Romans' with the appointment of Richard, Earl of Cornwall, brother of Henry III in 1257, and he had failed to secure election as emperor, so the proposal was as challenging to Henry as it was romantic. Tunstall had told him that if he were to accept election this would be an admission that England was subject to the Empire – a dangerous notion that would be 'a perpetual prejudice' to his successors. 'The Crown of England', said the Bishop in a phrase that was to become famous, 'is an empire of itself' and further dignities were incongruous and irrelevant. Yet Henry was not convinced, as for him the Holy Roman Empire was 'the monarchy of Christendom', the highest honour (the Papacy apart) to which a sovereign could aspire.

Effectively the election campaign began with Maximilian's apoplectic stroke in 1517, and it was known that Francis I of France would challenge the Hapsburg candidate, the Archduke Charles, Maximilian's grandson, who had become King of Spain the previous year. The Pope disliked the idea of a French Emperor almost as much as he disliked the Hapsburg claims to the territorial power of the Church, and hopefully cast around for a third candidate. Wolsey wrote to him in extremely cautious terms, to find out whether Leo X would bless Henry's candidature; if so he might be prepared to stand. Four months went by after Maximilian's death before Henry committed himself to intervening in the election by sending Richard Pace to Germany to attempt to win support from the seven electors. Of the three candidates, who would continue their personal rivalry for another quarter of a century, Henry reckoned himself the most suitable and convinced himself that seniority counted, for he was by now twenty-eight, with ten years' experience of ruling a kingdom, whereas Francis I was three years his junior and had only been King of France for four years, and Charles was a stripling of nineteen. From the first days of Francis' accession Henry had been jealous of him and the Venetian, Pasquilio, had found himself asked a whole series of questions about the rival when Henry came across him breakfasting in a bower in the gardens at Greenwich. 'The King of France, is he as tall as I am?' (there was little difference). 'Is he as stout?' (he was not). 'What sort of legs has he?' (spare). Then Henry opened the front of his doublet and put a hand on his thigh, saying, 'Look here! And I have also a good calf to my leg'. Henry in 1519 felt he *looked* imperial.

Wolsey was sick with dysentery when Pace was given his instructions and remained lukewarm about the whole venture, for he thought it utterly unrealistic of Henry to imagine the German princes and archbishops would prefer an outsider to a Hapsburg. In any event it was Charles' credit with the Fuggers' bank that decided the election at Frankfurt on 28 June. The Archbishop of Mainz had asked 52,000 florins for his vote and then increased his price to 120,000, and the sums Pace could offer so late in the bidding were derisory to the seven men selling their votes. Henry would have to content himself with playing the role of 'arbiter of Europe', which the Cardinal had devised for him, without an imperial title.

In the spring of 1519 there was a minor palace revolution, for a number of the privy council felt it was high time the behaviour of the young men of the King's Chamber was checked. Henry had from the earliest days of his reign maintained at court a small group of men of his own age whose company he enjoyed. He was gregarious by instinct and the gentlemen of the Privy Chamber formed something of an exclusive club with the King as president. Men like Sir Nicholas Carew and Sir Edward Neville jousted with him, endeavoured to beat him at tennis and to win money from him at dice; they formed the stage army for court masques, rode closest to the King on progress, shot with him at the butts, drank, jested and sang with him into the night. Inevitably some of them became over-familiar and senior counsellors thought they were clipping the divinity that hedged the King; these 'young minions' were 'too homely with him and played such light touches with him that they forgot themselves'. Some of these knights, including Neville and Sir Francis Bryan, had been recently at the French court on a diplomatic mission where they found Francis I much more roisterous and unbuttoned than Henry. Each day they had accompanied him to ride, disguised, through the streets of Paris, 'throwing eggs, stones and other foolish trifles at the people'. When they came back to Greenwich they tried to carry on with their high-spirited tomfoolery, laughing at staid courtiers, mimicking high officials and behaving with anything but courtly manners. When people lifted reproving fingers, the young bucks ran down the prim ways of Henry's court and English traditions, and said everything must be done on the French model.

They over-reached themselves. One day in May the council meeting on its own at Greenwich decided to request Henry to put a stop to this intolerable effrontery. The Cardinal, Norfolk, Worcester and Sir Thomas Boleyn were the most outspoken critics and they found the King did not argue with them; he was obviously sorry to discipline the 'young minions' by banishing them from court, but he saw the point of the council's complaints and agreed to a purge of the Privy Chamber. The Lord Chamberlain was required to summon the offenders and tell them they were to be sent away from court for a season. Carew was despatched to govern a fort in Calais, while Bryan, Neville, Sir John Peachy, Sir Edward Poyntz and Sir Edward Guildford were dismissed from their posts in the Chamber and warned to pay attention to the other offices they held in the country. In part, clearly, the purge was an attempt to reform the household administration by stopping duties

from being discharged by deputies that was to lead in a few years time to the issue of the Eltham Ordinance. The places of the young bloods were taken in the Chamber by Sir William Kingston and the three Sir Richards – Wingfield, Jerningham and Weston – making 'four sad and ancient knights', men of Wolsey's choosing who were not Francophile in outlook.

Henry himself took the hint, decided it was high time to put away childish things, give up gambling and devote his abilities to public business. Norfolk was sure his monarch had begun to lead a new life, and when Francis I heard of these changes he sneered, 'You will find a new world in England' and feared the *entente* was cracking. Too much must not be read into the political significance of the 1519 purge. The gentlemen of the Chamber sent packing were not, as one ambassador wrote, some of Henry's chief lords; they had some influence with the King, but no power. The direction of affairs lay still with Wolsey, though Henry was, after the events of May, more inclined to take an active part in the formation of policy. In any event the banished knights were necessarily to be included in the great entourage to mark an extension of the *entente* between England and France at the Field of Cloth of Gold.

The idea of a summit meeting between Henry and Francis between Guisnes and Ardres in June 1520 was hailed as a turning-point in Anglo-French relations, which would bury old enmities and bring about an *entente cordiale* that would foster universal peace. Rivalry and suspicion must remain until the two Kings had actually met, their courtiers and ladies had mingled for a month, and each had sworn not to shave his beard until the meeting had taken place. Henry had, in fact, to break his vow, because Catherine disliked his unshaven appearance and the Queen Mother of France excused him, since love was not shown in men's beards, but in their hearts. The aim of the meeting, said Sir Richard Wingfield, the ambassador in Paris, was for the monarchs to 'make such an impression of entire love' that shall 'never be dissolved, to the pleasure of God, their both comforts and the weal of Christendom'. So rich were the costumes and pavilions of both courts that the name 'Field of Cloth of Gold' came naturally as the only accurate description of the gathering; it was sheer coincidence that the scene of the meeting had anciently been called the Golden Vale. It was to be, said contemporaries, the eighth wonder of the world.

Wolsey had been commissioned by both kings to make the arrangements for the meeting and it is hard to believe that he looked on it as anything other than a stage for his own greater glory. The Field of Cloth of Gold had many facets: it was a political conference, an athletics meeting, with jousts, tournaments and wrestling, a festival of music and drama and a series of

The meeting of Henry VIII and Francis I at the Field of Cloth of Gold, June 1520, as depicted in a stone monument at Rouen.

Right Opening page of the ratification of the treaty of perpetual peace between Henry and Francis I, made at Amiens, 18 August 1527. This copy, from a set of three ratifications in England, has never been reproduced before. With the portrait of Francis are depicted the arms of France and his personal badge – a salamander – with the motto *Nutrisco et extinguo*.

Overleaf The Field of Cloth of Gold, the lavish Renaissance setting for the meeting of Henry and Francis I in June 1520, between Guisnes and Ardres. This narrative picture, possibly by Hans Roest, shows various incidents as if they were taking place simultaneously. In the left foreground Henry and Wolsey arrive in procession; in the centre background the two sovereigns meet, while in the distance a tournament is in progress. The fountain (right foreground) provides free wine for all.

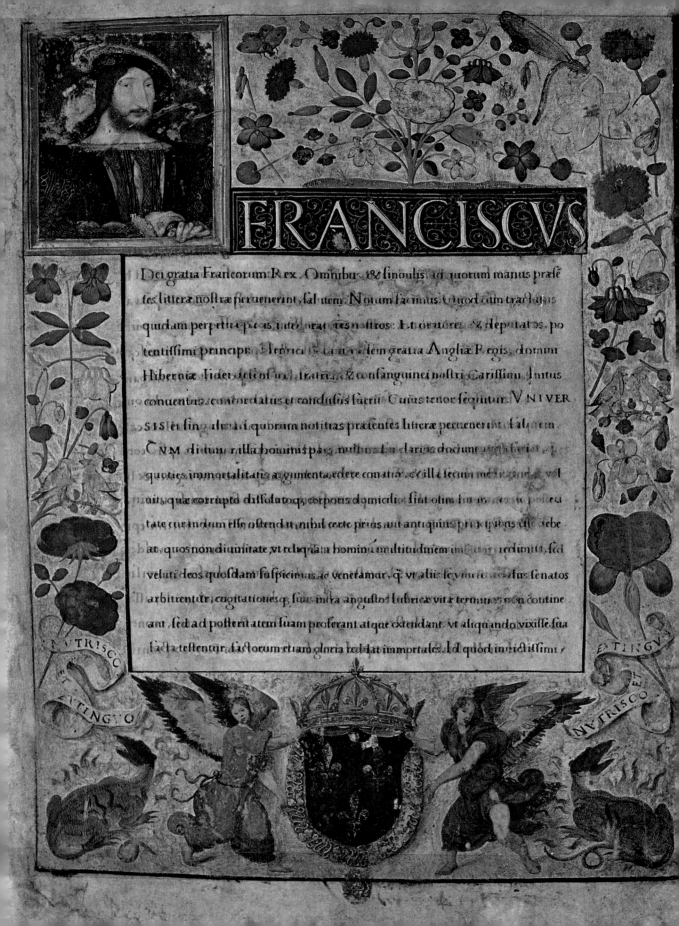

FRANCISCVS

Dei gratia Francorum Rex. Omnibus & singulis, ad quorum manus præsentes litteræ nostræ peruenerint, salutem. Notum facimus Quod cum tractatus quidam perpetuæ pacis, inter oratores nostros Et oratores & deputatos, potentissimi principis, Henrici eiuslem gratia Angliæ Regis, domini Hiberniæ fidei defensoris, fratris, & consanguinei nostri Carissimi, Initus conuentus, concordatus et conclusus fuerit. Cuius tenor sequitur. VNIVERSIS et singulis ad quorum notitias præsentes litteræ peruenerint, salutem. CVM dictum nulla hominis pars, nullo est a clarius documento fuerit, quoties immortalitatis argumenta edere conatur, et illa secum meditando, vel init, quæ corrupto dissolutoque corporis domicilio sint olim in immortalitate curandum esse ostendit, nihil certe prius aut antiquius principibus esse debebat, quos non diuinitate, vt reliquam hominum multitudinem imbutos, redimitis, sed veluti deos quosdam suspicimus ac veneramur, q vt aliis seiunctis rebus senatos arbitrentur, cogitationesq suas intra angustos lubricæ vitæ terminos non contineant, sed ad posteritatem suam proferant atque extendant, vt aliquando vixisse sua facta testentur, factorum etiam gloria reddat immortales. Id quod inuictissimi

state banquets. The administrative arrangements for transporting over 5,000 English men and women, who formed or supported Henry's court, across the Channel with all their requirements for a month made plans for a summer progress in the southern shires seem elementary by comparison; and the expedition was only possible because England still held a bridge-head at Calais. The place where the kings were to embrace was, in fact, within the English 'pale'. Provisions costing £8,839 and another £1,568 for wine and beer were assembled at Calais. The utmost care was taken over transporting the thoroughbred Neapolitan horses for the jousts and the steel mill at Greenwich which was dismantled and set up at Guisnes with other forges for repairs to swords and lances.

Because Guisnes Castle was pronounced unsuitable for the royal lodging, ambitious plans were made for a very large temporary palace to be built of brick and timber, close by, and an army of workmen strove to beat the calendar. In the end the idea of a banqueting house was abandoned in favour of a vast, highly ornate tent, yet the palace proper still included three chambers for the King on the first floor, the largest being more spacious than the White Hall at Westminster, with separate apartments for Queen Catherine, and there was even a secret passage to take Henry to a privy lodging in Guisnes Castle itself to take his ease. Wolsey had a suite next to the King's and the Duchess of Suffolk, as Dowager Queen of France, was assigned quarters next to Catherine's. These buildings, with a chapel 'painted blue and gold', and a porter's lodge, formed a quadrangle. The whole was made resplendent by heraldic painters like John Rastell (who had married Thomas More's sister) for Garter King of Arms had prepared a book with all 'hearts, fowls, devices, badges and cognisances' relevant to the occasion. The canvas roofs were 'gilded and garnished' inside and out and Alexander Barclay, the black monk, was given leave of absence to devise mottoes and sayings to be painted on the banqueting house and apartments. Allegory and symbolism were thus in evidence on every side. A notable feature of the palace was the amount of glass. The state apartments were hung with the richest tapestries and fitted out with Turkey carpets, chairs of estate and gold and silver plate brought across by the Lord Chamberlain's men. From two gilt pillars, bearing statues of Cupid and Bacchus, flowed streams of malmsey and claret respectively, free for all. In all this there was intense competition with the French preparations at Ardres. Reports on the progress of the French pavilions spurred on the English workmen to excel and there was welcome relief at Guisnes when it was heard that the roof of the principal French pavilion had been torn off by a high wind. The chief courtiers had been assigned rooms in Guisnes Castle, the others were found accommodation in the encampment of nearly four hundred tents that Richard Gibson, master of the King's hales, tents and pavilions, had erected in neighbouring fields. But Gibson's *tour de force* was the banqueting house, 'the most sumptuous ever', covered outside by cloth painted to resemble brickwork, *à l'antique* and decorated inside with cloth of gold and silver, interlaced with the Tudor colours of white and green. One Italian thought this English palace so superb that even Leonardo could not have surpassed it, another compared it to the fairy-tale palaces of Ariosto's *Orlando Furioso*. If showmanship was all, the Cardinal's men had brilliantly achieved the right setting for their King and their master.

Left The Royal Salt, a superb example of Renaissance craftsmanship, which Francis I presented to Henry.

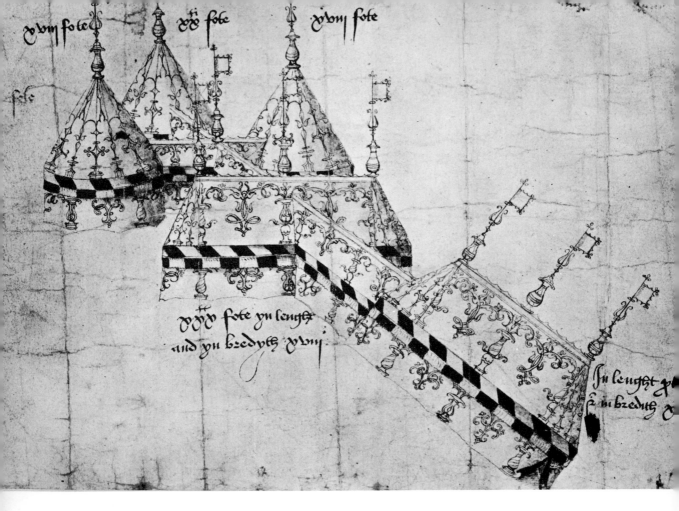

Henry took with him on this peaceful expedition to France 114 nobles, ecclesiastical peers and gentlemen, comprising Wolsey, Archbishop Warham, the dukes of Buckingham and Suffolk, the Marquess of Dorset, ten earls, five bishops, twenty barons, four knights of the Garter and seventy knights. Also in his retinue were Secretary Pace, the master of the Rolls, twelve chaplains, twelve serjeants at arms, all the kings of arms, heralds and pursuivants, 200 guards, seventy grooms of the Chamber and another 266 additional household officers. All of these brought their own servants: Wolsey extravagantly allowed himself 12 chaplains, 50 gentlemen, and 237 servants, though he only permitted the two dukes to bring 140 men apiece and the Archbishop of Canterbury a mere 70. The entire King's retinue amounted to 3,997 persons. In the King's absence, the government of the realm was entrusted to Lord Treasurer Norfolk and the Bishop of Winchester, both glad to be separated from the Cardinal. The Queen's retinue of 267 included the Earl of Derby, Bishop Fisher of Rochester, the Duchess of Buckingham, six countesses and twelve baronesses who with their servants numbered 1,175, bringing a grand total of 5,172 men and women, requiring the services of 2,865 horses. Never before had the English court moved abroad in such strength and in such style.

Petty rivalries provoked a series of disputes about the number of attendants each king should bring to the Field, about the date of the meeting

Drawing of the tents erected by Richard Gibson for Henry's encampment at the Field of Cloth of Gold, 1520.

A sword belonging to a member of the Imperial guard, left in England following Charles v's visit to Henry in June 1520, and found on the bed of the River Thames.

and the exact place where the monarchs should embrace, and there were thorny problems of precedence and etiquette and the rules under which the jousts were to be held. Most of these awkward questions were amicably settled, but there was a much greater cause for friction in that Charles v arrived at Dover from Spain on 26 May for discussions with Henry, which they agreed to continue at Calais after the Field of Cloth of Gold was over. The French were intensely suspicious of these developments, which effectively prevented the meeting between Francis and Henry from being more than a spectacular display of national rivalry.

Despite the exceptional preparations being made at Calais and Guisnes for the festivities and the fact that most of the household officials were already out of England, the Emperor was royally entertained at Dover and Canterbury during his five-day visit. At the state banquet at Canterbury 'love-lorn youths' waited at table on the Spanish ladies and, we are told, some of the Spaniards were quite overcome by amorous pursuits, like the Count of Capra, who fainted and had to be carried out. The old Duke of Alva opened the ball by dancing the *Gloves of Spain* to the tune of the fife and dancing in the Spanish fashion continued until daybreak. Charles left Sandwich for Flanders and Henry embarked at Dover for Calais on 31 May. In fact there is no evidence to convict Henry of duplicity in his negotiations, for Charles found he could not draw him to join the coming struggle against Francis.

On Corpus Christi Day Henry and Francis, supported by the greatest of their courtiers rode to opposite edges of the Val d'Or at the signal from cannon. For a tense moment they waited, as if in full battle array, and then, as trumpets sounded, the sovereigns galloped forward to the appointed place and, still mounted, embraced.

There followed feats of arms in full pageantry, with elaborate symbolism, so the men could show off their martial prowess before their ladies watching from the galleries. The challenge was in three parts: jousting at the tilt, a tournament in the open field and finally a combat on foot at the barriers, all conducted according to very precise rules, with an elaborate system of scoring. Contestants in the lists had to present their shields and issue challenges at the Tree of Honour, an artificial affair of hawthorn and raspberry (symbols of the kings) decked out with a miscellaneous array of fruits and leaves. There was a tricky moment when there was doubt among the heralds about which monarch should first hang his shield and in which position, but Henry settled the matter by causing Francis' arms to be placed on the right and his own on the left, equally high. The words of a three-part song written for Queen Catherine by William Cornish, perhaps for this very occasion, embody the conventions of the Challenge:

> My sovereign Lord for my poor sake
> Six courses at the ring did make:
> Of which four times he did it take:
> Wherefore my heart I him bequest,
> And of all other for to love best
> My sovereign Lord . . .

It is worth remembering that though the kings and their parties were the authors of the challenge, at no time did they take part in any joust or combat against each other, so that personal rivalry was avoided. When on the spur of the moment Henry asked Francis to wrestle with him, he found himself thrown to the ground in a masterly way by his opponent and was much put out. He did, however, acquit himself well in the archery contest. While the English ladies were watching the jousts they drank rather freely, passing round a large flask of wine, which each put to her lips, and also drank out of large cups, that circulated at least twenty times among them and the French nobles who kept them company; and it was the English custom of sharing the same cup, rather than the amount of wine consumed that shocked foreigners. At one banquet King Francis surpassed himself with a display of gallantry by going round the hall cap in hand kissing all the English ladies in turn, 'save four or five that were old and not fair standing together'.

At noon on Saturday 23 June a solemn mass was celebrated by Wolsey in a temporary chapel erected on the site of the lists. The choirs of the English and French Chapels Royal sang alternately and Cornish had trained his gentlemen and children to perfection; they may well have in-cluded in their repertoire a motet by Fayrefax, who was present. Before the benediction, Richard Pace faced the illustrious congregation to deliver a Latin speech on the theme that the mass heard by the two courts was to the honour of God and the Court of Heaven, to confirm good friendship, and that to mark the occasion the Cardinal would grant plenary indulgence and absolution to all present. During the mass a firework in the shape of a dragon, intended for the evening's St John's Eve festivities was accidentally set alight and caused some confusion. Afterwards Wolsey laid a foundation stone for a chapel of Our Lady of Friendship to be jointly built and main-tained by the kings of England and France. The chapel was never built. At the end of the festivities a treaty was signed confirming the proposed marriage between Mary Tudor and the Dauphin, and for ending French interference in Scottish affairs, but neither aim was achieved.

Already, before Henry had returned to Calais for his secret talks with the Emperor, Francis was preparing for another war and in 1522 Henry would enter the Hapsburg-Valois struggle as Charles's ally. Before then John Fisher, Bishop of Rochester, had preached a notable sermon, contrasting heavenly and earthly joys, in which he looked back at the high junketings and 'midsummer games' of the previous June. The cost of it all had brought monarchs and men nearer poverty, for 'never was seen in England such excess of apparelment before, as hath been used ever since'. The bill for the jousting clothes topped £3,000. He remembered the strong winds blowing dust into everyone's faces and clothes, wrecking tents and shaking the strange houses built for pleasure. As Erasmus had foretold the great gather-ing between Henry and Francis achieved nothing; the attempt at camara-derie was a sheer charade and this striking late flowering of a departed chivalry was irrelevant to the problems of a nationalistic Europe.

With Wolsey's courts at Hampton and York Place rivalling the King's in attracting aspirants to power, at times Henry felt himself deserted by officials and councillors. While he did not object to being relieved of various tasks of government, he did resent being ill-served and had it made known that courtiers must not desert him. One summer morning in 1522 Richard

Sampson had ridden to Windsor and found the King in a peevish state. Besides Master More, he asked to be sent to him 'some personages about him as well to receive strangers that shall chance to come, as also that the same strangers shall not find him so bare, without some noble and wise sage personages about him.' Once in 1520 Ruthal had gone to Wolsey's manor of the More to await the Cardinal's arrival, but found himself summoned to attend the King, then on progress in Berkshire and Wiltshire, as there were too few councillors with him, so the bishop had somewhat reluctantly to join in the 'goodly pastimes and continual hunting'. Sometimes the boot was on the other foot; the Cardinal had asked Suffolk and Devon to join him, but Suffolk excused himself, because Henry needed his company as he had 'but four or five attendants on him'. Since various of the great officers of state, the Lords Chancellor, Treasurer and Privy Seal, the Steward and Chamberlain, might be absent on important affairs, an order was made in 1526 for ensuring a regular quorum of 'councillors attendant on the King'; those so nominated were John Clerk, by now Bishop of Bath and Wells, William Knight, the new Secretary, Sir Thomas More, who had become Chancellor of the Duchy of Lancaster, and the Dean of the Chapel. 'Two of them at the least to be always present every day in the forenoon by 10 a.m. at the furthest and at afternoon by 2 p.m. in the King's dining chamber, or in such other place as shall fortune to be appointed for the Council Chamber.'

Apart from important public occasions, such as the entertainment of special embassies and the distribution of the royal Maundy, King and

Motet by William Cornish, master of the children of the Chapel Royal.

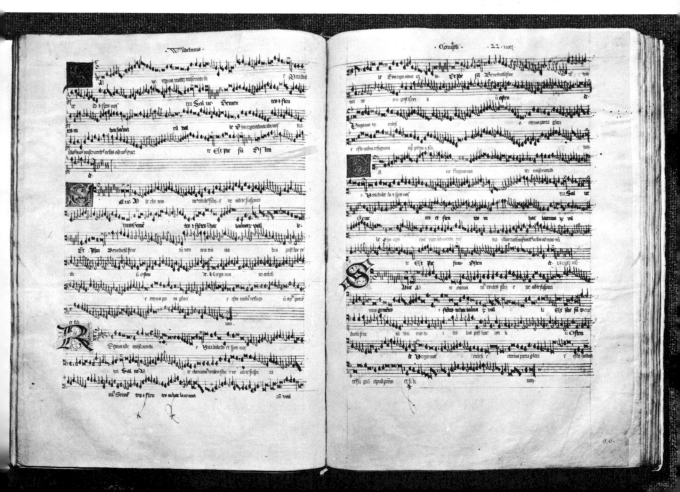

Cardinal were, in fact, very rarely together. Henry saw more of Wolsey at public worship or round the banqueting table than he saw him for private discussions. Each kept his own court. The Cardinal never accompanied the King on progress and his appearances at Greenwich and Richmond were infrequent. As a result a massive correspondence grew up between them, in which the key intermediary was the King's Secretary, who read out many of the letters forwarded by Wolsey and wrote out the replies; Wolsey's own letters Henry would generally read himself. The Secretary was often abroad on diplomatic business and Wolsey would provide a substitute. Richard Pace, a humanist and linguist of note, had been Secretary to Cardinal Bainbridge and had got into Wolsey's bad books at the time of his master's death, but Wolsey recognised his ability and took him into his own service until 1516, when he became Secretary in succession to Bishop Ruthal, now Lord Privy Seal. His Latin translation of Plutarch's *Moralia* was published in Venice in 1522, where he was on an embassy, and soon sold out. The men who acted as Secretary during Pace's absences from England with one exception had all been trained in the Cardinal's service – Richard Sampson, one of his chaplains, Sir William Fitzwilliam, whom King Henry had taught to hunt when he was a cupbearer, but whom Wolsey had singled out to be treasurer of his own household, and Brian Tuke, who had begun his career as a clerk of the Signet but now had a footing in both courts as governor of the King's posts and as Secretary to the Cardinal until, in 1522, he became French Secretary to Henry. Pace's successors as Secretary were Dr William Knight (1526) and Stephen Gardiner (1529), each of them trained at York Place. The exception was Thomas More.

More, who had entered public life with diffidence, made an immediate impression on Henry. Whenever he was at court he would send for More for invigorating conversations in his Chamber on a wide variety of topics quite unconnected with government and the two of them would often sup together informally or be joined by only the Queen. More at times found it uphill work to make Henry concentrate on his correspondence; he conveyed to Wolsey the King's admiration for the Cardinal's great labour when merely reading through the letters he had penned occupied him for over two hours and both Wolsey and More knew he had not the stamina for such feats of writing. Once, when Wolsey wanted speedy answers, Henry laughed at More: 'Nay, by my soul, that will not be; for this is my removing day for Newhall; I will read the remnant at night.' After dinner he signed two letters but procrastinated with the others. Henry did not relish the paperwork of the palace when there were more interesting pursuits on hand and Pace was amused that one day he excused himself from despatches on the grounds that he had to say matins and on the morrow said he must go off with the hounds, and when he returned he insisted on supper first and then tried to dodge the chore. The Pope may well have thought that Wolsey made Henry 'go hither and thither' and force him to sign papers without knowing their contents, but Leo x never appreciated just how hard it was to obtain the sign manual. Was it so surprising that later in life Henry resorted to having a wooden stamp made bearing his normal signature? Minor ailments, like headaches, would always be used as a good pretext for a holiday from despatches. Much of the frustration could have been avoided had Wolsey been regularly at Henry's side and by 1520,

Thomas Linacre, physician and humanist (d 1524). Henry appointed him a royal physician on his accession, and in his last months Linacre acted with the Spanish philosopher Vives as tutor to Princess Mary.

to speed decisions Wolsey would himself make a précis of foreign letters for the King's eyes. Letter writing was for Henry 'somewhat tedious and painful' and the Cardinal had to shame him into writing in his own hand to his sister Margaret, for 'women must be pleased'. The strength of his later passion for Anne Boleyn can be gauged by the number of letters he sent her. Yet despite Henry's lack of application for those aspects of kingship that bored him and despite his devotion to the chase and the Church, he was reckoned a vast improvement on the King of France who never rose before 11 a.m.; spent three hours with his mother and as long with his mistresses or out hunting, so that 'by day it was impossible to obtain an audience of him'. It was with the Cardinal, not with Henry, that it was difficult to obtain an audience.

The young hooligans of the Chamber had not in fact seduced their sovereign away from scholarly pursuits and Erasmus continued to be impressed by the intellectual development of the King and the way in which he attracted men of learning to his service. 'You would say', commented Erasmus, 'that Henry was a universal genius. He has never neglected his studies; and whenever he has leisure from his political occupations, he reads or disputes – of which he is very fond – with remarkable courtesy and unruffled temper. He is more of a companion than a King.' In another letter he wrote 'there are more men of learning to be found in Henry's court than in any university' which was 'an example to the rest of Christendom for learning and piety'. It was 'a museum more than a court' and while the humanist had little love for the courtier's life he would have been glad to return had he still been young. There was scintillating company there. Besides Henry himself there was Catherine, 'a miracle of learning, but not less pious than learned', Thomas Linacre, the King's physician, More, Master of the Court of Requests and a privy councillor, Colet, a regular preacher, Mountjoy, the Chamberlain, Richard Pace, the King's Secretary, and other humanists like Tunstall, the Master of the Rolls, and John Stokesley, the King's confessor. When More was promoted, Erasmus wrote to Tunstall: 'I should deplore More's fortune in being dragged to the court, but that under such a King and with so many learned men for companions and colleagues, it may seem not a court, but a temple of the Muses.' The French diplomats visiting Greenwich amazed Francis I's court when they returned to Paris by describing the important position Henry accorded to '*les savants*' and praised the elegance of the conversation they heard.

Thomas More, whom Colet reckoned the one genius of the kingdom, was himself a lawyer's son. His father had removed him from Oxford when he discovered Thomas was learning Greek, a subject which the elder More regarded as one of dangerous modernity, and he had placed him at Lincoln's Inn to read law. For four years he had considered whether he had a vocation to enter the priesthood, but in the end he had decided to pursue a career at the Bar, and fortunately, to marry, for his house soon became an international centre for humanist studies. Though he had written a moving elegy on Queen Elizabeth of York, his first work to attract serious attention was a translation of the Italian biography of Pico della Mirandola (1510) and the English lawyer identified himself closely with his subject, the master of the Platonic Academy in Florence, who had renounced the world to follow the reforming friar Savonarola. Later on Erasmus would write: 'In

More's household you would realise that Plato's academy was revived, except that in the academy the discussions concerned geometry and the power of numbers, whereas the house at Chelsea is a veritable school of Christian religion.' It was inevitable that so brilliant a lawyer, fast acquiring an international reputation as a scholar, should find himself drawn to the King's service and the court. Wolsey was so impressed by his advocacy in a commercial suit in the court of Star Chamber, which he won against the Crown in 1516, that he straightaway employed him in negotiations with various French merchants. From Calais More wrote to Erasmus: 'You are a wise man in keeping yourself from being mixed up in the busy trifles of princes; and it shows your love for me that you wish me rid of them; you would hardly believe how unwilling I am' to undertake such work. This mission brought him preferment at court – a seat on the King's council and the post of a master of Requests, in which he sat as judge in the 'Court of Poor men's Causes'; yet the visit to Calais also set the stage for the opening pages of *Utopia*, published later that year.

Utopia, a tract for the times, professed to be a conversation the author and his friend Peter Giles had held in Calais with a certain 'Raphael Hythlodaie' who described his recent travels to that ideal state, the island of Utopia. Here was a new-style Platonic Republic whose social organisation *ad mundum* pointed at the follies of Henrician England. In Utopia there was religious toleration, there was no poverty and no crime. Such laws as were framed were humane and were administered without need of professional lawyers. There was no distinction between town and country; more remarkable there was no money, and love of finery and pomp, like the pursuits of gambling and blood sports, were reckoned signs of social malaise. To bring home the criticism even more, there were no inherited titles and 'the court', if one could call it such, devoted itself to the pleasures of the mind. Laced with whimsy, presented in the decent garb of exquisitely-written Latin, this was a formidable essay on the abuse of power, the most powerful plan for social justice since the Gospels, and its publication lifted More to the Olympian heights.

Ten years before Holbein painted his portrait, Erasmus described More as having an open face with a clean complexion, set with blue-grey eyes and set off with auburn hair and a thin beard. Despite his wealth he lived modestly, abstaining from wine and rich fare and, though hardly a soul knew it, he wore a hair-shirt next to his flesh. He was, wrote the grammarian Robert Whittington, 'A man of an angel's wit and singular learning. I know not his fellow. For where is the man of that gentleness, lowliness and affability? And as time requireth, a man of marvellous mirth and pastimes, and sometimes of as sad gravity. A man for all seasons.' Just as More was in his character the antithesis of the vainglorious Cardinal, so his supremely happy family circle, in touch with the sovereigns of the intelligentsia, was in marked contrast to Wolsey's court at Hampton. Alice, his second wife, too old to begin studying Latin, was constantly at his side, urging him to be less of a dreamer, yet there was no incongruity. In 1521 when More became under-treasurer and was knighted, his eldest daughter, Margaret, a scholar in her own right, married William Roper, a member of the house-

Sir Thomas More, by Holbein.

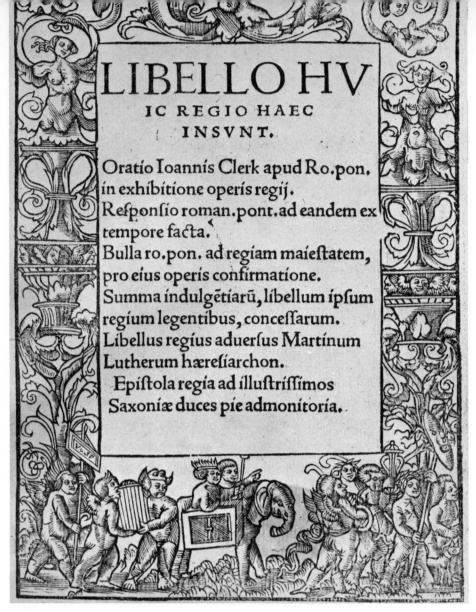

LIBELLO HV
IC REGIO HAEC
INSVNT.

Oratio Ioannis Clerk apud Ro.pon.
in exhibitione operis regij.
Responsio roman.pont.ad eandem ex
tempore facta.
Bulla ro.pon. ad regiam maiestatem,
pro eius operis confirmatione.
Summa indulgētiarū, libellum ipsum
regium legentibus, concessarum.
Libellus regius aduersus Martinum
Lutherum hæresiarchon.
   Epistola regia ad illustrissimos
Saxoniæ duces pie admonitoria.

Henry VIII's book attacking
the ideas of Martin Luther.

hold trained to the law, whom he had looked on as a son long before he became a son-in-law and had argued him out of his Lutheran tendencies. Soon after the Mores moved to Chelsea Henry paid them an unexpected visit and walked in the garden for an hour after dinner with his arm round Sir Thomas's neck. Roper was never more proud of his father-in-law, as he told him later that night, but More, deeply moved, answered that there was nothing to be proud about 'for if my head could win him [Henry] a castle in France . . . it should not fail to go.' As Norfolk warned him, it was 'perilous striving with princes'. Against his will, More's own life and that of his family had become intimately involved with King and court. Soon after Henry's visit to Chelsea he became appointed Chancellor of the Duchy of Lancaster and the same year there was a double wedding at Willesden when his daughter Elizabeth, nineteen, married William Dauncey, the son of a knight of the Body to the King, while her younger sister Cecily married Giles Heron, son of the treasurer of the Chamber.

Hans Holbein the Younger of Augsburg, who had worked in Basle for seven years as a member of the printers' guild, found patronage declining before the chill winds of the Reformation and Erasmus suggested he should visit England 'to scrape some angels together.' It seemed the most natural thing in the world for More to take the artist, with his distinctive Northern style so different from the Italians working for Wolsey, under his wing at Chelsea at the end of 1526. 'Your painter, dearest Erasmus,' he wrote, 'is a wonderful man, but I fear he will not find England so fruitful as he had hoped. Yet I will do my best to see that he does not find it absolutely barren.' More found him modest employment in executing some decorative painting for the master of the Revels, who was to provide a temporary banqueting house at Greenwich. He then commissioned him to paint portraits of himself, Dame Alice and his daughter Margaret Roper as well as a great family group, for which he made many preliminary studies (now at Windsor). Thanks to this support and introductions to Archbishop Warham and Sir Henry Guildford, the courtier, who sat and paid for portraits, Holbein was able to return to Basle next year and buy a house. Four years later he was to return to England permanently.

Henry was staying at Abingdon in 1521, with More in attendance, when he heard that a society of Trojans had been formed in neighbouring Oxford to oppose the introduction of the study of Greek. Lenten preachers at the university church had attacked humanism as likely to lead to heresy and one of them from the pulpit at Abingdon waxed long on the same theme. Afterwards Henry appointed Sir Thomas More to hold a solemn disputation with the man on the use of Greek, and once More had opened his case the don realised his own foolishness and fell on his knees to beg the King's pardon, excusing himself by saying that his words had been prompted by the Spirit. 'Not the Spirit of Christ', Henry intervened, 'but the Spirit of Folly'. Had Mr Preacher not read any of the works of Erasmus? he asked. 'Why then, you are a foolish fellow to censure what you never read.' He was allowed to depart, but the King ordered that he should never again preach before him. The man had completely misjudged the King's attitude and would have been dumbfounded had he known that Henry had recently taken part in a disputation himself, defending the use of 'mental and *ex tempore* prayer' against those who advocated that laymen should stick to the formal periods written for them by churchmen.

Wolsey had introduced the King to the works of Thomas Aquinas and suggested he tackle Duns Scotus as well as steep himself in the Early Fathers, possibly because he hoped such studies would help him to take his mind off politics. In 1517, however, Luther's *Theses* brought theological questions into the forefront of politics and Henry decided to write a tract against the monk of Wittenberg. Wolsey encouraged him, asking Pace to copy out Luther's *De Captivitate Babylonica* for the King, with a copy of the papal bull excommunicating him. Henry perhaps saw himself as the *Deus ex machina* that Erasmus had hoped would end the tragedy begun in Germany. His *Defence of the Seven Sacraments*, written in Latin, was a topical book, completed rather hurriedly, with some help from More, Fisher and Lee, and others who knew Hebrew and the byways of patristic studies, but turned by the King's pen into a most effective essay in Catholic polemics. The theology was dull, as orthodoxy so often is, but the style was lively. The future head of the English Church regretted in after years writing not a few purple passages such as this: 'What serpent so venomously crept in as he who calls the Most Holy See of Rome "Babylon", and the Pope's authority "Tyranny" and turns the name of the Most Holy Bishop of Rome into that of "Anti-Christ"?' Even more unfortunate was to be his championship of the indissolubility of marriage: 'The insipid water of concupiscence is turned by the hidden grace of God into wine of the finest flavour. Whom God has joined together, let no man put asunder.' On some days he had had to put off hunting and put aside all despatches while he wrote, verified his references and polished his Latin prose, and the Pope marvelled that he had found the time for this composition.

There had been various royal authors down the years in Western Europe, but Henry was the first to catch the flood tide of printing. As part of the publicity for the book there was a carefully stage-managed ceremony at St Paul's Cross on 12 May 1521 where, after John Fisher, Bishop of Rochester, had preached a notable sermon, Luther's works were burnt, while the Cardinal of York held for the crowd to see a manuscript copy of the King's tract. It was soon in print and copies were sent to Rome, including a magnificently bound volume for the Pope himself, and editions printed on the Continent made it a best-seller. In his dedication to Leo x in which Henry offered 'the first offspring of his intellect and his little erudition', he said he had felt it was his duty as a Christian prince to study how best to extirpate Lutheran heresy and now must testify his zeal for the faith by writing, 'that all might see he was ready to defend the Church not only with his armies, but with the resources of his mind.'

Henry's motives had not been entirely disinterested, for he was anxious to outshine the Emperor and the King of France at the papal curia and it had always irked him that whereas the former sovereign was the 'Holy' Emperor and the 'Most Catholic' King and the latter the 'Most Christian' King, he, the most loyal and orthodox son of the Church, lacked a title. Long before Luther's *Theses* there had been talk of bestowing a papal title on him – 'Protector of the Holy See', 'King Apostolic' and even 'Orthodox' were mentioned. Henry's book made a papal title inevitable and Leo x asked him for his views; as a result he settled on 'Defender of the Faith' and on 11 October 1521 the Pope's bull was issued bestowing the coveted title 'Fidei Defensor', an addition to the English royal style which was destined to survive not only the breach with Rome but even the turmoils of our most worldly of centuries. It was confirmed by the 'golden bull' in 1524 and though neither document made the title hereditary its use by subsequent kings and queens was to be warranted by an Act of Parliament of 1544. Such was a just reward for his labours and, as Wolsey was not slow to point out, Henry had shown himself to be an example to all Christian princes. A man who rushed to the defence of the Church in this way would have made a far better Holy Roman Emperor than Charles v and, there was the veiled hint, that the Cardinal who had encouraged his sovereign to action would make a worthy Pope. A good deal of the kudos had been reflected on Wolsey. Long after Wolsey had gone Henry found his youthful tract rather a liability, for its argument tied him to various doctrinal statements he could not easily retract.

One effect of Henry's resolution to pay more attention to public affairs and devote less of his time to amusements, following the removal of the 'young minions' in 1519, was his personal investigation of the running of his household, which led to his requiring the Cardinal to undertake drastic reforms. 'The King's pleasure is that his household from henceforth shall be put in honourable, substantial and profitable order, without any further delay.' Alas, Henry lost interest and it was not until 1525, when a financial crisis demanded retrenchment, that Wolsey had worked out the details, which were embodied in the Eltham Ordinance endorsed by King and council the following January. This recognised two basic weaknesses in the time-honoured system: there were too many officials at court, many of them without any definite job to do, and the frequent absence of royal servants, notably accountants on special duties such as purveyance for the army, robbed the Lord Steward of professional men essential for the good administration of his department. In short there were too many of the wrong people in the Chamberlain's list at court and too few of the right people in the Steward's list.

Henry had been lavish in granting posts in his Chamber so that there were far too many carvers, cupbearers, ushers and sewers, and all of them brought their own servants to court, to be housed and fed at the King's expense; even when some of the masters were absentee sinecurists, their servants hung on to the privilege of free board and lodging at court. Those with duties to perform too often collected their fees but discharged their

The Golden Bulla of Pope Clement VII, affixed to the papal bull of 1524, which confirmed Pope Leo X's bull of three years before, granting Henry VIII the title of Defender of the Faith, in recognition of his book against Luther.

functions by deputies and the ranks of hangers-on were swollen by servants of servants of royal servants. Brawling was commonplace among this army of pensioners, and the King's Guard was in no better state than his Chamber. Some lines of Aeneas Sylvino Piccolomini on the miseries of a courtier's life were fruitily translated at this time by the black monk, Alexander Barclay, who was no stranger to conditions at Greenwich and Richmond:

> 'And sometimes these courtiers them more to incumber
> Sleep all in one chamber near twenty in number.
> Then it is great sorrow for to abide their shout
> Some fart, some flingeth, and other snort and route
> Some boke and some bable, some commeth drunk to bed,
> Some brawl and some jangle when they be beastly fed,
> Some laugh, and some cry, each man will have his will,
> Some spew and some piss, not one of them is still.
> Never be they still till middes of the night,
> And then some brawleth and for their beddes fight.'

The chronicler Hall remarked that the 'great number of the yeoman of the guard were very chargeable and . . . there were many officers stricken in age which had servants in the court, and so the King was served with their servants and not with his own.' The supernumeraries were now dismissed, with suitable pensions as recommended by Sir Henry Guildford, the controller, so that the gentlemen of the Chamber, for instance, were reduced from one hundred and twelve to twelve, the sewers from forty-five to six and the grooms of the Chamber from sixty-nine to fifteen. 'Alas, what sorrow and what lamentation was made when all these persons should depart the court', but if the men dismissed could no longer cheat their sovereign, men said they would pillage the countryside! Henceforth ability was to be the sole criterion for filling posts at court and a ladder of promotion was devised, with weight given to seniority. Regular attendance was now obligatory, unless leave of absence had been granted, and no duties could be performed by deputy; in particular no serjeant of arms, herald, messenger, minstrel, falconer, huntsman or footman was to bring to court 'any boys or rascals'.

These reforms intimately affected King Henry. He was to have his Privy Chamber 'and inward lodgings reserved secret, at the pleasure of his Grace, without repair of any great multitude' – except for the favoured few, no courtier was to presume to cross the threshold. The staff of the Chamber were to be circumspect, careful of their language and 'expert in outward parts'. At any one time there were now fifteen of them on duty, headed by the Marquess of Exeter, Henry's first cousin, 'who has been brought up since childhood with the King'. Henry Courtenay, born in 1498, who had succeeded to his father's earldom of Devon in 1511 and taken Buckingham's place as a knight of the Garter, had been appointed 'privy councillor immediately attendant on the King' in the autumn of 1525, a few months after his promotion to the marquisate of Exeter. Under him were six gentlemen-in-waiting, two gentlemen ushers, four grooms, a barber and a page. The gentlemen-in-waiting were Sir William Taylor, Sir Thomas Cheyney, Sir Anthony Browne, Sir John Russell, Henry Norris and William Carey; the ushers were Roger Ratcliffe and Anthony Knevett, and the grooms were

William and Hirsam Brereton, Walter Welsh and John Carey. Besides Penny the barber, there was Francis Weston, a page-boy of fourteen, who in ten years' time was to lose his head as a putative lover of Anne Boleyn. These officials of the Chamber were to be 'loving together and of good unity and accord, keeping secret all such things as shall be done or said in the same.' They were not to be curious about the King's movements, not to gossip about his pastimes and habits, the company he kept, his 'late or early going to bed, or anything done by his Grace', or they would incur the King's displeasure. The gentlemen-in-waiting spent the night on the pallet inside the Chamber, to be ready in the morning to dress the King, but of the six, only Norris attended Henry in his bedchamber. The ushers reported by 7 a.m., to guard the door during the day, and the grooms by that hour had swept the Chamber, put down fresh straw and laid and lit the fire. Each morning the King's doublet, hose and shoes (though not his gown) were brought to the Chamber door by the yeoman of the wardrobe of robes and handed to one of the grooms, who would warm the garments by the fire and then deliver them to the gentlemen-in-waiting; for no groom or usher should presume to lay hands upon the royal person or interfere with the preparations for his dressing. Whenever the King was away from the Privy Chamber, the staff should not immoderately gamble at dice or cards – as happened in the groom porter's house; they could play at cards or chess, provided voices were not raised and that immediately the sovereign returned they abandoned their game. Penny, the barber, must be ready each morning with water, cloths, knives, combs and scissors, to trim King Harry's beard and hair and, because of his daily contact with him, he was required not only to be scrupulous about his cleanliness but to avoid bad company.

In the Lord Steward's 'below stairs' departments, officials were required to attend to their specific duties and no other, so that for the future it would not be possible for a clerk of the royal larder to be away from court arranging for military provisions. The laziness, which Barclay had taunted, seemed to go with the Tudor household livery – 'They have no labour yet are they well beseen, Barded and guarded in pleasant white and green' – was now outlawed. The establishment of each department was set down, with the wages and allowances for each individual and a precise statement of his or her duties. The scullions who washed up the crockery had been found to be working in most unhygienic conditions, and as most of them worked naked, the rest clad in garments of 'vileness', the master cooks were now allowed twenty marks a year to provide them with proper clothes. Leavings from the dinner plates and the dregs from tankards and glasses were no longer to be left in the courtyard for flies and vermin, but must be collected after every meal under the supervision of the almoner's staff and given to the beggars at the gate. No dogs were to be kept within the palace buildings, 'other than some few spaniels for ladies', but had to be left in the kennels, so that the palace remain 'sweet, clean and well-furnished' and the keeping of hawks, ferrets and other animals required a royal permit. There were rudimentary arrangements to prevent embezzlement and to ensure economy in fuel and lighting. Every morning by 9 a.m. the remains of all candles and torches were to be collected for re-use, instead of being pilfered or thrown away. Specimen menus were set down for each rank in the ladder of court society and there were detailed instructions about the allocation of horses; significantly 'a cardinal' when lodged at court was allowed stabling for twenty-four horses, a duke for no more than eighteen.

Changes of such magnitude involved changes in command. The old Lord Chamberlain, the Earl of Worcester, had been getting decrepit and had been too feeble either to play a part in bringing in the reforms or in trying to obstruct their introduction. Lord Sandys, the treasurer of Calais, was appointed to succeed him and, in fact, Worcester died in April 1526. In place of Sir Thomas Boleyn, Sir William Fitzwilliam became treasurer of the Household and Edmund Peckham replaced John Shurley as cofferer. Master Shurley had gone about his duties in his own quaint way and when Wolsey was working out details of the reforms had gone off to his Sussex home for the summer, setting a lamentable example to his staff.

By ancient custom all men and women who had lodgings at court were to take their main meals together in the King's hall, grouped with their servants into messes, yet just as Henry dined in state in the hall only on red letter days and fed most of the year in his Privy Chamber with his personal attendants, so other officials took to dining in their own lodgings, inviting their own guests to their table at the King's expense. By 1526 this practice of 'sundry noblemen, gentlemen and others' delighting 'to dine in corners and secret places' had become quite out of hand and as a result much of the food sent up to the hall was wasted or misused. From now on the number of tables in lodgings was limited to those of the Lord Chamberlain, the vice-Chamberlain, the Captain of the Guard and the Lord Steward, and it was to the last table that councillors, henchmen and the Steward's senior staff repaired. At one stroke the number of hangers-on who had found ways of feeding free was drastically reduced and it was possible to make stricter control over the amount of food supplied. At the same time the list of those receiving the traditional allowance of 'bouche of court', consisting of a daily ration of firewood, candles, bread, wine and beer sent to their rooms, was pruned and the amounts were firmly fixed according to rank.

Wolsey's ordinance achieved notable economies and introduced a new principle of service to the Crown which should have strengthened the *esprit de corps* of officials, high and low; yet unfortunately his reforms did not go far enough, for there was no real provision to guarantee they would be fully implemented and the notion of the chief officers of the household (steward, treasurer and controller), achieving these ends by meeting round the Board of Green Cloth only once in the whole year, shows a surprising lack of administrative grasp. It was not until thirteen years later that the root of this problem was tackled through forming an adequate organisation, with stricter control by the Board of day to day affairs.

There had never been a subject wielding so much power and living in such magnificence as the Cardinal. Two great crosses of silver were carried before him in procession, the first, a double cross, like the cross of Lorraine, as Legate, the other as Archbishop and the crucifers were the tallest priests in the realm, and also before him were borne two silver pillars and two gilt poleaxes; a handsome page walked bareheaded behind his master bearing the great seal in a silk purse. Out of doors Wolsey wore the cardinal's red-tasselled hat, but in church it was carried in procession and placed on the high altar. He rode on a mule, symbolising humility, yet the beast was decked out with costly red and gold trappings. Nearly a thousand persons were entered on his household roll, gentlemen and yeomen, chosen for their height and features no less than for their competence and devotion to Wolsey's service, grooms and clerks, and pages and choristers who valued their places at his court as the key step in a ladder of preferment that he controlled. This army of servants wore his distinctive crimson velvet livery, embroidered with a cardinal's hat – the device that even decorated his gilded bed posts. The food and other alms given to the poor who loitered at the gates of York Place and Hampton Court made the relief offered at royal palaces seem mean by comparison. Whereas Henry was always accessible, the Cardinal was withdrawn, and not even a peer of the realm could obtain an appointment except through his secretary and few were lucky enough to secure an audience before the fourth attempt. At banquets he was always served first, because he was the Pope's own representative, yet he was held in repute 'seven times more than if he were pope'; for he was 'the proudest prelate that ever breathed'.

There was a higher honour yet that Wolsey felt was his due, the papacy itself, which he had coveted for many years, and his fitness for the tiara was not far short of his ambition to wear it. In 1520 he felt assured of French support at the next election and soon the Emperor Charles v had pledged his influence, while Henry was naturally as anxious as Wolsey himself, since to have an English pope would redound to his own power and glory, and the fact that there had been no Englishman elected since Nicholas Brakespear in the twelfth century made the prize all the more worthwhile. When Leo x died in December 1521, Wolsey even offered to pay Spanish troops to overpower the conclave in Rome, but Charles double-crossed him and secured the election of his old tutor as Adrian vi. There was talk that Wolsey should entice Adrian to England where he might find the climate too severe to survive. In fact Adrian died in Rome in 1523, but Wolsey fared even worse at his second attempt, failing to secure a single vote, and once again it was the Emperor's candidate, Guilio de' Medici, who was elected as Clement vii. Adrian was the last non-Italian pope and the cardinals at Rome had disliked his asceticism; their college would not tolerate another outsider and the voice of the Defender of the Faith was drowned by the imperialists. Wolsey had never had a chance, for he failed to appreciate that the papacy had already become an Italian state. He had told Henry that he 'would rather continue to serve him than be ten popes', yet he took the second rebuff badly and never forgave Charles v. As a consolation prize he was made Legate for life, on the understanding that he would be merciful to the English friars. At the beginning of 1529 there were rumours in London that Pope Clement was seriously ill and some said he had died, and as Wolsey was now desperately clutching at straws to settle the matter of the King's divorce from Catherine, his chance of being elected as successor to the man who had blocked the divorce proceedings seemed a marvellous stroke of fortune. Eighteen years before Wolsey had said he looked on Rome as the hub of his own and his King's affairs, and now he desperately looked on attaining the papacy as the only means of satisfying his sovereign's wishes. But Clement recovered and within the year Wolsey had fallen from power.

In November 1518 Catherine gave birth to another stillborn child and it now began to seem unlikely that Henry would have a son by her. Though he pledged himself to go crusading against the Turks in return for the gift of a male heir born in wedlock, Catherine's confinement of 1518 was to be her last, and there were soon rumours about the succession. If Princess Mary married a Valois or a Hapsburg there was the terrible risk of England becoming an appendage to a Continental power and an unmarried Mary seemed an even greater hazard for the peace of the realm. Inevitably people commented about the claims the Duke of Buckingham might put forward to the Crown and the Duke became a marked man. His chancellor at Penshurst reported to Wolsey that he had heard the Duke lament the execution of the Earl of Warwick in the last days of the fifteenth century and God was now punishing Henry for his father's ruthlessness 'by not suffering the King's issue to prosper, as appeared by the death of his sons'. There was much else besides, hearsay or invention. Buckingham and Wolsey were poles apart, and the Duke was looked on as the spokesman of the higher nobility who resented the Cardinal's power, and once in a public ceremony, when he was holding the basin for the King to wash his hands, Buckingham deliberately spilt water into Wolsey's shoes. Wolsey now related to the King Buckingham's alleged treason and Henry pounced, ensuring that the Duke was found guilty by his peers of constructive treason and executed in May 1521, his only crime being descent from King Edward III.

Potential claimants and pretenders could not hope for anything more than rough justice under the Tudor monarchy. Edmund de la Pole, Earl of Suffolk, had been executed eight years earlier for his nearness to the throne and when Henry heard that his younger brother, Richard, self-styled Duke of Suffolk, had been killed at the battle of Pavia in 1525, fighting by the side of Francis I who was himself taken prisoner, he was overjoyed. The death of 'the White Rose of England' seemed a cause for especial celebration and he marked it by holding an investiture on 18 June. His illegitimate son by Elizabeth Blount became Duke of Richmond and Earl of Nottingham and of Somerset, he was assigned a full establishment of his own and was effectively being groomed for the succession. The Earl of Devon, who had become close to Henry since Brandon's match with Mary, was advanced to the marquisate of Exeter; the King's young nephew, Henry Brandon, became Earl of Lincoln; Henry, Lord Clifford, who had begun as a page and continued his service in defending the North Country against the Scots, was promoted to Earl of Cumberland; and Thomas Manners, a favourite of the King's from the days of the battle of the Spurs, became Earl of Rutland. There were two further creations: Sir Robert Radcliffe, a hard-working courtier who had lived down the disgrace of his father's execution for rising with Perkin Warbeck thirty years before, was made Viscount Fitzwalter, while Sir Thomas Boleyn, increasingly sent on diplomatic missions since leaving the post of treasurer of the Household, became Viscount Rochford. Boleyn's elder daughter, Mary, had married William Carey, a gentleman of the Privy Chamber, in 1521 and had for some years become the King's mistress, but in 1525 there was not the slightest hint the younger daughter, Anne, would before long hypnotise Henry by her beauty.

June 1525 marked a turning-point in the relations between King and

Hampton Court Palace, King Henry's drawbridge and gateway, with his personal emblems and arms.

Cardinal and their respective courts. Wolsey was forced to abandon the Amicable Loan, a euphemistically styled tax that was imposed without parliamentary sanction for meeting the costs of a proposed mission to France, and the undercurrent of opposition to the Cardinal swelled. Ballads against him circulated more freely:

> A great carl he is and fat,
> Wearing on his head a red hat.

In Oxford he was endowing Cardinal College on the site of St Frideswide's Monastery and was planning fresh alterations to the More. His own wealth emphasised the King's straitened circumstances and it was in June 1525, too, that Wolsey deemed it politic to present Hampton Court, with its rich contents to his sovereign to sustain himself in his exceptional position. Henry, who had long envied the Cardinal's great house, did not hesitate to accept so lavish a gift – the greatest, it was said, an English subject had ever made, though Wolsey still made occasional use of the residence himself.

Gradually Henry transformed Hampton, and this was not just a matter of replacing Wolsey's personal emblems with the royal arms, but a wholesale extension. Henry's great hall, with its elaborately carved roof and musicians' gallery, took five years to complete and to finish it by then masons and carpenters worked by candlelight. Antonio Toto, whom Wolsey had attracted to England, was soon painting religious pictures to embellish the palace, while Henry Blankston of Cologne was busy with decorative paintings and Galyon Hone, the Fleming who had become the King's glazier, was to be occupied at Hampton for a full ten years. Although the Cardinal's kitchen was forty-eight feet long it was thought too small for catering for a king, so a second kitchen was added. At this time, too, the chapel was embellished with a wonderful fan-vaulted wooden ceiling. Henry naturally needed facilities for sport for which Wolsey had made no provision and to the north of the palace laid out a tilt-yard, larger than that at Greenwich, though all that remains of it today is a single tower, from which the ladies of the court had watched the champions in safety. Nearby he built a closed tennis court, with twelve windows, protected by wire netting, to let in the light.

Wolsey did not consider his wings had been clipped, however, and it seemed indeed that his stature on the Continent reached a new zenith in 1527, as a result of the Hapsburg-Valois struggle in Italy. Francis I, now free from his capture at Pavia, though his eldest sons remained hostages in Spain, looked to the Cardinal as his chief support against Charles V. On St Valentine's Day Sebastian Giustinian, by now the Venetian ambassador in France, delivered an oration before the French King in which he described Wolsey as that great Lucifer following the course of the sun, King Henry VIII. This 'most invincible Lucifer' was one of the brightest stars in the heavens, 'a divinity on whom the greatest reliance might be placed on earth', since his authority was equal to that of the King's. And then, three months later, Imperial troops sacked Rome while Pope Clement remained a refugee from the Holy City at St Angelo, a puppet of the Emperor. Wolsey saw his role as that of saviour of the Church universal, the greatest of prelates, a truly international figure above the strife who might impose a permanent peace settlement.

The roof of the Great Hall at Hampton Court, built by Henry from 1525–30.

Yet within two years Lucifer had fallen, cast down by his master whom he had failed. As a desperate gesture to save himself Wolsey made a greater benefaction than Hampton Court, and his York Place became Henry's Whitehall. The proud prelate, despite his exceptional power in Church and State and his unprecedented legatine authority from the Pope, had shown himself incapable of securing for Henry the divorce he demanded, to enable him to marry Anne Boleyn, and Wolsey's grand edifice as arbiter of Europe and *alter rex* of England, collapsed like a house of cards. Lucifer the bringer of light had been transformed by his King into Lucifer the doomed archangel, cast into everlasting torment. Like a king, Wolsey had already planned his tomb and commissioned Benedetto da Rovezzano of Florence (who had worked in France on the tombs of the dukes of Orléans) to devise one that should be no less superb than the tomb Torrigiano had made for Henry VII, and like a king he intended burial at Windsor. Work had begun on the sarcophagus of black marble on which would lie a recumbent statue of the cardinal in golden bronze, and at the corners of the platform on which it was to stand were to be four great pillars of bronze, nine feet high, each supporting an angel bearing a candlestick, while another four angels were to kneel at the head and foot of the tomb, bearing the legatine pillars, the archiepiscopal cross and the cardinal's hat. It remained unfinished, like all Wolsey's work.

King Henry's kitchen at Hampton Court, which dwarfed the kitchens built for Wolsey.

The ornate ceiling of the Chapel Royal, Hampton Court.

98

3 Lady in waiting

'Mademoiselle Boleyn has come to the Court at London and the King has set her in a very fine lodging, which he has furnished very near his own. Greater court is paid to her every day than has been for a long time paid to the Queen.'

Cardinal Du Bellay, French Ambassador in London (Dec. 1528)

There was to be another court, to challenge Queen Catherine's household within the palace itself, and to extinguish the Cardinal's rival court. Some time between the end of 1525 and the middle of 1526 Henry fell passionately in love with Anne Boleyn. She refused the undignified role of mistress that had satisfied both her elder sister Mary, during the previous four years, and Elizabeth Blount before her, as she had set her heart on a crown. Catherine refused to acknowledge that her marriage to her royal brother-in-law had been unlawful and would not give up her crown and her husband for a nunnery, while Wolsey failed to obtain from the Pope the divorce which Henry insisted was his natural right. In consequence 'the King's Great Matter', fraught with immense consequences, dominated the life of the English court for six years.

The Boleyns had been adept at social climbing. Anne's great-grandfather had been a London mercer who became Lord Mayor in 1457, but her grandfather had given up commerce for developing his estates in Norfolk from his mansion at Blickling and had married Margaret Butler, the Earl of Ormonde's daughter. Sir Thomas Boleyn, her father, who was a younger son, looked higher and succeeded in allying himself to a Howard, for when Thomas, Earl of Surrey was still in disgrace for fighting on the wrong side at Bosworth and consequently deprived of his estates, he was in no position to frown on marrying one of his eighteen children to a wealthy landowner, with a fine home at Hever in Kent. Boleyn money helped the Howards and Butlers in their hours of difficulty and proved a remarkably sound investment. Elizabeth Howard bore Sir Thomas three children and though their dates of birth and even their order in the family remain uncertain it is most probable that Mary was born in 1503, George in 1505 and Anne two years later. Already, before the full restitution of the Howards, Sir Thomas Boleyn had succeeded in making his mark at court so that he had been created a knight of the Bath at Henry's coronation and was soon employed

Anne Boleyn: portrait by an unknown artist.

Hever Castle, Kent, the home of the Boleyn family; a view from the west.

The Habsburg Charles v, Holy Roman Emperor (1519–55), a portrait by Titian.

on diplomatic missions which enabled him to give his elder daughter the opportunity of experience in foreign courts. Mary went first to spend some months at Brussels under the wing of its brilliant Regent, Margaret of Austria, and then in 1514, when Mary Tudor went to France to marry Louis XII, the eleven-year-old girl was included in her train as a maid of honour. When Louis sent most of the English ladies home, Mary Boleyn was allowed to remain at court and on the King's death she stayed on at the palace with the new Queen of France, who was herself a mere seventeen. Queen Claude's household was then the most exclusive finishing school for young ladies in Europe and after Sir Thomas Boleyn became Henry's ambassador to France he arranged for Anne, by now aged twelve, to join her sister. Here she learnt the graces of deportment, dancing, polite conversation and high fashion and the intricacies of etiquette, and according to tradition Henry VIII first set eyes on both Boleyn girls at the Field of Cloth of Gold. Mary Boleyn already had gained (or rather had already lost) a reputation among the French gallants before she returned to Hever, for years afterwards Francis I remembered her as 'a hackney'. Mary married William Carey, one of the Privy Chamber, and almost at once became the King's mistress.

Anne had stayed on in Paris until she was called home in 1522, when a fresh war with France threatened, and a place was found for her at the English court, where her father was now treasurer of the Household,

though she spent much of the year at Hever Castle. Having spent the impressionable years of adolescence under Queen Claude, Anne seemed more French than English by upbringing and a French poet wrote that she was such a graceful maiden that no one would have believed she was in fact English. At a pageant masque given by Wolsey for the Imperial ambassadors in March 1522, Anne Boleyn was one of the beautiful maidens imprisoned in the 'Château Vert', duly rescued by the King, appropriately playing the role of 'Ardent Desire'. She knew sufficient from her sister about Henry's desires, and it was his liaison with Mary that helped their father's elevation to the peerage as Viscount Rochford in June 1525, on the same day that Henry Fitzroy became Duke of Richmond. An avaricious man, eager to rise higher as much for the sake of the money that important offices brought in as for the ambition of holding them, Sir Thomas was prepared to sacrifice any daughter who could increase the King's favour towards his family.

Henry had by then despaired of Catherine producing a son and the honours lavished on the six-year-old Richmond marked him out as heir presumptive to the throne, while his half-sister, Princess Mary, herself only nine, was required to leave her mother to go to Ludlow Castle and hold court as Princess of Wales. Catherine complained of these indignities to herself and Mary, but worse was to come, for Wolsey now took the opportunity of removing from the Queen's household staff three women he knew to be against him and as Henry refused to countermand the Cardinal, she was now seriously isolated from her friends. Even before the King discovered Anne he was contemplating a divorce from Catherine, to enable him to marry someone who could give him a legitimate heir.

Mistress Boleyn was no dazzling beauty, ripening in her teens to fluster every man who set eyes on her, as Bessie Blount had been. Her strong points were her raven black hair and her black, almond-shaped eyes; some thought her neck too long and her complexion too sallow for an Englishwoman, others would find nothing in her appearance to praise but went out of their way to remark on the rudimentary sixth finger on her left hand – a sinister sign suggesting a sorceress, they said – which she was able to conceal with her other fingers and by deft use of the folds of her dress. Perhaps the most balanced picture of her is that of an Italian, in 1532, when she was twenty-six: 'Mistress Anne is not one of the handsomest women in the world; she is of middling stature, swarthy complexion, long neck, wide mouth, bosom not much raised and, in fact, has nothing but the English King's appetite, and her eyes, which are black and beautiful'. Yet she exercised an unprecedented fascination over Henry that can scarcely be explained in rational terms and so used was he to getting his own way that the more unattainable she seemed, the more desperately he wanted her as wife and Queen. With her vivacity she had dared to insist on marriage.

Henry was not the first to fall under her spell, for a Kentish neighbour's son, young Thomas Wyatt, secretly already a poet, had cause to regret his marriage at seventeen to Lord Cobham's daughter, when he saw his cousin Anne again after her long sojourn in France. Wyatt's father, Sir Henry, who had been in the Tower long ago for resisting the pretensions of Richard III, had been a councillor since 1509, and was now treasurer of the Chamber. Thomas was often at court with him, became appointed an esquire of the

Sir Thomas Boleyn, Earl of Wiltshire and Ormonde (1477–1539), Lord Privy Seal and father of Anne Boleyn.

Body and showed himself to the King's delight to be an accomplished courtier as wit, lutanist and deviser of masques. Later he left on a mission to Italy under Sir John Russell and although he was kept busy when Russell broke his leg there was still time to immerse himself in Renaissance literature and begin a detailed study of Petrarch's sonnets. Almost to the end of Anne's life Wyatt continued to flirt with his cousin and he wrote a whimsical verse 'Of his Love, called Anna' that was not published until many years afterwards.

> What word is that, that changeth not
>   Though it be turn'd and made in twain?
> It is mine Anna, God it wot,
>   And eke the causes of my pain,
>   Who love rewardeth with distain;
> Yet is it loved; what would ye more?
> It is my health, and eke my sore.

The story is told by Wyatt's grandson that one day, in 1527 or 1528, the poet playfully stole a locket from Anne, which he insisted on keeping as a trophy, and the same week the King confiscated a ring of hers which he thereafter wore on his little finger. Playing bowls with Wyatt and others a day or so later, Henry declared he had won the final throw, pointing to the wood with the ringed finger and, with a knowing look at Wyatt, said 'I tell thee it is mine'. Wyatt at once countered by asking leave to measure the throw, to claim it as his, and took off the locket to use it for measuring the distance between the wood and the jack. Henry felt he was trumped and strode off, muttering he had been deceived. Before long Thomas would be penning his poem 'The Lover despairing to attain unto his Lady's grace, relinquisheth the pursuit', with the fearsome logic of the final lines:

> Who list her hunt, I put him out of doubt
>   As well as I, may spend his time in vain!
>   And graven with diamonds in letters plain,
> There is written her fair neck round about:
>   'Noli me tangere; for Caesar's I am,
>   And wild for to hold, though I seem tame.'

Another, more serious suitor, was Sir Henry Percy, heir to the earldom of Northumberland, who was serving an apprenticeship in politics in Wolsey's household. Percy fell head over heels in love with Anne Boleyn and, one gathers, she would gladly have married him, but he was already engaged to Lady Mary Talbot, the Earl of Shrewsbury's youngest daughter. When the youth asked Wolsey if this match could be broken off he was firmly rated for his foolishness, and when he persisted in his obstinacy the Cardinal sent for the Earl who took his son back with him to the North. This incident accounts for Anne's venomous dislike of Wolsey and perhaps the reason for his acting so forcibly was because he knew the lady had already attracted the King's attention.

Most of the batch of love-letters between Henry and Anne belong to 1527. Henry complains of their being apart, counts the days till they see each other again and sends her his warmest affections and his portrait done in a bracelet; 'Written with the hand of that Secretary who in heart, body

A holograph letter from Henry to Anne Boleyn, September 1528, telling her of the imminent arrival of Cardinal Campeggio, whom they both expected to annul Henry's marriage with Catherine of Aragon. He tells Anne, 'I would you were in mine arms, or I in yours, for I think it long since I kissed you'.

and will is Your loyal and most ensured servant, H autre AB ne cherce R.'

Her replies have not survived, though she sent him a present of a jewelled 'ship in which the solitary damsel is tossed about', and yet her answers to his professions of love were surely ambiguous as well as discreet, with a dash of the provocative. Henry in desperation asked – (though the questions so hard to ask outright, were decently veiled in French) – that

you will expressly certify me of your whole mind concerning the love between us two. For of necessity I must ensure me of this answer, having been now above one whole year struck with the dart of love, not being assured either of failure, or of finding place in your heart and grounded affection. Which last point has kept me for some little time from calling you my mistress, since if you love me in none other sort save that of common affection, that name in no wise belongs to you, for it denotes a singular love, far removed from the common. But if it shall please you to do me the office of a true loyal mistress and friend, and to give yourself up, body and soul, to me . . . I will take you for my only mistress, rejecting from thought and affection all others save yourself, to serve you only.

Anne was playing for the highest stakes; it was to be marriage, or nothing at all and, once Henry had grasped that, he became convinced he only wanted her as a wife and the mother of England's heir; indeed he soon saw himself as the chivalrous knight protecting the same 'virtue' that she had so vigorously defended herself. Neither realised their affair would drag on so long unconsummated. In February 1528 he had told her that with the negotiations now in hand 'shortly, you and I shall have our desired end', yet however slight the delay, it would be 'not so soon as I would it were'. All the unexpected difficulties Henry encountered in achieving his divorce from Catherine over the next five years merely made him long more fervently for Anne as a true wife. Their trysts became known to those with their eyes and ears open and even in August 1527 Mendoza was writing from London to

Charles v: 'In truth the King is so swayed by his passions . . . It is generally believed that if he can obtain a divorce he will end by marrying a daughter of Master Boleyn.' Anne became installed in apartments near her lover's and Catherine put on a brave face of knowing nothing about their relationship. That autumn Anne refused to leave the Chamber when Wolsey was announced for private discussions with Henry and she said to the messenger in a pique, 'Where else is the Cardinal to come? Tell him that he may come here, where the King is'. For decency's sake she often supped by herself and at Windsor Henry would have courses sent down to her room. When she asked Thomas Heneage to write to Wolsey to send her tasty fare such 'as carps, shrimps or other', he asked the Cardinal to excuse his boldness in passing on the request – 'it is the conceit and mind of a woman'. She was imperious even now.

The great disrupter of the ordered life of the court was the plague and when it forced Henry and Anne to be apart, as in 1528, the King dwelt on his great loneliness – 'wishing myself (specially on evening) in my sweetheart's arms, whose pretty dukkys I trust shortly to kiss', as he fondly told her. That hot summer brought a severe epidemic of the 'sweating sickness', and the court broke up, for Henry was terrified of falling a victim himself. The symptoms were frightening, for the danger-point could swiftly be reached: 'One has a little pain in the head and heart; suddenly a sweat breaks out and a physician is useless, for whether you wrap yourself up much or little, in four hours, sometimes in two or three, you are despatched without languishing.' Henry left Greenwich in a hurry with a handful of attendants for Waltham and as one of Anne's own maids had caught the infection he sent her to Hever Castle, her father's home, where indeed she was ill herself, as well as her brother, and he wrote tenderly, sending her one of his physicians, Dr Butts. He reminded her that women escaped the infection more readily than men and that no woman from the court – and few outside it – had actually died of the plague. Her uncle, Lord Treasurer Norfolk, caught it but survived, yet three of Henry's most favoured friends from the Chamber died – Compton, Poyntz and William Carey, husband of Anne's sister Mary. Eighteen members of Archbishop Warham's household died within four hours and Wolsey, who had escaped to the More, little less alarmed than his master, lost a score of retainers. Henry moved on from Waltham to Hunsdon Manor, in Hertfordshire, which he had purchased in 1520 specifically as a country retreat from the plague, and here he seemed quite safe; 'Laud be Jesu', wrote one of his faithful followers, 'the King's Grace is very merry since he came to this house, for there was none fell sick of the sweat since'. From Hunsdon Brian Tuke wrote to the Cardinal, on the King's behalf, advising him to follow his own procedure for avoiding infection: keep out of all places where there is the slightest risk, and if anyone falls victim, move on speedily to another residence, freshly cleansed. 'His Highness desireth your Grace to use small suppers and to drink little wine . . . and once in the week to use the pills of Rasis', and if he did become ill he was to ask his physician to prepare a posset with clarified herbs that would help him to sweat moderately and continuously

By the spring of 1527 study of the Scriptures had convinced Henry that in the eyes of the Church he was a bachelor. To him the interpretation of

Leviticus chapter xx verse 21 was absolutely clear: he had been living in sin for eighteen years with his deceased brother's wife and God had given judgment by denying him a son. This burden on his conscience was becoming unsupportable and he prayed for relief. He saw at last the significance of the 'protest' he had been made to enter, about marrying Catherine, in 1505 and questioned the validity of the papal bull. No argument, no word of consolation from the Pope himself, would satisfy Henry. He needed a son born in wedlock, who could ultimately succeed to his throne unchallenged and to provide England with this male heir, he must have his marriage with Catherine annulled to enable him to marry again. It was fortuitous in his view that he had already found a successor in Anne, with whom he was deeply in love, but he was absolutely sure that the need for a legitimate son came before any desire for Anne. Nothing would shake him from his new-found conviction that Catherine had never been his lawful wife; and he would not see that the very argument on which he was rejecting Catherine made Anne an equally unsuitable successor, for Anne's sister Mary had been Henry's mistress.

A plan was agreed upon whereby, early in May, Wolsey and Warham came to Greenwich Palace requiring Henry to appear as a defendant in the Legate's Court at York House on the 17th to answer the validity of his marriage. These collusive proceedings were kept secret, especially from Catherine, and the proctors appearing for and against the royal union were all discreet members of the King's household. Wolsey found the marriage open to doubt and pronounced the case so complicated that it must be submitted to eminent theologians and skilled canon lawyers. This meant that the Pope's consent must be secured. As the Spanish ambassador had caught wind of the affair, on 22 June it was decided that Henry must tell Catherine himself of their need to separate, and as he had feared she was tearful and obstinate.

He had left it too late. Already while the court was in session news came of the sack of Rome, leaving Clement VII at the mercy of Charles V and Catherine saw as her salvation a direct appeal to her Imperial nephew. She commissioned Francesco Felipez, a sewer in her household, which he had entered long ago as a page, to travel secretly to Spain and a passport was secured for him. He eluded arrest and by the end of July was at Valladolid conveying Catherine's troubles to the Emperor, as a result of which it was clear that the proceedings would be removed from London to Rome. The most now that Clement would do for Henry was to agree to a dispensation permitting his remarriage *if* his marriage with Catherine should prove to be invalid.

We need not pursue the labyrinthine diplomacy of 'the King's Great Matter'. Henry assured Clement of his fidelity and reverence for the Apostolic See and asked for his aid as a favour 'which ought not and cannot be justly denied to our piety'. At different times, in an attempt to avoid taking responsibility, the Pope suggested Henry should obtain a sentence from the English courts, re-marry and subsequently test the validity of that union at Rome, but the King saw no merit in a scheme that left in doubt the legitimacy of children by a second marriage. Clement also worked hard to persuade Catherine to enter a nunnery, but to no avail, and only when all efforts at compromise failed he at last issued a commission jointly to Wolsey

Pope Clement VII, Guilio de' Medici, who ruled the papacy 1523–34.

and Cardinal Campeggio, with secret instructions to the latter to proceed as slowly as possible and forbidding him to pronounce an opinion without further orders. Once, in 1519, Wolsey had kept Campeggio waiting, but now the boot was on the other foot; it was not until October 1528 that he arrived in England and not until 31 May following that the Legatine Court opened at the Blackfriars. Henry's sister, Margaret of Scotland, had succeeded in having her broken marriage with the Earl of Angus annulled, to enable her to marry Henry Stewart – 'a shameless sentence from Rome', remarked her brother – for it outraged his sense of decency, and while he tried to cut the Gordian knot of his own matrimonial tangle, he lectured Margaret in high terms on the divine ordinance of inseparable matrimony.

Conflicting biblical teaching about a man's relations with his widowed sister-in-law provided a field day for theologians of the Reformation era, who were well-versed in the niceties of controversy and tended to find in the Scriptures just those statements which would confirm the positions they had already taken up. For years learned men would argue whether or not the words of Leviticus had been abrogated by the teaching of Deuteronomy, whether or not the law of Moses was binding on Christians, whether or not the Bible was giving anything more rigid than general theoretical guidance in matrimonial affairs. In the welter of opinions the chance of Henry receiving a straightforward answer to his own practical problem was remote, though he never could understand why this should be.

Campeggio was lodged in the Duke of Suffolk's London house, which made an uneasy residence, for Suffolk was one of Henry's staunchest partisans and a key witness, since in November 1501 he had attended young Arthur on the morrow of his wedding and with Dorset and Sir Arthur Willoughby provided circumstantial evidence that the Prince's marriage with Catherine had been consummated. Catherine had protested at the competence of the Legatine Court, largely because she was sure of Wolsey's partiality, yet she duly appeared and made a moving appeal to the plaintiff, not the judges, to protest now at the fate of being cast aside. She had been 'a true, humble and obedient wife, ever comfortable to your will and pleasure. . . . This twenty years I have been your true wife and by me ye have had divers children . . . And when ye had me at the first, I take God to be my judge, I was a true maid without taint of man. And whether this be true or no, I put it to your conscience'. There was more, but Henry kept silent, and when the Queen had finished she curtseyed and left the great hall.

On 23 July the court at the Blackfriars was crowded, for a judgment was expected. Henry himself, courtiers, bishops and nobles hung on the Italian's words, when the King's proctor demanded sentence. Campeggio rose and in a brief statement announced that the court would be adjourned until 1 October, for the vacation. This was more than mere procrastination. All interpreted it as ending the King's chances of obtaining a divorce through a papal court and signalling Wolsey's fall. Suffolk spoke what was in Henry's mind when he banged his fist on the table and cried out, 'By the mass, now I see that the old said saw is true, that never a cardinal or legate did good in England.' Henry retired to Greenwich and before the end of the week had appointed Stephen Gardiner his Secretary. The King had heard that Clement had definitely signed the revocation of the suit to Rome and in this new situation he decided to summon Parliament to meet in November

The seal of Cardinal Lorenzo Campeggio, sent by Pope Clement VII as legate to preside with Wolsey over the ecclesiastical court at Blackfriars to hear the matrimonial dispute between King and Queen.

and also to accept the advice of a Cambridge cleric, Thomas Cranmer, that he should seek the opinion of the universities on the question of his divorce.

Wolsey was denied access to his master and after fifteen years of unprecedented power was to be pushed aside. 'The Dukes of Norfolk and Suffolk and others lead the King to think that he has not advanced the King's affairs as much as he could have done', wrote the French ambassador. The King's attorney preferred an indictment against the Cardinal in the Court of King's Bench for receiving bulls from Rome in contravention of the Statutes of Provisions and Praemunire and he acknowledged himself liable to the penalties. On Sunday 17 October he was dismissed from the chancellorship when Norfolk and Suffolk came to York House demanding the surrender of the great seal, but Wolsey required written authority from the King, so the dukes returned to Windsor and it was not until the next day that he delivered the seal to the master of the Rolls. He retained his archbishopric of York and set out for the north to the diocese he had never visited and was preparing for his enthronement at York Minster the following November when he was arrested for treason, in that he had asked both Francis I and Charles V to intervene with Henry to save him. He was spared a state trial, with the verdict a foregone conclusion, as he died on his slow progress south, at Leicester Abbey, on 29 November. Never again would England tolerate a cardinal's rule, for the wave of anti-clericalism was unprecedented.

The Church the Cardinal had embodied was rich, worldly and uncaring and everyone had his or her own private grudges. The laws administered by the ecclesiastical courts, which governed more than half of a layman's life, were oppressive and the fees heavy, whether it was for a poor man's burial, for the probate of a merchant's will or for a matrimonial cause. The priests, so long a caste apart, freed from the secular courts, now began to be hated for their exclusiveness, said Reginald Pole, and Cardinal Campeggio, fearing the danger from Parliament, implored Henry to save the Church from ruin.

With the end of Wolsey, those who had led the pack to hound him reaped their rewards. When he had been slow to leave London for York in 1529, Norfolk had ordered Thomas Cromwell, Wolsey's steward, to tell him 'If he go not away, I will tear him with my teeth.' Suffolk's name was suggested for the chancellorship, but Norfolk objected, for it would have given too much power to an already powerful councillor, so instead Suffolk became Lord President. Anne Boleyn's father was advanced to the earldom of Wiltshire and appointed Lord Privy Seal. As an ecclesiastic, Bishop Tunstall was reckoned quite unsuitable for the chancellorship and so the great seal passed to a layman and common lawyer of distinction, Sir Thomas More, whom Henry knew well and respected.

Even shorn of the cardinalate and all the other clerical posts and powers which Wolsey had engrossed, the Lord Chancellor was still the first minister in the kingdom and More was an obvious choice, for he was a man of international reputation. He had at first refused. The King's Great Matter weighed heavily on his own scruples, but Henry assured him that he need play no part in this, which would be handled only by servants 'whose consciences could well enough agree therein'. Let the new Chancellor 'look first unto God, and after God unto him'. Chapuys considered 'there never was or will be, a Chancellor as honest and so thoroughly accomplished as he.' Yet Henry was not to keep his promise and after two and a half years More felt he could no longer retain his high office in all conscience and quitted public life. Even then Henry would not let him alone. He could not allow the humanist to take a neutral position, but said he must declare himself; if he would just genuflect before the altar of Henrician supremacy, all would be forgiven, but Thomas More steadfastly refused to take the Oath of Succession and was to be caught by the full vigour of a new Treasons Act.

For the sake of appearances King and Queen were together for a few important occasions but Catherine mostly kept to her own apartments. When they dined together in state on St Andrew's Day, 1529, she told him he was treating her badly, for he rarely invited her to sup with him and never set foot in her quarters, so he defended himself by reminding her that she remained mistress in her own household where she could 'do what she pleased'. The conversation drifted to the proceedings in the Legatine Court and Catherine held her own in argument about the Pope's power. Exhausted by the scene, Henry crossed over to visit Anne, hoping for some words of comfort, but she was as irritable as Catherine, telling him the Queen would always get the better of him in argument and what was wanting was action. She told him that in waiting for him to become a free man, she had said farewell to her youth and looks 'to no purpose at all', when she might have made an advantageous marriage. Those were, truly, exasperating days for the three of them. Only a month before Henry had brought Anne secretly to York Place to view the mansion that the Cardinal had speedily vacated, and the fine tapestries and plate were shown to them. The splendour of it all thrilled Anne and she told Henry that this should be their London house, for there were no quarters there suitable for Catherine. Great changes were put in hand to enlarge the new Whitehall and satisfy Anne's fastidious requirements. Neighbouring houses were compulsorily acquired to extend the site and make room for gardens. 'All this has been done', reported Chapuys to Charles v, 'to please the lady, who likes better that the King should stay' in Whitehall than anywhere else, 'as there is no lodging in it for the Queen.'

Wyngaerde's view of Whitehall Palace, from the River Thames.

Henry was to put his acquisition of York Place on a legal footing with the next archbishop of York, but meanwhile development proceeded and in the year beginning April 1531 he spent £8,151 2s. 7d. on rebuilding what he now regarded as Anne's palace, but which was destined to become the principal setting for the Tudor monarchy. When he left it, the new Whitehall would extend over twenty-three acres – twice the size of Pope Clement's Vatican. His chief surveyors, Thomas Heritage and Thomas Alvard, were ordered to demolish the old buildings at Westminster Palace that had never been repaired following the great fire, eighteen years before, and to take down the royal mews at Charing Cross, which disfigured the site Henry wanted to develop. Materials from these buildings and from the old manor of Kennington were to be used where appropriate at Whitehall. Abbot Islip of Westminster was prevailed upon to exchange with the King various properties that the Abbey owned on the east and west sides of King Street, including the Axe Brewery, for lands and an advowson outside London. Thomas Swalowe rode around the shires taking up workmen for the King's service and soon there were 382 labourers demolishing old houses that hampered the proposed extensions, and Thomas Cromwell chided the Abbot of Bury St Edmunds for retaining masons and other craftsmen that were required at Westminster. Caen stone came not only from Normandy, but also from Wolsey's college at Ipswich, and other materials were removed from the Cardinal's former properties at Kingston and Esher; for instance the new gallery at Esher was taken down in sections, carted to Westminster for re-assembly in St James's Park and erected at Whitehall as the Privy Gallery. Henry's instructions were that the principal lodgings were to be fully furnished and ready for occupation by mid-October 1532, as their principal residence.

Wolsey's memory had to be effaced and so in place of the device of a cardinal's hat, Whitehall was embellished inside and out with the King's arms under crowns imperial, supported by royal beasts. On the new gate-house, built across the highway from Charing Cross to Westminster (sub-sequently called the Holbein Gate) were 'two fleur de lys in freestone with large branches of roses, together with the King's posie', wrought under-neath. All the bay windows bore the King's badges, so that Henry could indeed stamp Whitehall with his own personality, and with all this heraldic painting there was much work for immigrant artists, like Lucas Horenbout from Ghent. It was essentially a waterside palace. Henry constructed a new embankment on the Thames, running about one hundred and sixty feet west of the present Victoria Embankment, as a safeguard against flooding, with his own Privy Stairs; the existing Whitehall Stairs had been a public landing place and no more than the Cardinal did the King contemplate inter-fering with this amenity or stopping the right of access through the Palace to Whitehall Gate. The fact that people could walk at will through the precincts gave Whitehall quite a different character from Greenwich or Richmond, for apart from the large number of courtiers and officials for whom there were lodgings in the palace, there were always ordinary folk about to form the 'gallery' at both semi-private and public events, rather than to be on hand as a stage crowd.

The Whitehall gateway, blocking the road, linked the old buildings with the new and over it ran the wooden Privy Gallery, taken from Esher, and at

'The Holbein Gate', Whitehall – also known as the 'Cockpit Gate'. The theory that it was designed by the artist is unfounded, for it was almost finished in 1532, before Holbein entered Henry's service. Possibly at a later date he had rooms over the gate-way.

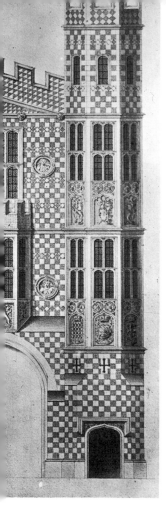

A reconstruction of the plan of the Tudor Palace of Whitehall, superimposed on a modern street plan of the vast area it covered.

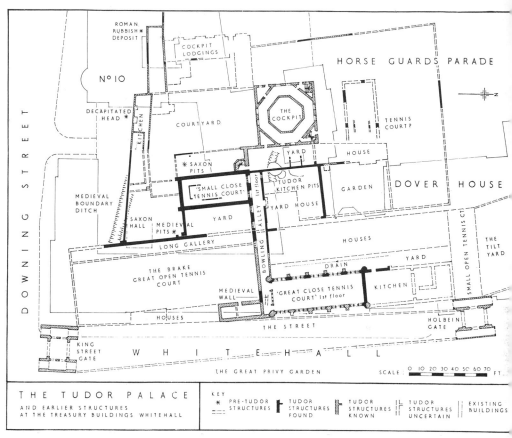

THE TUDOR PALACE
AND EARLIER STRUCTURES
AT THE TREASURY BUILDINGS WHITEHALL

KEY
* PRE-TUDOR STRUCTURES

TUDOR STRUCTURES FOUND
TUDOR STRUCTURES KNOWN
TUDOR STRUCTURES UNCERTAIN
EXISTING BUILDINGS

the eastern end this joined the Stone Gallery, running south. Above this Stone Gallery was built the Long Gallery, with a ceiling that was later to be decorated by Hans Holbein. At the southern end of the highway, along which again there was public access, was now constructed the King Street Gate. South of the Privy Gallery lay the orchard, and north of it the Privy Garden, which was laid out as one of the earliest formal gardens in England. Only the north-east of the entire site had been occupied by Wolsey's palace and Henry necessarily kept the chapel and great hall, but built over the rest of the grounds there in a piecemeal way. Besides a study there was also the King's library and immediately underneath were the chambers assigned to Anne, with the fine desk Henry had had gilded for her. Among the courtiers to be allocated the first sets of rooms available were Anne's father, now Earl of Wiltshire, and the faithful Thomas Heneage. As other buildings went up around the courtyards accommodation was gradually found for greater numbers of courtiers and officials than at any other English palace, or indeed at any other official residence in the world. On the west side of the street, overlooking the park, were built the cockpit, the tennis court and (on the site of the present Horse Guards) the tilt-yard.

This palace of Whitehall, symbolising the power of the new monarchy, was to be regally completed over the years, with additional buildings sprawling over the site. Nor was this all. To round off the site on the west

Henry in 1532 acquired the hospital of St James, which stood in open fields. This was by foundation a religious house for leprous women who, despite their affliction, lived 'chastely and honestly in divine service'. It was still a lonely spot, rather suited for an isolation hospital, yet leprosy was by then mercifully rare and only three widows and an aged spinster were living there, each receiving the traditional allowance of £2 12s. od. and a quarter of a barrel of best beer a year. Henry dissolved the foundation, pensioned off the women, pulled down the hospital and next year started building another palace round four courts. Over the gateway was a clock tower, with octagonal turrets, designed by John Molten, and decorated with the Tudor rose and the initials 'H' and 'A'; and soon a much more splendid chapel than Wolsey's building at Whitehall would rise here. The new palace, five minutes walk across the park from Whitehall, retained the name of the hospital's patron saint, St James.

Few can remain impartial in matrimonial disputes and so Henry's decision to put away his Queen initially split the court, just as it divided subjects at large. In the royal family itself, Henry's sister Mary stood by the Queen, while her husband, Suffolk, was one of Henry's chief supporters. Norfolk never ceased from furthering the chances of his niece to become Queen, and yet his Duchess, sickened by his liaison with their children's laundress, Bess Holland, remained faithful to Catherine. By birth a Stafford, the Duchess never could forget the execution of her father Buckingham, England's premier duke, in 1521 on charges trumped up by Wolsey for being too near the Crown in blood; if all the world tried to draw her over to Anne's side, she said, she would never give in and, indeed, she was to refuse to attend Anne's coronation. It was, however, hard for many to resist the pressures which the King could exert and for every John Fisher who stayed loyal to Catherine there was an Edmund Bonner and a Stephen Gardiner who went over to Henry. 'Leave of absence is never refused from court to those who take the Queen's part', it was noted in 1531 and once Catherine was banished to the More, and then to Ampthill, Henry could begin to make drastic reductions in her household, though even that November she was attended by '30 maids of honour with 50 more young ladies to wait at table' and 200 others in the wings. Too few of the royal household stuck to their principles like Controller Guildford. He had been rated by Anne Boleyn for his opposition to her and she warned him that when she became Queen, as she was certain she would, she would have him dismissed, but Guildford resigned his office forthwith and refused Henry's request to reconsider his decision. Despite Henry's support from the universities, led by men like Robert Wakefield the Cambridge canonist and Hebrew scholar (whose pupils included Reginald Pole), the most distinguished humanists were against him – More and Fisher, Polydore Vergil and Louis Vives, and even, because views on the divorce cut across religious lines, William Tyndale.

Relations between Henry and Catherine were still maintained for formal occasions during the first half of 1531 and they still visited one another 'every few days' for the sake of appearances. Once, at dinner in hall, they talked about Mary who was ill and Henry reproved Catherine for not looking after her properly, so the next day she asked him to visit the Princess, but he answered roughly that, 'she might go and see the Princess

St James's Palace – the gateway and Clock Tower, built by Henry in 1533.

Anno Dⁿⁱ M.cccc.xxvij
Ætatis Suæ xl a

Left Sir Henry Guildford (1489–1532), master of the Horse and later controller of the Royal Household. In this portrait by Holbein he is wearing the collar of a knight of the Garter and is holding his staff as controller.

if she wanted, and also stop there'; but the Queen made it clear that she would not voluntarily leave her husband for Mary or for anyone else in the world. When the court moved to Windsor that summer Catherine was still in residence, but on 11 July Henry left the castle stealthily, very early in the morning, for an extended hunting expedition and Anne rode with him. He did not say a farewell to his wife, though he was never to see her again. Perhaps she, too, sensed this was the end, for she wrote to him to let him know how concerned she was at not being able to talk with him at his departure, but all to no effect, as before the King returned to Windsor she was ordered by the council to vacate her apartments and move to Wolsey's former house at the More. She was forbidden either to write to Henry or to see her daughter and her household establishment was to be whittled away. She was now 'scantily visited by courtiers' and her little court at the More

Right A view of Windsor Castle during Henry's reign, as used in the background to a picture illustrating the biblical story of Jeptha's daughter.

THOMAS. CRANMER, BI
. MARTIR .

became a home of lost causes. Out of a total expenditure of £2,952 she had to meet in 1534, only £283 went on the wages of her officials and servants and less than £60 on running costs of her hall and chamber. Princess Mary felt the pinch too, and had to remove her household from Beaulieu, which was now assigned to Anne's brother, George.

By New Year's Day the imperious Anne had been 'lodged where the Queen used to be, and is accompanied by almost as many ladies as if she were Queen.' At times she annoyed Henry even more than Catherine had done, for ever rubbing salt in the wound by asking if they ever were likely to be married. There were indeed occasions when her sheer arrogance and forthright manner of speaking to him astonished the King, who told Norfolk that she was not at all like Catherine, 'who never in her life used ill words to him'.

From now on Anne was constantly at Henry's side, while Catherine moved on a final slow progress of distant royal manors at Ampthill, Buckden and finally Kimbolton, with little more than a confessor, a physician, an apothecary, Lady Willoughby and two other women – even fewer about her than in the days as Princess at Durham House twenty-five years before, yet still stiffly regal, while her marriage was annulled and England was severed from Rome. In the letter dictated from her deathbed, to Henry in January 1536 she asked God to pardon him for his sinfulness, 'for the which you have cast me into many calamities and yourself into many troubles' and pleaded with him to be a good father to Mary and preserve her rights. Even as life was so surely ebbing she implored him to look after her maids of honour, whose wages were again in arrears, and to be sure to provide them with their rightful marriage portions.

The chief penalty Henry paid for his affair with Anne was being cut off from his daughter, who had been affianced in turn to the Dauphin, to Charles v and then to other members of the house of Valois. The later parallels drawn between Catherine of Aragon and Mary have tended to obscure the characteristics which Mary inherited from her father. She had much of the precociousness of all Henry's children and he was proud of her. She could play the virginals when she was four and soon began a strict regimen of study according to plans drawn up by Vives. Being sent from court under the care first of the Countess of Salisbury, then of Lady Shelton, was at least in obedience to the Spanish philosopher's principle that 'Cherishing marreth sons, but utterly destroyeth daughters.' Henry would dearly have had Mary back at court, to see her regularly and spoil her, even at the risk of countless arguments about her mother, yet Anne Boleyn was adamant: since Mary aroused so much affection in her father, her presence was a constant threat to Anne's supremacy, for so long as Catherine lived she might attempt a reconciliation with Henry, and so Mary was kept away from court. The rivalry between Catherine and Anne was inevitably to be continued in the next generation by their respective daughters.

To take his mind off the divorce Henry had taken up gambling again. In January 1530 he lost £450 at dominoes at Greenwich and Whitehall and ran through £100 at cards and dice against the gentlemen of the Chamber, with occasional games of Pope July, Imperial and Shovelboard, of which the rules are forgotten, but there were always stakes. Anne caught the gambler's fever, but he encouraged her to keep her stakes low by giving her

no more than £5, and all in groats, 'for playing money'. He now invariably
betted with his opponents at bowls and tennis. Ten years back spectators of
the royal tennis game had thought it 'the prettiest thing in the world to see
him play, his fair skin glowing through a shirt of the finest texture', but now
he was less obviously the champion, his footwork slower though his striking
power still tremendous, and the sport somewhat debased by the cash nexus.
Young Francis Weston, a groom of the Chamber, consistently beat the
King at four angels a game and when he took Anne Pickering as his wife
Henry gave him ten marks and ominously wished him better fortune in
marriage than he had found; among his debts when Weston went to the
scaffold four years later, for allegedly treasonable relations with Anne
Boleyn, was a sum owing to Mistress Hannesley, wife of the keeper of the
tennis courts, for tennis balls she had supplied. To his great satisfaction
Norfolk beat Henry at bowls on May Day 1532 for a stake of £21, while
Anne who was keen to take up the game was beaten rather unchivalrously
by the sergeant of the cellar.

Anne chiefly enjoyed the hunting expeditions from Windsor, Hampton
and further afield, partly because this was essentially a royal sport, and one
that Queen Catherine had loved, so that she grew especially jealous when
she was excluded from the chase; but also because on these informal
occasions Anne had Henry more or less to herself, for often there would be
no more than the master of the Horse and a couple of attendants riding
with them into the country. Henry chose her bows and arrows and bought
her a fine pair of hunting gloves, but her performance was not distinguished
for he had to compensate a tenant whose cow had been killed by Anne's
greyhounds. A decade before Richard Pace had said that the King spared
'no pains to convert the sport of hunting into a royal martyrdom', and his

A tennis ball excavated
from the foundations of the
modern Treasury Building,
Whitehall, on the site of
the 'small close tennis court'.

keenness had not been blunted, though instead of the army of courtiers who had then ridden in his company the pastime was now shared by a few hand-picked friends. Some saw a political motive in these hunting progresses, since they might accustom folk in country districts to seeing Anne in Henry's company and prepare them for the time when she would become Queen; and Chapuys, the Imperial ambassador, made the most of tales that in various villages Anne had been hissed as she rode by and that in one district their reception had been so hostile that they had turned back.

Before he defied Pope and Emperor by marrying Anne, Henry wanted to assure himself of the support of Francis I and planned a state visit to France in the autumn of 1532. He particularly wanted Anne to be with him, for he was sure she would make a most favourable impression on the French court, and in preparation she was buying 'costly dresses' in the French fashion that she had herself introduced to England. This had caused a stir, for Polydore Vergil had noted that a garb adapted 'from many most wanton creatures' in Francis' court was 'singularly unfit for the chaste' in Henry's. Henry now gave her a great many jewels of his own and ordered Catherine to surrender her own jewellery.

Before leaving England he decided Anne should have a title and on the first Sunday of September before mass was sung in St George's, Windsor, she was created Marquess of Pembroke. At this ceremony the King was attended by the dukes of Norfolk and Suffolk and the French ambassador, while Anne was supported by the countesses of Rutland and Sussex and had her mantle and coronet carried by Norfolk's daughter Mary, who would soon marry Henry's natural son, Richmond. In the chapel Anne knelt before the King who invested her with the mantle of crimson velvet, furred with ermine, and placed the coronet on her head; to make it easier for him she had not put up her hair but wore it long. To support her new dignity she was granted lands worth one thousand pounds a year and the Latin patent was read out by Garter King of Arms while she remained kneeling. Then she curtseyed and retired to her chamber before morning service began.

Some thought her elevation to the peerage meant that she would never now become Queen, but others considered that Henry might well marry her while they were in France. Their visit from 11–29 October was on a much smaller scale than the Field of Cloth of Gold, yet Henry's train included as many as 2,773 men and women. French courtiers commented very favourably on the King's 'maîtresse d'hôtel', resplendent in cloth of gold and a blaze of diamonds, and thought the marriage could not be postponed much longer. That Christmas Henry lavished all manner of gilt cups, flagons, goblets, bowls and chandeliers on Anne, which she put on show in her apartments at Whitehall, and a month later they were married.

Francis I had advised Henry to marry Anne without further ado and see how Pope and Emperor would react. Since marriage at long last seemed a foregone conclusion, perhaps it was in December 1532, if not the previous month, that Anne finally agreed to cohabit with Henry, though they may indeed have been living together as man and wife since her elevation to the marquisate in September. At any rate by mid-January she was pregnant and could insist on marriage to prevent their child from being born out of wedlock; but since Henry was dependent on the Pope for the bulls providing

Thomas Cranmer to the Archbishopric of Canterbury, as Warham's successor, he dare not risk a public ceremony. Their most clandestine marriage was performed early on 25 January by an unnamed chaplain in the presence of a handful of inner courtiers who were sworn to secrecy. This, the quietest of all royal weddings, was not at all what Anne had contemplated, yet diplomacy demanded it. Cranmer himself knew nothing about it for a fortnight. Henry at once seemed more relaxed and in his happiness could not help giving broad hints to courtiers. On 24 February Anne entertained the King and the greatest in the land to dinner in her chamber at Whitehall, proud of her tapestries and gold plate. Henry asked old lady Norfolk, 'Has not the Marquess a grand dot and a rich marriage, as all that we see and the rest of the plate belongs to her?' Two days before, as she had come out of her apartment, she noticed among the waiting courtiers her old flame, Wyatt, and cried out to him with excitement that for three days she had 'such a violent desire to eat apples, as she had never felt before, and that the King had told her it was a sign that she was with child.' She could no longer keep silent about her triumph and though she hotly denied that she was pregnant, Wyatt and the others readily grasped the truth, and Anne knew it, turning away from her audience, with a burst of hysterical laughter, leaving them 'abashed and uneasy'. She might almost have known that Pope Clement's bulls for Cranmer had been signed a few hours before and were on their way to England. He was consecrated Archbishop on 30 March and presided over a Convocation which, despite Fisher of Rochester's brave stand, was duly subservient. Within a few days Catherine was told of the marriage and that being Queen of England no longer she would revert to the status of Princess of Wales. Finally on Easter Eve, 12 April, Anne was attended in greater state than Catherine had ever enjoyed, preceded by trumpeters, with sixty ladies in her suite as she went to service at the Chapel Royal and was publicly prayed for as Queen. Next month at a special ecclesiastical court at Dunstable Cranmer gave judgment that Henry's marriage to Catherine had been null and void from the very beginning and subsequently declared the validity of Henry's union with Anne.

Once the announcement was made, Anne had truly become Queen Consort and homage was paid her as Henry's wife, even though in Hapsburg despatches she still featured in cipher as 'the Lady' or more earthily as 'the King's wench' or 'the English concubine'. The relations and adherents of the Boleyns now secured their pickings at court. Anne's brother George, Lord Rochford, became an esquire of the Body and master of the Buckhounds and moved into the royal manor of Newhall. Sir Francis Bryan, a cousin of Anne's and loyal servant of Henry's down the years, could at last reap the patronage he felt his due, while young William Brereton, who had shrewdly worshipped the rising sun, was rewarded with a key post as page of the Chamber where his daily contact with the King enabled him to acquire grants of lands and offices in Wales worth £1,200 a year. For lesser men in the Boleyn livery the years of weary waiting, pacing the long gallery at Whitehall or the chapel courtyard at Greenwich, in the hope of catching the King's eye for a place of profit at court were over and they established themselves with remarkable speed. Perhaps the most remarkable example of pluralism, despite all that the Eltham Ordinance had decreed, was Henry

Norris, who had begun as a page of the Chamber when Anne was still being schooled in courtly graces by Queen Claude, and so impressed Henry by his loyal service that he became senior esquire of the Body and the one household official allowed in the King's bedchamber. Yet Norris's advancement did not become spectacular until the arrival of Anne, whom he supported from her earliest days at court, and thus he was enviably placed to profit by further patronage in offices and lands from his master. 'To him that hath was it given' was the motto of the Tudor court and Norris's preferment seemed unending. He became groom of the Stole, master of the Hart Hounds and of the Hawks, Black Rod in the Parliament House, 'graver' of the Tower of London, collector of the subsidy in the City of London and weigher of goods in the port of Southampton. He was also appointed chamberlain of North Wales, and keeper or steward of a score of castles, manors and parks and, though this was not in the King's gift, high steward of Oxford University. Most of these offices Norris performed by deputy. His prime post in the Chamber brought in a mere £33 6s. 8d. a year, but the others made up the total fees and annuities to £400, and there was nearly as much coming in each year from lands Henry had leased or granted him. The changes in personnel at court always brought consequential changes in local administration and land ownership.

To make up for the indignity of a secret marriage, Anne was to be accorded a splendid coronation, since long ago she had insisted to Henry that if she married him she should be crowned 'in the same church and with the same ceremonies used by English Queens'. On 29 May the Lord Mayor, sheriffs and aldermen of London, answering the King's request to receive his 'most dear and well-beloved wife Queen Anne', went down the river to Greenwich to escort her barge with due pageantry from the Palace Stairs to the Tower. In attendance were Suffolk, Dorset, her father and many other nobles and bishops, and as she was rowed upstream ships fired their salutes. The occasion was enlivened by a water carnival, with singers, instrumentalists, tableaux and fireworks. This journey to the Tower, and the procession by litter through the London streets on the Saturday, were for Anne a personal triumph. It was for this that she had waited for six difficult years. For once Henry was not the principal actor; indeed he was off-stage most of the time, being rowed incognito from Greenwich in advance of Anne to be ready to greet her with a kiss by the waterside. At the traditional eve of coronation ceremony at the Tower, eighteen knights of the Bath were dubbed – the first since 1509 – and among them were Dorset, Derby and young Francis Weston.

Next day Anne made her state entry through London to Westminster in an open litter of white cloth of gold, drawn by two palfreys in white damask, and over her was a canopy borne by four knights. Prominent in the procession were the French ambassador and his suite, the Duke of Suffolk, High Constable of England for the day, and Lord William Howard, deputising for his brother of Norfolk, who was abroad. Anne's personal badge, the white falcon, was to be seen in every street. The pageantry had been devised by John Leland, the King's antiquary, and Nicholas Udall, the headmaster of Eton, who had also written the Latin verses declaimed at appropriate halts, extolling the Queen's beauty and virtue and fervently praying that she might give birth to a prince, and the same theme was

Design for a triumphal arch for Anne Boleyn's coronation procession 1533; probably by Holbein.

elaborated in the set tableaux. One scenic display of Apollo and the Muses was apparently devised by Hans Holbein, now permanently settled in London, where he was establishing himself as a portrait painter among the wealthy merchants of the German community. In this set-piece Urania went so far as to refer to Anne's pregnancy, while at Cornhill, more delicately, the figure of 'St Anne' was honoured and her fecundity praised. Rhenish wine ran from a marble fountain at the corner of Gracechurch Street and at different stages on the traditional route massed choirs of 'angels and virgins' praised the new Queen. When she finally reached Westminster Hall she found the great door decorated with verses reminding her how beautiful she was. After refreshment she withdrew to disrobe and afterwards went by barge to the Privy Stairs of Whitehall to join Henry.

Next morning, Whitsun Day, the procession formed in Westminster Hall ready to move across to the Abbey for the coronation itself. The folds of the heavy robes concealed Anne's altered figure and all eyes were on the string of pearls, 'bigger than chick peas', round her neck. Before the high altar, to

Westminster Hall; the setting for Anne's coronation banquet, 1533, and for her trial three years later.

the sound of 'Vivats', Archbishop Cranmer placed St Edward's crown on her head, but as it was so heavy, it was soon replaced by another crown made specially for her.

At the conclusion of mass the procession re-formed to return to the Hall for the coronation banquet. As with the service in the Abbey, Henry was absent, but he viewed the banquet with various ambassadors 'from a little closet out of the cloisters of St Stephen's.' The countesses of Oxford and Worcester throughout dinner stood by Anne's throne and from time to time 'did hold a fine cloth before the Queen's face when she list to spit or do otherwise at her pleasure.'

The Imperial ambassador described the ceremonies and festivities as 'cold, meagre and uncomfortable and dissatisfying to everybody' and others detected a reluctance on the part of Londoners to shout 'God Save the Queen' and bare their heads as she passed in procession. Her fool, who had travelled as far afield as Jerusalem, is said to have reproved lukewarm spectators by crying out, 'I think you have all scurvy heads and dare not uncover.' Some laughed openly at the large initial letters 'H.A.' that were a feature of every street corner decoration, making a jeering 'Ha, ha!' at the woman who had arrived at the throne *via* the royal bed. The same commentator thought the litter was so low that the ears of the last mule in the team looked from one angle as if they belonged to Anne herself; and of course he added that the Crown ill became her and a wart disfigured her.

It was to counter such impressions that propaganda of a new kind was devised, in the pageantry itself and in the official reporting of it. There had been nothing on this scale for Henry himself in 1509, yet despite the visual impact of the scenes enacted, to make doubly sure that the message was relayed Wynkyn de Worde issued a pamphlet by royal authority describing Anne's triumphal entry and putting on record the Latin verses and English ballads written in her honour.

After the coronation and the tournaments that followed in the new tilt-yard at Whitehall, the King and Queen moved on to Greenwich, where there was great rejoicing and mirth among a smaller circle of courtiers. Sir Edward Baynton, Anne's chamberlain, wrote to her brother, Lord Rochford, now Warden of the Cinque Ports, about the 'pastime in the Queen's chamber', where Lady Wingfield was mother of the maids of honour. If any men that had gone home from court, he wrote, had left behind 'any ladies that you thought favoured you, and somewhat would mourn at parting of their servants, I can no wit perceive the same by their dancing and pastime they do use here.' For Anne, her family and friends, no less than for Henry and his companions from the Privy Chamber, there was intense relief that the Gordian Knot had been cut.

Norfolk had found his niece as difficult as his master, and his habit of sighing got worse. At one time Anne had been urging him to marry his eldest son, Surrey, to Princess Mary, and then she had changed her mind. The Duke feared that unless Surrey were to be married off, men would say he was being kept in readiness as a husband for the Princess and would accuse the Howards of designs upon the Crown, so he did not raise objections when Anne found a bride for the boy in Frances Vere, daughter of the Earl of Oxford. They were both sixteen when they married in April 1532. Norfolk refused to accept responsibility for his estranged wife's behaviour

in boycotting Anne's coronation and was himself conveniently out of the country on diplomatic business, though his old mother was delighted to be in the limelight again. It was only serious illness that excused the absence from court of Mary of Suffolk, the Dowager Queen of France and after the festivities Suffolk hastened back to her bedside at Westhorpe Hall, carrying a message from Henry that went far towards a reconciliation with his sister. As a widower Suffolk was utterly lost and looked around with indecent haste for a fourth wife; nor did he look very far. His own son, Henry, Earl of Lincoln, was betrothed to Catherine, heiress of the late Lord Willoughby, and now Suffolk arranged for this to be annulled so he could marry the fourteen-year-old girl himself. It was a bizarre match, quite apart from the great difference in their ages, for Catherine's Spanish mother was the most loyal of Catherine of Aragon's ladies and was even then in attendance on her at Ampthill, while Suffolk was the King's courtier *par excellence*, who had stayed afloat in the stormy political waters, ever since his return from France in 1515, by tying himself securely to Henry. He arranged for his marriage to be celebrated at court on Sunday 7 September 1533, but these nuptials were destined to be overshadowed by a greater event, for on that very day at Greenwich Queen Anne was in childbed.

Above left Charles Brandon, Duke of Suffolk, courtier and intimate of the King.

Above right Lady Willoughby de Eresby, whom Charles Brandon married as his fourth wife in 1533, when she was fourteen.

Right Detail from the symbolical painting of Henry and his family, after Holbein, showing a part of Whitehall Palace – the only known contemporary illustration – with a maid.

4 The image of God

'Squire Henry means to be God and do as he pleases.'

Martin Luther

'Henry has rare endowments both of mind and body, such as personal beauty, genius, learning etc., and it is marvellous how he has fallen into so many errors and false tenets.'

Carlo Capello (1535)

That summer of 1533 Henry had kept his progress 'about London, because of the Queen'. He had bridled his anxiety and testiness to show her as much kindly consideration as he could and even stopped meeting the council at Greenwich to save Anne from the least worry about public affairs. A superb bed, which had once formed part of the ransom for a French prince taken in the wars, to be freed, was brought out of the treasury and set up in Anne's bed-chamber at Greenwich for her lying-in. The Supreme Head of the Church had been assured by astrologers that the child would be a boy in his own image, and was utterly confounded when in the afternoon of 7 September his Queen was delivered of a baby girl. It was not for this that he had defied the Pope. 'God has forgotten him entirely, hardening him in his obstinacy to punish and ruin him', commented Chapuys with satisfaction, and when three days later the baby was christened Elizabeth, after her grandmother, by Archbishop Cranmer, her godfather, Henry could not bring himself to be present. There were few signs of public celebration and the whole proceedings were described as 'very cold and disagreeable to the court and to the city'. Yet after the long series of disappointments over Catherine's stillbirths and miscarriages, Henry took comfort in the fact that the child lived and, as after Mary's birth, reckoned it was only a matter of time before she had a brother. With scant concern for the mother's feelings or the infant's welfare, he established a separate household for the new Princess of Wales and early in December she was taken to Hatfield to be placed in the care of Lady Bryan.

Yet if Anne had, for the present, failed to present Henry with a son, her marriage with him had been the root cause of his enhanced power. While Wolsey had ruled Henry had been largely uninterested in government, but once his own marriage with Catherine became the central issue in politics

Jane Seymour, Henry's third Queen (1536–7); portrait by an unknown artist.

he had every reason to bestir himself; and yet no more than the Cardinal could he find a way out of his difficulties. Henry had harnessed the intense anti-clerical and less widespread anti-papal feelings in England, especially in Parliament, to bring down the Church, yet separation from Rome was very far from his mind until the beginning of 1532 at the earliest. To achieve a divorce from Catherine he would lessen his kingdom's dependence on the Papacy, much as the King of France had done, but he would certainly not countenance the overthrow of the Pope's temporal and spiritual authority. The clergy had meekly submitted in 1531 to the threat of *praemunire*, paid their fines and recognised Henry as 'their singular protector only, and supreme lord, and as far as the law of Christ allows also Supreme Head', but he still had no intention of denying the Pope's spiritual supremacy.

Late in 1531, when Thomas Cromwell (whose career is discussed below, pp. 179–86) entered the inner circle of councillors, a more decisive policy was planned. Once the trusted servant of Wolsey, he had ably defended his master and succeeded in having the attainder against him dropped. Henry, who soon afterwards began to employ him, was quick to realise that here was a layman with a genius for public affairs, and he now placed his trust in a servant who proposed to expel the Pope from England as forcibly as he had expelled his own Queen from his household. Loyalty, hard work and skill in handling people were qualities that impressed Henry and his new minister, unlike Wolsey, had no great appetite for position and wealth, living modestly at Bermondsey and waiting until 1536 for even a knighthood. There was not the slightest danger of Thomas Cromwell establishing

Seating plan for the opening of Parliament, held at the Blackfriars, 1525; drawn by Garter King of Arms.

a rival court. Cromwell has had a bad press ever since the days when Cardinal Pole identified him as 'the messenger of Satan' and men who mourned the execution of More never doubted for a moment that Cromwell deserved *his* end, for realistic administrators and astute political managers have little romantic appeal. Yet it was Thomas Cromwell more than any other man who brought the new monarchy into being to give an entirely new dimension to kingship.

In 1532 Cromwell used his skill to turn Parliament against the Papacy and to force the English clergy to accept the King's control of all legislation. He helped draft the first Annates Act, designed to deprive the Pope of the first fruits of benefices, but the force of the Act was diluted by the insertion of a clause postponing its coming into operation until a further attempt at negotiations with Rome had been completed. In that same April, when the clergy submitted to Henry VIII, Cromwell became master of the King's Jewels, and a few days later his friend Sir Thomas Audley replaced More as Lord Chancellor. There was still talk about browbeating the Pope into granting Henry's wishes and schemes were suggested for Parliament to endorse a divorce decree pronounced by the Archbishop of Canterbury; yet Cromwell was sufficiently clear-sighted to realise that the days of compromise and negotiation had passed. Henry's proposed confiscation of papal annates was having no more effect on Pope Clement than his threats of excommunication on the King. At last in April 1533 Parliament passed an Act Restraining Appeals to Rome – all appeals, not merely Queen Catherine's – and this statute vigorously declared England's national sovereignty. The following session saw the final severance of the English Church from Rome, while other legislation, devised by Cromwell, completed the revolutionary process. Henry was supreme in his own domain, and Cromwell assured him that plunder of the Church would make him as rich as any king in Christendom.

The preamble to the 1533 Act Restraining Appeals forms a political tract that firmly denied there was any novelty about the foundations of the New Monarchy.

Where by diverse, sundry, old, authentic histories and chronicles [it ran] it is manifestly declared and explained that *this realm of England is an empire*, and so hath been accepted in the world, governed by one supreme head and King, having the dignity and royal estate of the *imperial crown* of the same, unto whom a body politic, compact of all sorts and degrees of people divided in terms and by names of spirituality and temporality, be bounden and owe next to God a natural and humble obedience. . . .

The imperialist theme was developed in Polydore Vergil's *History*. Born in Urbino, Polydore had come to England at the turn of the century as sub-collector of those papal taxes that Henry was to abolish. He became naturalised and soon had his feet on the ladder of clerical preferment, leading to several prebends and the archdeaconry of Wells. Polydore had a flair for historical research and an ability to write a telling narrative. By 1533 he had reached the death of Henry VII and the time was ripe for publication; the first edition, dedicated to King Henry, was printed in Basle. The friend of Erasmus and enemy of Wolsey, he had toiled long in gathering materials and polishing his style, and his work was a milestone in English historiography. He tackled the Dark Ages and medieval times in a new spirit, so that his *History* was different in kind as well as degree from the old monastic and civic chronicles. Moreover, the naturalised papal collector proved himself to be more nationalist and anti-papal than any Englishman and his *History* proved to be a powerful piece of propaganda for Henry's ecclesiastical supremacy; it was the heaven-sent up-to-date version of the 'authentic histories', to which the Act Restraining Appeals alluded. The 'Crown Imperial', Polydore asserted, derived from Constantine in the days before the Church had been tainted by papal corruption, and English kings had inherited the same crown to be masters in their own dominion, in ecclesiastical no less than in secular affairs. To the reader of Polydore Vergil, then, the breach with Rome was not a revolutionary act, but a restatement of England's sovereignty, which had always existed, despite the accretions of papalism, and was accordingly a return to pristine freedom, not a novel liberation.

Others took up the same theme. In his tract on Obedience, Bishop Gardiner stated that God had established kings who, 'as representatives of his image unto men, he would have to be reputed in the supreme and most high room and to excell among all other human creatures.' By contrast, Lord Morley in 1534 stressed the novelty of Henry's supremacy. He praised the monarch as 'an ark of all princely goodness and honour', who was not only 'the noblest King that ever reigned over the English nation' (and the use of that phrase speaks volumes) but also '*pater patriae*, that is, the father of our country, one by whose virtue, learning and noble courage England is newborn, newly brought from thraldom to freedom.' The image of the truly nationalist monarch had been created and, as we shall see, the artists in Henry's service sharpened the image and were able to preach more effective sermons on the divine right of the King of England to rule than the politicians and theologians.

Henry was adamant that his decisions over Anne and the Church, ratified by Parliament, should be unreservedly supported by the whole body of his people. At the end of March 1534 his leading subjects began taking the oath to the succession, as the statute enjoined, and to all that the Act of Succession involved. Sir Thomas More and Bishop Fisher of Rochester, the first to refuse the oath, were the two people whose support Henry most wanted. For him to have this token of their unreserved allegiance would indeed show him to be on the side of the angels, but for them to oppose him would undermine his position. Both men had recently been caught up in the affair of Elizabeth Barton, the Nun of Kent, who had immediately voiced popular protest at the divorce from Catherine, though they had escaped serious consequences. It mattered nothing to More that the Abbot of Westminster should remind him that the entire Parliament had taken the oath; he was not, he replied, bound to conform to the assembly of one realm against the general council of Christendom. He would swear his allegiance to the succession if, and only if, the oath could be so framed that it did not imply he was also giving his personal sanction to the repudiation of the Pope's authority or the invalidity of Henry's marriage to Catherine. More had no illusions about Henry, for he had seen with terrible clarity where his political revolution was leading him, and it was for this that he had resigned the Woolsack in May 1532 on the day after the clergy had submitted. When Cromwell summoned him from the Tower he reiterated his loyalty to King Henry: 'I am the King's faithful subject and daily bedesman. I say no harm, I think no harm, but I wish everybody good. And if this be not enough to keep a man alive, in good faith I long not to live.' He would neither assert nor deny the royal supremacy, but if he were forced to make a choice between imperilling his soul or endangering his body few doubted the outcome.

The early martyrs of the Act of Succession included John Houghton, Prior of the London Charterhouse, and Richard Reynolds of Syon Monastery, a scholar of distinction, who were both executed at Tyburn on 4 May 1535 for refusing the oath. Six weeks later John Fisher of Rochester, who had so firmly taken Catherine's part, was brought for trial as a traitor. Though emaciated from his confinement in the Tower, he would not waiver; Henry King of England, he maintained, was not and could never be Supreme Head on Earth of the Church of England. For his execution on 22 June he left off his hair shirt for his finest clothes – 'Do'st thou not mark that this is our wedding day', he reproved his doubting servant, 'and that it behoveth us therefore to use more cleanliness for solemnity of the marriage?' Fearlessly he addressed the crowd that had gathered to watch and pray, assuring them that he was being led to death for wishing to preserve the honour of God. One who was present thought the frail old man was 'a very image of death, and (as one might say) Death in a man's shape and using a man's voice.'

Only after Fisher's execution was More brought to trial, when further attempts to get him to genuflect before the Supreme Head of the Church had failed. Dame Alice, his wife, could not see why, for the sake of a mere oath, he allowed himself to be shut up indefinitely in a wretched prison. 'Is not this house as nigh heaven as mine own?' he retorted. 'But she, after her accustomed fashion, not liking such talk, answered, "Tilly, vally, Tilly, vally".' Even Meg Roper, his favourite daughter, took the oath, yet in all humility he saw himself as the voice of conscience that must speak out against the world, the flesh and the devil. He told his judges that he prayed God preserve him in his opinion, even to death. When Richard Rich perjured himself by twisting words More had said into a malicious statement against the King, he asked the court to believe his own version and pay no attention to a man who was 'a great doer and of no commendable fame'. Compromise, scepticism, the easy way were alien to his nature. At the last a messenger from the King required him to speak no more than a few words of farewell to the world at his execution and, loyal even in the presence of the axe, he obeyed. More had always talked with those closest to him about the future life with the strong conviction of a man for whom the life of the spirit was real and pressing. While Anne Boleyn was relieved that her chief enemy next to Catherine of Aragon would trouble her no more, Henry knew that England would never see his like again, and feared that More's stand on principle would be widely interpreted as the most powerful witness against his rule.

Never popular, the stock of Anne and her family, which would have been redeemed by the arrival of a prince, fell further. 'There is little love for the

John Fisher, Bishop of Rochester, by Holbein.

TL Epuscop de rofestez

one who is Queen now, or for any of her race', wrote a Frenchman, and though it was probably wishful thinking, some claimed to see clear signs that Henry was 'already tired to satiety of this new Queen', before many months. Yet though he might amuse himself with a mistress there was certainly no danger of Anne being abandoned while there was still hope of more children. In April 1534 she told him she was again pregnant and her constant irritability, leading to outbreaks of violent temper, both convinced him that she was with child and was in no condition to be entrusted with the powers of Regent, so he cancelled his visit to France and instead they went on a leisurely progress of the Midland counties. Henry had told Chapuys quite confidently that he would soon have a son, but at the end of the progress, in which he had shown something of his old tenderness, Anne had to admit to him that her hopes had been false, and he felt badly cheated, even felt justified in beginning another affair that lasted through the winter. At a ball given for a special embassy from Francis I Anne momentarily broke down as she saw Henry in animated conversation with her new rival – her name has not come down to us – and vented her hysterical laughter on the Admiral of France.

After Christmas 1534 Henry was discussing with Cromwell and Cranmer the chances of getting rid of Anne without having to return to Catherine. To salvage their fortunes the Boleyns, even more anxious to retain the position and wealth Anne had brought them now that she was in danger of losing her influence with the King, brought to court a pretty cousin of Anne's, Madge Shelton, daughter of the governess to Princess Mary. Their scheme worked, for Madge became at one stroke one of Anne's maids of honour and reigning mistress. If Anne thought her a foolish girl for giving herself to Henry too easily, she was furious at this new infidelity, and it was not surprising that she was reported to be looking haggard and worn. On edge, she even dared to reprove her husband for his conduct and was told she must 'bear with it as one of her betters had done'. Anne now intrigued with Lady Rochford, her sister-in-law, to secure the withdrawal from court of Mistress Shelton, 'whom the King had been accustomed to serve daily', but their conspiracy foundered and Lady Rochford was dismissed from her post in the Bedchamber. The Queen became even more spiteful and vindictive towards Mary and demanded that her ears be boxed 'for the cursed bastard she is'; she had the Princess's jewels confiscated and at times talked of having her poisoned.

Anne did not have to look far if she sought compensations for Henry's neglect, for there were young men at court, nurtured in the school of chivalry, who were eager to profess they worshipped the ground she trod upon, fluttering round her like moths round a naked candle. Of course she still clutched, like Henry, to the chance of bearing a son and in the autumn of 1536 began another pregnancy. While she took care of herself at York Place, he went on progress and visiting Wolf Hall, in Wiltshire, fell in love with Jane Seymour, the daughter of the house, who soon put Madge Shelton out of his mind.

The Seymours, a family with landed interests long established in Wiltshire, had sound aristocratic connexions. Jane was the daughter of Sir John Seymour who had served with the King in France in 1513 and had been at the Field of Cloth of Gold, and her mother, a Wentworth, was descended

Edward Seymour, Queen Jane's brother, created Earl of Hertford, 1537; on Edward VI's accession he was to become Lord Protector as Duke of Somerset.

138

from Edward III. What appealed most to Henry about the Seymours was that they were prolific and though, as was usual, not all their children had survived infancy, boys outnumbered girls. Edward Seymour, born in 1506, had been a page to Mary Tudor as Queen of France and then, after service with Wolsey and in Richmond's household, he had become an esquire of the Body to the King; he had been rising in royal favour since he accompanied Henry to Boulogne in 1532 and probably it was he who had persuaded his sister Jane to change her allegiance from serving as lady-in-waiting to Catherine of Aragon to joining Anne's shadow court. Jane had been born about the year of Henry's succession, so she was somewhat older than Anne had been when the latter had first aroused Henry's passions. Not that Jane was remarkable in appearance or accomplishments. Of middling height, 'nobody thinks that she has much beauty', wrote Chapuys, who had no desire to disparage her. 'Her complexion is so fair that she may be called rather pale. She is a little over twenty-five. You may imagine', the ambassador added, 'whether, being an Englishwoman, and having been long at court, she would not hold it a sin to be still a maid – at which this King will perhaps be rather pleased, for he may marry her on condition that she is a virgin and when he wants a divorce he will find plenty of witnesses to the contrary'. Modesty was a useful attribute and one which her brother Edward and his friends from court, Nicholas Carew and Thomas Elyot, urged her to preserve, despite the artificiality of life at court. Whereas Elizabeth Blount and Mary Boleyn had accepted the King's advances only to be cast aside, Anne had held out for a Crown, and the way the wind was blowing Jane could expect to do likewise.

When the news of Catherine's death at Kimbolton on 8 January 1536 reached Whitehall Henry was overjoyed. At last the heart of opposition to his policies had stopped beating and the Emperor no longer had an excuse for interfering in English affairs. In the worst possible taste Henry celebrated the death of the woman who had been his devoted wife for twenty years by dressing in yellow satin, with a white feather in his cap, to begin a new round of festivities – almost a second Twelve Days of Christmas. He conducted little Elizabeth to chapel with great pomp, made a fuss of her at dinner and afterwards carried her in his arms, showing her off to one courtier after another. Anne, too, wore 'yellow for the mourning' and was delighted at the favour paid to the Princess, but she did not join in the dances because of her pregnancy, nor did she share Henry's relief at the news from Kimbolton. She was still far too vulnerable, despite Catherine's death, and while her father, Wiltshire, said it was a pity that Mary was not also dead, Anne made an attempt at a rapprochement with the Princess as a line of defence. There were too many whispered rumours at court and she felt they all concerned her.

People assumed the moral standards of the Queen's apartments could be no better than those of the King's. The whole tone of the court had sadly declined since the days when Erasmus and the Venetian Giustinian had praised it so highly. That Eustace Chapuys should find it hard to believe in 1536 that Jane Seymour was a virgin, because she was an Englishwoman who had 'been long at court', speaks volumes for the altered standards; and Anne, who was in a position to safeguard the reputations of her own ladies, had not made any effort to show that 'pastime in the Queen's Chamber'

was any better than courtiers expected.

In mid-January 1536 Henry, wearing heavy armour, had a serious accident while riding in the lists at Greenwich. An opponent unhorsed him and as he fell the mailed horse fell on top of him, so that he lay unconscious for two hours and for a time his life seemed in danger. Norfolk carried the news to his niece and, according to her, the shock was so great that it brought on a miscarriage and on 29 January she aborted of a foetus that 'had the appearance of a male' of fifteen weeks. Anne knew that after this further failure she would not be given another chance. Ironically this happened on the very day on which Catherine of Aragon was buried. When Henry at last came to her bedside he said harshly that he now saw that God would not give them a son. Anne tried to explain how frightened she had been about his fall in the lists, for she loved him more than Catherine had ever done, she said, and because of this could not bear seeing him making advances to other women. He stalked out of her bed-chamber saying he would talk to her later, but the same day he whispered in a trusted ear that when he had married Anne he had been 'seduced by witchcraft and for this reason considered it null. It was evident because God did not permit them to have any male issue, and that he believed he might take another wife.' Others at court now said the Queen must have 'a defective constitution'.

It was to please Jane that Henry appointed Edward Seymour a gentleman of his Privy Chamber. A month later, when the King was still looking for a valid excuse to part with Anne, he sent his new love a purse of sovereigns with a love letter. Jane had been trained well enough to make capital out of the incident, for she kissed the letter the messenger brought to Greenwich but returned it to his hands unopened, and on her knees charged him to take the purse back to Henry, telling him she came from an honourable family and her virtue was untainted. Her greatest treasure, she said, was her honour and so she would not accept the royal gift, but if Henry wanted to give her a present 'let it be when God should send her some good and honest husband.' All this was duly reported to the King who was so impressed that the next time he saw Jane he praised her exceptional modesty and, as proof of his own honourable love for her, undertook not to speak to her again 'except in the presence of one of her relatives.' Within a day or so Cromwell was required to vacate his rooms at Greenwich Palace and here Jane's brother Edward was installed with his wife, so that Henry could come 'through certain galleries without being seen' to meet his lover, duly chaperoned. A warning of the impending fall of the house of Boleyn was the St George's Day election at Windsor, when Anne's brother, Rochford, was passed over in favour of Sir Nicholas Carew, the close friend of Edward Seymour. But in the whispering gallery of politics it was not Henry's affair with Jane that caused surprise, but Anne's own conduct. Cromwell's spies picked up gossip at court easily enough, and threaded it together into an unseemly chronicle. On 24 April Henry appointed a commission led by Cromwell and Norfolk to discover sufficient evidence against Anne to bring about her downfall.

Now that Henry never took her hunting Anne passed the time with her lap dogs and singing birds and discussed with her ladies-in-waiting and maids of honour the fashions that John Matte, her tailor, was creating for her. In the highly-charged atmosphere of court life, where chivalrous service could by a glance or a gesture be transformed into passionate devotion, the young men played the dangerous game of flirting with the Queen, lightheaded as ever and eager for flattery and affection. Her coquetry comes through in the household accounts of the last months of her life, which detail purchases of orange tawney silk for one night-gown and 'garnish of Venice gold, wrought with chainwork' for embellishing another nightgown. Anne spent 2s. 8d. for two lengths of fine needle riband for rolling up her hair and considerably more with Baven, the bed-maker, for two tassels of Florence gold and deep gold fringe of Venice for decorating her 'great bed'. Right at the end she was asking her saddler to make new leading-reins with great buttons and long tassels for her mule, fussing about expensive caps that needed altering for her 'woman fool', and garnishing with green riband a pair of clavichords on which perchance Mark Smeaton played.

On the day that Rochford failed to be elected a knight of the Garter,

Virginals reputed to have belonged to Anne Boleyn. The case is of later date, probably Italian work.

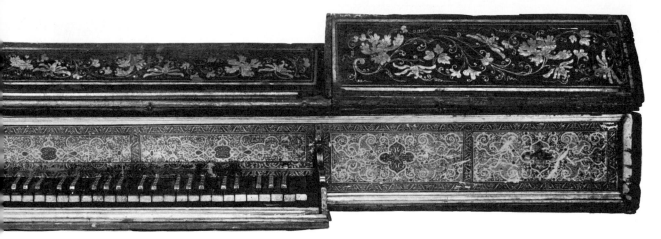

Anne was at Greenwich, chiding Sir Francis Weston of the King's Chamber for neglecting his own wife and paying marked attention to her maid of honour, Madge Shelton (not so long ago Henry's mistress) who was to marry Henry Norris, the principal gentleman of the Chamber. Weston blurted out that he loved someone in her household more ardently than either his wife or Mistress Shelton and, being pressed to divulge the name, said to Anne 'It is yourself'. Nor was he without a rival for he reckoned that Norris himself came often to the Queen's apartments more to catch sight of Anne than to talk with Madge Shelton. Anne later cross-questioned Norris why he delayed marrying her cousin and then, when he hesitated, gave her own views: he seemed to her to be waiting for dead men's shoes and if anything were to happen to the King, such as his accident last January, 'he would look to have her for himself'. Playful bandinage, perhaps, but exceedingly dangerous. Was it surprising that before they parted Anne should ask Norris to be sure to contradict any rumours against her honour? Within the week she found Mark Smeaton, a groom of the King's Chamber and a noted lutanist, in her rooms and asked him why he was so sad. He answered it was of no importance and then she said to him 'You may not look to have me speak to you as I should to a nobleman, because you be an inferior person.' 'No, no! A look sufficeth me', he found himself saying and hastily added 'and so fare you well.' This indiscretion was overheard and soon Smeaton was being examined by Cromwell at Bermondsey and then, put on the rack in the Tower, he confessed to adultery with the Queen.

On May Day there was the customary tournament at Greenwich, with Norris and Lord Rochford, the high priests of chivalry, among the challengers. Anne, it is said, dropped her handkerchief from her balcony to Norris, as a token of her affection and her husband, noting the incident, interpreted it as an unmistakable sign of her infidelity; before the afternoon was out Norris, for years Henry's most trusted companion and the one official allowed to enter his bedchamber, was under arrest, and next day Rochford was sent to the Tower. Norfolk, Fitzwilliam, Paulet and others examined Anne in the council chamber at Greenwich, when she was told that Smeaton and Norris had both confessed to adultery with her. When she tried to defend herself her uncle shook his head many times, muttering 'Tut, tut, tut.' She was told she must prepare for removal to the Tower, which she had not visited since the eve of her coronation, but before she left

Greenwich she was seen at an upper window fondling her daughter. Years afterwards a Protestant refugee from Germany vividly recalled the scene he had observed from the courtyard, while Anne attempted to plead with Henry. She left by barge to arrive at the Watergate of the Tower, not yet nicknamed Traitors' Gate, and babbled freely about her lovers, but her jailor Kingston wrote down all she said for Cromwell's benefit and as a result Sir Francis Weston and William Brereton, both gentlemen of the Chamber, were taken into custody. Of the five paramours with which Anne was credited only Smeaton, who had been racked, admitted misconduct; the others firmly denied the charges, though Henry had promised Norris a pardon if he would but confess to being Anne's lover. By a wide construction of the law their alleged adultery, and in the case of Rochford incest, was accounted high treason.

The King was convinced of the guilt of all five men. He reckoned there was ample proof that he had been cuckolded and made the victim of Anne's witchcraft, and in his rage none dared to persuade him otherwise. The more he considered it, the more certain he was that Anne was guilty, that she, like Catherine, had never legally been his wife. His own profligacy assured him that her behaviour had been utterly libidinous and he raved that she was a nymphomaniac who had had over one hundred lovers.

There had been flirting and an unabashed delight in collecting fulsome compliments from handsome young men, the endless game of giving and receiving tokens, love lyrics sung rather too passionately and dancing in a far from strait-laced style. The group had enjoyed themselves in their tinsel, fairy-tale domain, but emotionally they had been playing with fire, because it was Henry's wife who had been their goddess. An outsider could not but misunderstand the rules of the game and it was this alone that made the gross criminal charges plausible. It would have been difficult for Anne to have kept secret a single love affair, but for her to have been over three and a half years the mistress of five men, all extremely well-known, would have been impossibly hard to hide. Perhaps it was to find further evidence to bolster a weak case that led to Wyatt's arrest, but as her lifelong friend could provide no scrap of information of significance, and there was nothing to incriminate him, he was released after a few weeks.

The indictment against Anne, even allowing for its being shrouded in lawyer's Latin, did not mince words. Having been Henry's wife and queen for forty months and more, 'contemning her marriage, bearing malice in her heart against the King and following her frail and carnal lust, she did falsely and traitorously procure by means of indecent language, gifts and other arts ... divers of the King's daily and familiar servants to be her adulterers and concubines, so that several of them, by her most vile provocation and invitation, became given and inclined to the said Queen.' The document went on to particularise the charges: Henry Norris first had intercourse with her at Whitehall in the autumn of 1533, five weeks after Elizabeth's birth; William Brereton committed adultery with her on Christmas Day of that year at Hampton Court; in April 1534 Mark Smeaton and next month Sir Francis Weston had intercourse with her at Whitehall; finally her brother Rochford committed incest on 5 November 1535, after her last pregnancy had already begun. Anne was also accused of forbidding each of these five 'to show any familiarity with any other woman' – a crime not known to the law – of inveighing them to her will by presents and compassing Henry's death by promising to marry one of them 'whenever the King should depart this life, affirming she never could love the King in her heart.' If such were the terms of the indictment it was not strange that Chapuys should call Anne 'the English Messalina or Agrippina'.

Cromwell's timing of the state trials had been superb, for Anne was not called upon to face her judges until three days after the four commoners had already been convicted of adultery with her. At her trial she had recovered her composure and defended herself ably and Rochford, whose trial followed hers, made such a good defence that men were betting ten to one on his acquittal, until he admitted having said that the King was not able to have relations with his wife; 'that he had no virtue or potency in him'. Sister and brother were in turn found guilty, 'every lord and each after their degrees said guilty to the last'. Henry Percy, now Earl of Northumberland, perhaps the first and last man Anne had loved, had been too overcome to remain in Westminster Hall for the proceedings to finish, when Norfolk, with moist eyes, had pronounced sentence of death. Anne's tragedy and the rebellion of his brothers hastened Percy's early death the following year.

After Anne's condemnation Cranmer held a special court which determined that she had never been lawfully married to Henry, because of her pre-contract to Percy; but perhaps the most telling evidence before the Archbishop was Henry's old affair with Mary Boleyn. (Had Cranmer's court been held before the state trial, Anne could not, of course, have been convicted of adultery.) When Henry heard of the Archbishop's decision he felt his conscience greatly relieved, for as it was clear now that he had always been a bachelor, he had never in his life been guilty of breaking the Seventh Commandment. This was not spoken in jest; Henry meant what he said with complete seriousness, and he felt freed of a great burden, vowing like a penitent in the confessional to make a fresh start, taking on another

A gilt cup presented by Henry to the Company of Barber Surgeons of London.

wife, not because he was uxorious, but because he needed a male heir born in wedlock.

No-one had been more surprised than Cranmer at the turn of events. He had risen to preferment with the Boleyns and had crowned Anne but had known nothing of the whisperings at court. When he had heard of her arrest he had written a long letter to Henry to try and console him. 'I have never had better opinions of woman than I had of her', he wrote, for he had lived in the Boleyn household where the Gospel flourished. He would pray that she may be found innocent, but if she were in fact guilty of these heinous crimes then he, like any other true subject, would desire her punishment. There were some English clergy convinced that she could not possibly have been as abominable as her accusers alleged because 'she was a favourer of God's words', but the Archbishop did not share this view. He was not concerned to show mercy to a guilty woman, but to save the Reformation of the Church. Not many days before the Imperialist Chapuys had described Anne as 'the cause and the principal wet-nurse of heresy and Cranmer now feared that Henry, whose infatuation with Anne had been the occasion of the breach with Rome, might now forsake the reformed religion. He accordingly ended his letter to the King with the hope that 'Your Grace will have no less entire favour to the truth of the Gospel than you did before; for so much of your Grace's favour to the Gospel was not led by your affection unto her, but by zeal for the truth.' Cranmer visited Anne before her execution and heard her confession, but he pondered these things in his heart.

News of Anne's condemnation was taken to Jane Seymour by Sir Francis Bryan, one of the Boleyn cousinage, who had earlier picked a quarrel with Lord Rochford as a means of parting from the faction before it was too late. The manner in which he acted as messenger of these tidings earned him Cromwell's *soubriquet* of 'Vicar of Hell'. Henry celebrated the condemnation with a pageant on the river, where 'the royal barge was constantly filled with minstrels and musicians of the Chamber' and behaved like a man who had rid himself of 'a thin, old and vicious hack in the hope of getting again a fine horse to ride'. That evening at the house of John Kite, Bishop of Carlisle, he produced from his pocket a small book in his own hand, containing 'the tragedy about Anne he had predicted and written down'. He went off to sup with Jane, who was well served by caterers from his household. The day Anne was beheaded, Cranmer issued a dispensation allowing him to marry Jane, despite their affinity in the third degree; 'You never saw prince nor man make greater show of his horns, nor show them more pleasantly', noted Chapuys.

Anne had seen from her window in the Tower the executions of her alleged paramours and met her own death with dignity, for this time there were no hysterics, but a gentle speech on Tower Green on 19 May. She wore a grey robe of damask, cut low and trimmed with fur, and underneath a crimson kirtle and, to make it easy for her executioner, she put up her hair under a net, with a headdress embroidered with pearls. By royal command Cromwell, Lord Chancellor Audley, Suffolk and Richmond – reckoned heir presumptive to the throne – attended her on the scaffold. The night before she had tried to joke with the Lieutenant of the Tower, putting her hands

Thomas Cromwell, Henry's chief minister (1533–40); portrait by Holbein.

PARVVLE PATRISSA, PATRIÆ VIRTVTIS ET HÆRES
 ESTO, NIHIL MAIVS MAXIMVS ORBIS HABET.
GNATVM VIX POSSVNT COELVM ET NATVRA DEDISSE,
 HVIVS QVEM PATRIS, VICTVS HONORET HONOS.
ÆQVATO TANTVM, TANTI TV FACTA PARENTIS,
 VOTA HOMINVM, VIX QVO PROGRFDIANTVR, HABENT
VINCITO, VICISTI. QVOT REGES PRISCVS ADORAT
 ORBIS, NEC TE QVI VINCERE POSSIT, ERIT.

Holbein's design for
Queen Jane Seymour's
cup.

round her 'little neck', and saying it would not be difficult for the executioner. The expert brought over from St Omer now cut off her head with a
single movement of his two-handed sword. Henry spent the day quietly;
there was no feasting and the household expenses of £44 12s. were the
lowest for any day that year. He wore white for mourning for Anne and on
the morrow was betrothed to Jane, whom he married on 30 May in the
Queen's Chapel at Whitehall. A day at the end of October was selected for
her coronation, but in the event her crowning never took place because of
the plague.

Anne's father necessarily lost his office of Lord Privy Seal to which
Thomas Cromwell, the architect of the fall of the Boleyns, no less obviously
succeeded, and soon the Earl of Wiltshire was lamenting his diminished
income. Soon, too, Cromwell was consolidating his position by marrying
his son Gregory to Queen Jane's sister, Elizabeth. At Whitsun Sir Edward
Seymour was created Viscount Beauchamp, and became easily the most
influential of the gentlemen of the Chamber, securing close associates to the
posts formerly held by Norris, Weston and Brereton. In Queen Jane's
household there was, surprisingly, much continuity. Sir Edward Baynton
remained as vice-Chamberlain, the office he had held under Catherine of
Aragon, and would hold still under Anne of Cleves. Rochford's widow had
made her peace with the King and returned as a lady of the Bedchamber
before the end of the year and was destined to serve another two of Henry's
Queens after Jane. In the lower ranks the Seymours exercised their patronage and some of Anne Boleyn's menial servants, now replaced, were taken
on by the Lord Steward, like James of the Bottles.

Norfolk still clung to the Lord Treasurer's staff, despite the execution of
his niece, and he also survived the stupid designs of his half brother, Lord
Thomas Howard, who had unlawfully contracted to marry Lady Margaret
Douglas, the daughter of Queen Margaret of Scotland and the Earl of
Angus. To marry a niece of the King was to be aiming too near the Crown
of England, quite apart from the line of succession to the throne of Scotland,
and Lord Thomas was caught in the meshes of a new Treasons Act,
attainted and put in the Tower for the rest of his short life. The same July
died Henry's natural son, the Duke of Richmond, regarded by many as the
obvious heir to the throne. A consumptive youth, his health had noticeably
deteriorated in the previous two years, but there is no foundation in the
rumours that Anne Boleyn and Lady Rochford had tried to poison him.
Norfolk's daughter, Mary, had married Richmond and now the Duke was
required to take charge of his son-in-law's funeral arrangements. He was
ordered to wrap the body in lead and have it hidden in a farmer's waggon
for the journey from St James's to Thetford, where a secret burial took
place, for now that Mary and Elizabeth had been statutorily declared
illegitimate Henry feared there might be trouble if Richmond's death were
widely known. Some time later he turned on Norfolk, complaining that his
son had been buried without the honour due and there were rumours that
the Duke might lose his liberty, if not his head; but Norfolk was sure of his
ground. 'When I deserve to be in the Tower', he snapped, 'Tottenham will
turn French.'

Prince Edward as a baby,
painted by Holbein.

After a few days' honeymoon in the country Queen Jane accompanied
Henry in his barge from Greenwich to Whitehall on 7 June, which was the

149

occasion for further pageantry on the Thames. As they passed the Tower, where Anne had so recently met her death, four hundred guns saluted them and 'all the Tower walls towards the water-side were set with streamers and banners'. Next day Henry opened Parliament, which would place the succession in any children born to Jane and, as he left Whitehall in procession, she waved him farewell 'standing in the new gatehouse'.

Remembering Anne's imperious ways that had brought her so much unpopularity, Jane seems to have chosen for herself the part of a modest, shy woman, rather overwhelmed by the trappings of regality, even though her service at court had taught her a great deal about royal etiquette. She chose as her motto 'Bound to obey and serve', which was not unlike Catherine's 'Humble and loyal', but on an entirely different plane from Anne's 'The Happiest of Women'. When Chapuys was given his first audience at court after the wedding, he kissed Jane with the King's permission, and congratulated her on her marriage. Rather fulsomely referring to her predecessor's motto, the ambassador earnestly hoped the new Queen would realise it herself, by becoming the happiest of women. She seemed a little tongue-tied, so Henry came to her rescue, excusing her inexperience – 'She was not used to that sort of reception'. Cromwell spoke of her as 'the most virtuous lady and veriest gentlewoman that liveth' and certainly Henry was as convinced of Jane's purity as he had been of Anne's immorality. It was ridiculous to think that at forty-four he could not father a son by her.

Jane realised her essential role was as mother of England's heir, but immediately she wanted to act as peacemaker between Henry and Princess Mary, now twenty and still banished to Hunsdon. After Anne's execution the Princess had written to Cromwell: 'Nobody durst speak for me so long as That Woman lived', but now she asked him for the love of God to be her suitor to her father. As a result Norfolk, Sussex and Sampson, Bishop of Chichester, came to visit her, reproving her for her obstinacy in refusing to acknowledge Henry as Supreme Head of the Church. Norfolk told her that if she had been a daughter of his, he would have knocked 'her head against the wall until it was as soft as baked apple' – and the Duke meant every word of it – for she was a traitress, as Fisher and More had been. Mary now wrote asking for Henry's blessing, craving forgiveness for her offence and assuring him that she submitted to him 'in all things next to God'. But this was not good enough for a King ruling in the image of God and Henry was exceedingly angry; besides he knew that Cromwell, Exeter and other leading councillors were totally opposed to his having Mary degraded. Cromwell, with Chapuys' help, brought home to the Princess the great peril in which she lay, yet her submission was still not absolute. The Lord Privy Seal spoke out vigorously: 'If you do not leave all sinister counsels, I take leave of you for ever and desire you to write to me no more, for I will never think you other than the most ungrateful, unnatural and obstinate person living, both to God and your most dear and benign father.' He sent her a letter in the most grovelling terms which she copied out 'word for word' and signed on 13 June and in it acknowledged her 'merciful, passionate and most blessed' father to be Supreme Head of the Church, disavowed the Pope and declared her mother's marriage to him as incestuous and unlawful. Chapuys had assured her that the Pope would absolve her if she sent a secret protest

Title page of the *Valor Ecclesiasticus*, the valuations of church property in England and Wales – bishoprics and benefices as well as monasteries and colleges – prepared in 1535 by Cromwell's commissioners. The 'Valor' was often termed 'the King's Book.'

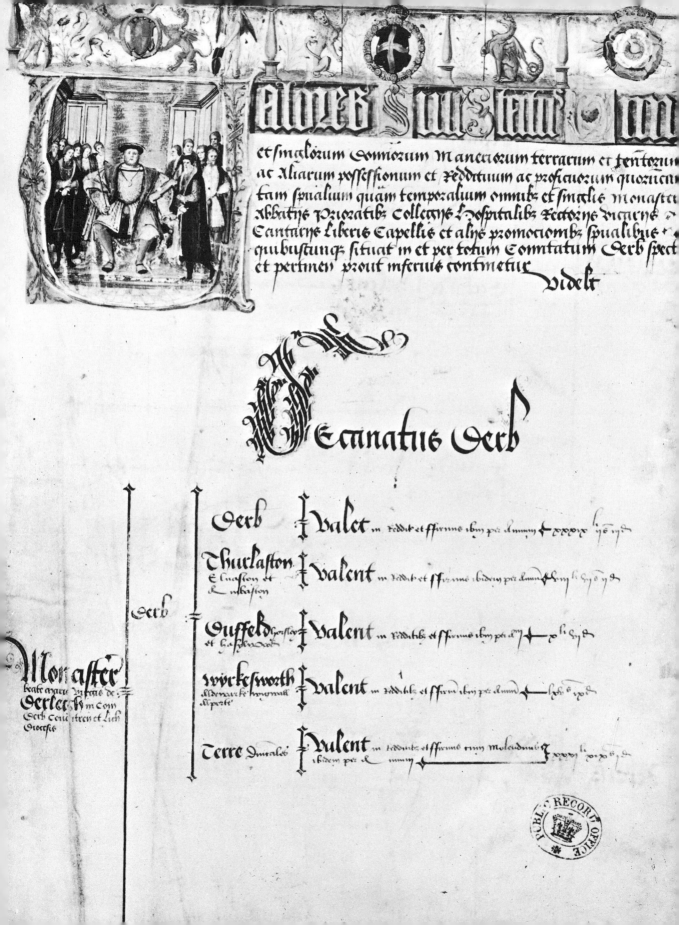

et singulorum comitorum maneriorum terrarum et tentorum
ac aliarum possessionum et reddituum ac proficuorum quorumcunque
tam spiritualium quam temporalium omnibus et singulis monasteriis
abbathiis prioratibus collegiis hospitalibus rectoriis vicariis et
cantariis liberis capellis et aliis promocionibus spiritualibus et
quibuscunque situat in et per totum comitatum Derb spect
et pertinen prout inferius continetur videlt

Decanatus Derb

Derb	Valet in reddit et firmis ibm per annum	lxxxix li xd
Thurlaston Elvaston et Ambaston	Valent in reddit et firmis ibidem per annum	lxxiij li ixs iiijd
Duffeld Horsley et Heage wood	Valent in reddit et firmis ibm per annum	xxv li xiijs
wirkesworth Aldemark Ironbrook Allport	Valent in reddit et firmis ibm per annum	lxvj li xd
Terre dominicales ibidem per annum	Valent in reddit et firmis cum molendinis	xxxvj li xs viijd

Monasterium
beate marie juxta de
Derlegh in com
Derb Covent tren et Lich
dioecesis

to Rome. Next day Mary was summoned to court and made to repeat her submission verbally before her father, 'most humbly lying at his feet to perceive his gracious clemency'. He still doubted her sincerity, but a little later when he descended on Hunsdon unannounced with Jane he could not conceal his affection for his elder daughter.

At the beginning of July the Queen gave her a valuable diamond and Henry, after years of neglect, brought her 1,000 crowns 'for her little pleasures, telling her to have no anxiety about money'. She now said how gladly she would serve his future children and pleaded to be taken back into the family: 'I would rather be a chamberer having the fruitions of Your Highness' presence than an Empress away from it'. Then, finally, she wrote as Henry commanded her to Charles V to inform him that, being guided by the Holy Spirit, she had willingly submitted to Henry, and she was allowed to return to the fold. Mary was now 'the first after the Queen and sits at table opposite her, a little lower down, after having first given the napkin for washing to the King and Queen'. Her little half-sister, also back at court, fed at a separate table. The reconciliation was complete and, enjoying his triumph, Henry reminded his councillors that 'Some of you were desirous that I should put this jewel to death', and Jane obediently took up her cue: 'That were a pity to have lost your chiefest jewel of England', and Mary, realising how narrowly she had escaped the full measure of Henry's wrath, fainted.

Cromwell's visitors had toured the country in the winter of 1534–5 to make a complete inventory of monastic and other ecclesiastical properties and revenues and their returns became consolidated in the *Valor Ecclesiasticus*, whose opening page, with the King in majesty decorating the initial letter of *Valores*, is reproduced on page 151. In Anne Boleyn's last days Parliament passed an act dissolving all those small foundations with a net annual income of under £200 and this began a revolution in English ecclesiastical life, in the structure of society and in the appearance of town and countryside no less far-reaching than the breach with Rome. The first suppression and the dissolution of the larger, wealthier religious houses which was to extend over the next four years brought Henry lands worth over £100,000 a year; but by selling or leasing many of these former monastic properties he gained perhaps £1,500,000, while those who acquired the spoils from him became committed to the Reformation settlement and the Tudor dynasty. Almost all of the larger grants went to men connected with the court; peers received 124 grants of land from the Court of Augmentations in these seminal years, other courtiers 183 grants and royal officials 147. To Thomas Cromwell himself went the property of St Osyth's Monastery, Essex, the lands of Launde Abbey in Leicestershire, extensive portions of the estates that had belonged in many counties to Lewes Priory, Sussex, and the Grey Friars at Great Yarmouth in Norfolk. Sir Anthony Browne, master of the Horse, was rewarded with vast tracts of Surrey that had been owned by Chertsey Abbey, Merton Priory, St Mary Overey in Southwark and Guildford Priory. Sir Philip Hoby of the Privy Chamber acquired Evesham Monastery in Worcestershire and his colleague Edward Harman the lands of Tewkesbury Abbey in Gloucestershire. Sir Thomas Cheyney, the treasurer of the Household, purchased on favourable terms

Hans Holbein – a self portrait painted in 1543.

NNES HOLPENIVS BA‧   SILEENSIS

PSIVS EFFIGIATOR   Æ: XLV‧

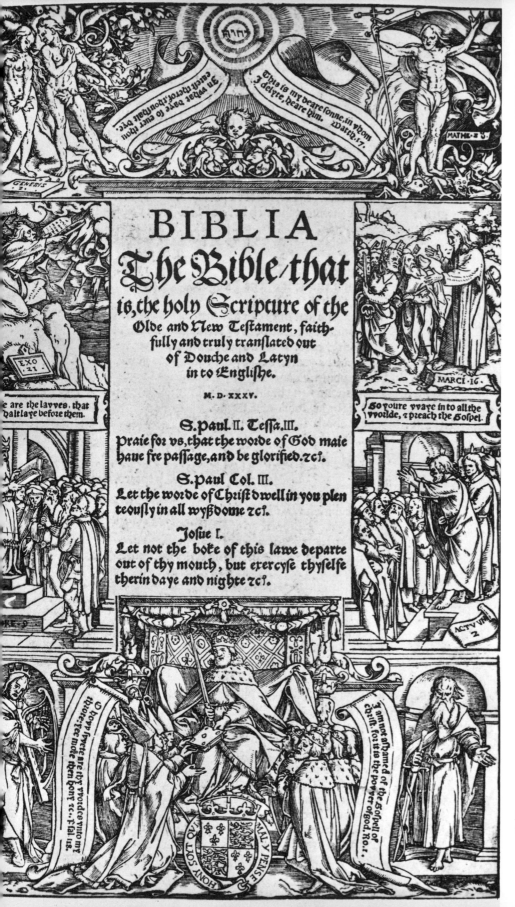

BIBLIA

The Bible, that is, the holy Scripture of the Olde and New Testament, faithfully and truly translated out of Douche and Latyn in to Englishe.

M. D. XXXV.

S. paul. II. Teſſa. III.
Praie for vs, that the worde of God maie haue fre paſſage, and be glorified. zc¹.

S. paul Col. III.
Let the worde of Chriſt dwell in you plenteouſly in all wyſdome zc¹.

Joſue I.
Let not the boke of this lawe departe out of thy mouth, but exercyſe thyſelfe therin daye and nighte zc¹.

Left Title-page of Coverdale's English Bible, 1535, depicting Henry in majesty, presenting the book to the bishops and lords.

Right Portrait of Henry VIII by Joos van Cleve.

the lands of Faversham and Boxley Abbeys in Kent, while the Duke of Norfolk and his son, Surrey, bought valuable sites in Norwich and considerable estates in East Anglia. The pattern was the same all over the kingdom. Families like the Cecils, Paulets, Russells and Wriothesleys paved the way for their remarkable rise to importance by the spoils they acquired, while in every shire there were men of middling rank, connected with the court, whose financial prudence and promise of continued loyal service to the Crown in the later 1530s enabled them to found 'official' county families.

Henry found it hard to take the rising of 1537 in Lincolnshire seriously and when the more widespread revolt broke out in Yorkshire and the north-west, under the name of the Pilgrimage of Grace, he underrated its leader, Robert Aske, failing to realise that the New Monarchy was being given its first testing by men, long restive, who were totally opposed to Henry's style of government. Queen Jane, apparently, pleaded with him on her knees to restore the lesser monasteries whose dissolution had provoked the rebellion, yet he bade her mind her own business and remember the fate of her predecessor. He asked to see Aske and he came on parole to court to explain the grievances of the rebels and set on paper the reasons for their solidarity. Henry was delighted with him and sent him back to Doncaster with a new crimson satin jacket. The King kept promising to ride north himself to direct operations, yet he never made the journey and after the rebels had been crushed and Aske, despite the promise of a pardon, had

been executed at York, Henry said he would spend his summer progress in those parts, to show himself to subjects who had never seen him, but he stayed in the south. To Norfolk, who had commanded the main army, he excused himself chiefly on grounds of ill-health: 'to be frank with you, which you must keep to yourself, a humour has fallen into our legs and our physicians advise us not to go far in the heat of the year.'

Ever since his fall in the lists in January 1536 Henry had been less energetic and venturous and never again took part in athletic tournaments. This was not his first serious accident, for in the tilt-yard in 1524 Suffolk had almost killed him, as in the excitement of trying out a new suit of armour made to his own design he had forgotten to lower his visor, and had the Duke's lance struck his face, instead of splintering his helmet, it would have been fatal. It is perhaps to that accident that the headaches the King suffered for a number of years should be ascribed. Though his leg may have given him trouble before 1536, it was probably the fall, curtailing the range and intensity of his exercise, which until then he had taken most seriously and regularly, that affected his leg and subsequently caused his obesity. Once historians attributed the ulcerous leg to syphilis, but there is not a shred of evidence for his enduring the painful administrations of mercury over protracted periods, which was the standard treatment in those days. Modern research suggests that Henry's affliction was either osteomyelitis – a septic infection of the thigh-bone caused by the jousting injury – or a varicose ulcer, produced by inadequate treatment of varicose veins, again exacerbated by the fall from his horse. The severe shock of his accident in the tilt-yard to a shin 'enclosed in steel, might readily result in just the injury required to break the skin over a varicose vein', and all was intensified through Henry's height, weight and girth. Over the years, with the primitive treatment then available, the veins became thrombosed, the leg swelled and a chronically painful ulcer developed on his thigh. Already in the spring of 1537 Lord Montague was daring to predict the King's early death: 'he will die one day, suddenly; his leg will kill him and then we shall have jolly stirring!' while a courtier noted that he 'goes seldom abroad, because his leg is something sore'. The affliction was to cause him intense pain for the next ten years.

Suddenly the political gloom vanished, making him able to bear his personal suffering more readily, for not only was the Pilgrimage of Grace suppressed, but Jane was pregnant. Overnight courtiers said they had never seen their master merrier: 'The King useth himself more like a good fellow than like a King' – a return to the early years of the reign, with bluff Hal diverting himself with his companions from the Chamber. On Trinity Sunday 1537 a *Te Deum* was sung in St Paul's 'for joy of the Queen's quickening of child', an unprecedented step in the chronicle of the English liturgy, itself reflecting the full significance of the royal supremacy.

It was in this summer of triumph that Henry commissioned Hans Holbein the Younger to paint on the walls of the Privy Chamber a fresco containing himself and Queen Jane, with his parents of York and Lancaster in the background, presaging the arrival of his heir. When Holbein returned to England in 1532, his friend More had already resigned the chancellorship and the artist had embraced the Dutch Reformist faith. Within the year he

Right Henry in middle age: a characteristic portrait after Holbein.

Overleaf left The Tower of London, with London Bridge in the background, in the early sixteenth century.

Overleaf right Nonsuch Palace, Surrey, as drawn by Hoefnagel in the later sixteenth century

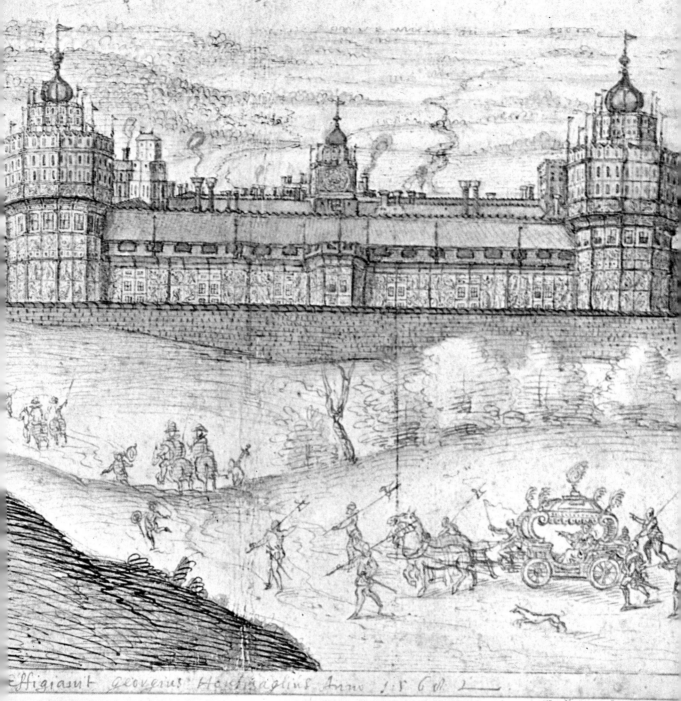

REGIVM IN ANGLIÆ REGNO APPELLATVM NONCIVTZ
Hoc est nusquam simile.

Effigiauit Georgius Houfnaglius Anno 1568

Right The Chatsworth cartoon of Henry VIII with his father in the background, intended by Holbein for the decoration of Whitehall.

Left Illuminated plea roll of the Court of King's Bench 1544, showing the King in majesty in the initial 'H' of 'Henricus' at the beginning of Hilary Term's pleadings.

had designed a pageant arch for Anne Boleyn's coronation procession and soon afterwards painted his portrait of Cromwell. It was Cromwell, the architect of the royal supremacy, who singled out Holbein, now permanently settled in England, as the man capable of giving visual imagery to the new monarchy, and in 1536 he was commissioned to devise a title page for Coverdale's translation of the Bible. His wood-cut was very different in kind from the formal portrait by Joos van Cleve, with the King holding a scroll enscribed 'Go ye into all the world and preach the Gospel.' Holbein enthroned Henry, holding the sword of justice in his right hand, giving the Book to his kneeling bishops with the left, and the other pictures on the title-page placed Henry unmistakably in the line of Old Testament prophets and New Testament apostles. This was the visual image of a King, personifying God on earth and its impact was more immediate than Coverdale's verbal rendering of the same message in his dedication: 'He only under God is the Chief Head of all the congregation and church.'

Holbein's fresco in the Privy Chamber, known today only through copies and made intelligible by the studies of Roy Strong, repeated the theme stridently, and by placing Henry with his parents he devised a 'monumental apotheosis of the Tudor dynasty'. Henry dominates the picture, with his legs astride, his feet firmly on the ground, the earliest 'definitive portrait' of the King, which Holbein continued to paint in various canvases, massive, jaunty, energetic, the symbol of earthly power. Only a great artist could convey Henry's personality so effectively and it has dominated posterity's idea of him; just as everyone's conception of the Last Supper since Leonardo worked has been coloured by his painting of the subject, so everyone associates Henry VIII immediately with the series of Holbein portraits, of which the figure in the group in the Privy Chamber fresco was the first. He towered over a timid Jane. And perhaps, as Mr Strong convincingly argues, the painting was rather more than a dynastic portrait and was executed on the upper part of the panelling in the room, to form a background to the throne on which the living Henry sat in state.

Jane was cossetted and pampered with dainties, unless it was a day of abstinence, for she shared with Anne Boleyn a taste for fine fare, especially venison and quails, but as the summer drew on and the plague became severe she feared her confinement. She took consolation in religious observances, meticulously observing the old church calendar, to Cranmer's concern. 'If in the court you do keep such holy days and fasting days as be abrogated', the Archbishop asked Cromwell, 'when shall we persuade the people to cease from keeping them?'

Hampton Court, enlarged and refurbished since the Cardinal's days, had been chosen for Jane's confinement and on 12 October, to end a difficult childbirth she was delivered of a son by Caesarean section. Henry was not at his wife's side for, frightened of the plague, he had been staying quietly at Esher – and not far away at Croydon there were three or four deaths a day – yet once the glad tidings reached him he rushed to her. He was beside himself with joy. 'We all hungered after a prince so long,' said Latimer, 'that there was so much rejoicing as at the birth of John the Baptist.' The infant was christened on the following Sunday when the number of attendants a courtier could bring to Hampton Court was limited according to his rank, to prevent too great a concourse which would be a

Hampton Court; the
astronomical clock made
by Nicolas Oursian

risk of infection. Edward's sisters, Mary and Elizabeth, helped by Lady
Herbert, carried his train. At an investiture later in the week Jane's elder
brother, Edward, was advanced to the earldom of Hertford and her younger
brother, Thomas, was knighted; the same day Fitzwilliam, the Lord Admiral,
became Earl of Southampton. In January 1511 Henry had ordered celebrations to honour a Prince of Wales who survived only a few weeks, but
twenty-six years later, Prince Edward lived on, to give him the heir for
which he had divorced Catherine and executed Anne. But the fact that the
baby lived put the fate of his mother quite in the shade. She had written
proudly to Cromwell announcing her son's birth, adding with equal pride
that it had been 'conceived in lawful matrimony'; yet twelve days later Jane
Seymour died 'through the fault of them that were about her, who suffered

Mistress Jak, Prince Edward's wet-nurse, by Holbein.

Hampton Court Palace. The medallions by Giovanni da Maiano for Wolsey can be seen on the gateway, but Wolsey's arms have been replaced by those of Henry VIII.

her to take great cold and to eat things that her fantasy in sickness called for.' In dynastic terms she had achieved all that was expected of her, and for this her name was revered in her own day and by later generations. Henry's grief was genuine enough. Twelve masses were said for her soul. Alone of his queens Jane was buried in St George's Chapel, Windsor, but he could not bring himself to attend the funeral, shutting himself up at Whitehall until a discreet period of mourning had passed, while Mary acted as chief mourner. He was to direct that when his time came to be called to his Maker his coffin should be laid beside hers.

Rigorous rules were enforced to safeguard Prince Edward's health. Just as 'God hath the devil repugnant to Him and Christ hath antichrist', so the baby Prince, despite his innocence, might have adversaries who wanted to endanger his person, ran the Ordinance. To approach his cradle even a duke needed a permit signed by the King and, because youths were reckoned careless and forgetful, no page was to be employed in the Prince's household. No member of his establishment was allowed to go to London during the summer months for fear of becoming infected by the plague or some other epidemic. The Prince's chamberlain or his deputy was to witness his daily bath and his being dressed, to supervise the preparation of his food and oversee the washing of his clothes. No precautions were too great, for on this one life depended England's future.

Even before Jane's funeral Henry was noted as being in good health and as 'merry as a widower may be'. Now that he had a son, would he remain a widower? Thomas Cromwell in conveying to the court of Francis I news of the Queen's death already had his mind on a further marriage for his master. 'Although His Highness is not disposed to marry again', he wrote, 'yet his tender zeal to his subjects hath already overcome his Grace's said disposition and framed his mind both to be indifferent to the thing and to the election of any person, from any part, that with deliberation shall be thought meet for him.'

The failure of the Pilgrimage of Grace hastened the downfall of the greater monasteries. Already in Anne Boleyn's last days Cromwell had established the Court of Augmentations to manage ex-monastic properties and administer their revenues, which indeed augmented the royal income by £32,000 a year. Yet the 304 lesser houses, with incomes of less than £200 a year merely sharpened the King's appetite for the untold wealth of the greater foundations. From 1537 onwards there was a stream of 'voluntary' surrenders to Cromwell's visitors by abbots and priors, eager to make the best terms they could, and the final Act of Parliament in 1539 was passed principally to endorse the surrenders that had already taken place and establish the King's title in the properties beyond all doubt, rather than to set in motion a new series of dissolutions.

There followed the destruction of the shrines of the English saints where pilgrims had worshipped down the centuries – St Thomas à Becket at Canterbury, St William at York and St Cuthbert at Durham – and Henry, though no opponent of the veneration of images himself, encouraged the iconoclasts because he wanted to lay his hands on the treasures adorning the shrines. Twenty-six wagon-loads of wealth were plundered from Becket's shrine and taken to the Mint and the bones of the saint who had

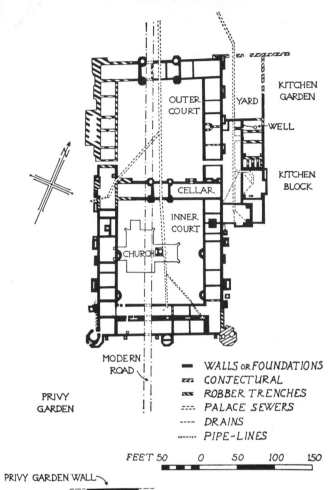

OUTER
COURT

YARD

KITCHEN
GARDEN

WELL

KITCHEN
BLOCK

CELLAR

INNER
COURT

CHURCH

MODERN
ROAD

PRIVY
GARDEN

━━ WALLS OR FOUNDATIONS
▱▱ CONJECTURAL
▨▨ ROBBER TRENCHES
∙∙∙∙ PALACE SEWERS
---- DRAINS
∙-∙-∙ PIPE-LINES

FEET 50   0   50   100   150

PRIVY GARDEN WALL

opposed Henry Plantaganet were scattered by order of Henry Tudor.

At last Henry had the wealth to indulge his passion for building on a grandiose scale, not just to enlarge a mansion begun by a Wolsey or to embellish his father's Richmond by piecemeal improvements, but to begin and finish a palace that would amaze the world. Such was that monument of royal ostentation aptly named Nonsuch, for it was designed from the first to be unique, certainly in England, and incapable of imitation, with its ornate chimney pots, its profusion of turrets and pinnacles, like an impression of Byzantium, and its costly carvings.

> That which no equal has in art or fame
> Britons deservedly do Nonsuch name.

Just as Henry had vied with Francis I at the Field of Cloth of Gold in the splendour of his temporary pavilions, so now, in 1538, he embarked on what was intended as an English answer to the French King's Chambord Château, which had been begun in the 1520s. The Surrey village of Cuddington was demolished – church, manor-house and every timbered farmstead – to make way for this triumph of fantasy.

James Needham, surveyor-general of the King's works, drew up plans for what was fundamentally a Gothic building that was to be overlaid with Classical decoration. It was built round two courts, the inner, containing the state apartments, which was completed first and was entered through a gatehouse and up a flight of steps. The half-timbered upper section of this inner court was 'garnished with a variety of pictures and other antique forms of excellent arts and workmanship', under the direction of Nicolas Bellin of Modena, who had worked with Primaticcio on the stucco decoration at Fontainebleau for Francis I; and Bellin himself carved and gilded the slate panels that covered the timber frescoes. William Cure of Amsterdam and Giles Gering saw to the intricate plaster work, with sculptures from classical mythology that amazed all beholders. The gateway was resplendent with statues of Roman emperors, yet these were dwarfed as one passed through to the inner court by a massive statue of King Henry, seated on his throne, trampling under foot a lion, the logical descendant of the gods and goddesses depicted in the plaster panels about him. 'Can harm befall the body politic, when its most sagacious King, wielding the sceptre, is protected on the right by the arts and virtues and avenging goddesses, on the left by the feats of Hercules and the tender care of the gods?' asked an ardent monarchist at the end of the century as he first saw the statue of Henry VIII.

The religious houses even provided some of the raw materials for Nonsuch. On 13 April 1538 neighbouring Merton Priory was surrendered to the King's visitors, yet only ten days later there arrived at Cuddington the first cartloads of hundreds of tons of stone, taken from the demolished priory. Chunks of Merton masonry were used in the palace foundations and broken pieces of sculptured angels and saints, once dedicated to the greater glory of God, formed the core of Henry's pleasure dome. Skilled and unskilled workmen from all over southern England were impressed for the King's service, so that five hundred and twenty men lived in tents, working late into the summer evenings to finish the palace as soon as possible. But the plans were too intricate and ambitious for speedy completion and it was

Left Pen and ink design for a mural decoration at Nonsuch Palace, about 1540.

not until 1541 that the inner court of Nonsuch was finally fit for the King to reside in, and Henry was never to see the outer court finished.

The park, covering 1,200 acres, was stocked with 1,000 deer, yet Nonsuch was very much more than a hunting lodge. From the outset it was devised as a great country palace, capable of housing great numbers of courtiers and attendants. Surprisingly, the banqueting-house was not part of the main building, but a timbered structure on a hill in the park. 'The very pearl of the realm', as Nonsuch became called, was stamped unmistakably with King Henry's personality. There was to be no other residence quite like it, just as there was to be no English King capable of rivalling Henry.

Comfort and convenience, as well as grandeur, were the hallmarks of Nonsuch, planned from its origin to be the most hygienic of all royal residences, to satisfy Henry's demanding requirements. A little can be gleaned about improvements to sanitation in the King's other houses. There was for the first time in 1533 a scourer of drains and sinks who worked his way round the palaces from Windsor to Whitehall, Hampton Court, Richmond, Greenwich, Eltham and back again, to keep the apartments safe from the most serious hazards. Among the duties of the King's apothecary was the supply of portable urinals, made of clay, at 3d. each. It was not until the very end of Henry's reign that we hear about 'a close stool for the use of the King's Majesty', when a new one was assembled by William Grene, the coffer-maker, at a cost of £6 8s. 1½d. This was a prodigious affair, with the seat, back and elbows of stout timber, padded with 3 lbs of down, covered with black velvet that was garnished with silk ribbon and fringe and tacked down by gilt nails. Grene's accounts specify a bowl and cistern, making it clear that this was not a movable closet but a water closet – and it was the first of its kind in the world.

Right Court musicians playing pipe and tabor, trumpet, harp and clavichord; an illustration from the King's own psalter.

Exultate Deo adiutori noſtro:
iubilate Deo Iacob

Sumite pſalmum : & date tympanum
pſalterium iocundum cum cythara.

5 The Flanders Mare

Above Christina, Duchess of Milan, a potential bride for Henry in 1538. The widow of Francesco Sforza, she was sixteen when Holbein painted her portrait in Brussels, and aroused Henry's interest in her.

Left Anne of Cleves by Holbein – the famous portrait which brought about her marriage with Henry.

'The Duke of Cleves hath a daughter, but I hear no great praise either of her personage nor beauty.'

John Hutton to Thomas Cromwell (1537)

'The state of princes in matters of marriage is far of worse sort than the conditions of poor men. For princes take as is brought them by others, and poor men be commonly at their own choice and liberty.'

Anthony Denny of the Privy Chamber (1540)

Even before Jane Seymour's burial in November 1537, enquiries were afoot for another bride for King Henry, who soon warmed to the idea of marriage-mongering that was destined to last a full two years. After his past experiences he understandably looked upon a further marriage as an 'extreme adventure' and was only prepared to embark on it to safeguard the succession. Although Edward appeared to be a healthy baby, the question of his survival was a constant worry and it would be provident for the King to beget a second prince. Moreover the widower's estate seemed unnatural to him and the recollection of his few blissful months with Jane, who had even succeeded in bringing him closer to both his daughters, led him to hanker after another honeymoon. On this occasion there was no potential English candidate, but no fewer than nine Continental ladies were seriously considered, and five of these agreed to sit for Holbein, whose portraits whetted the widower's interest. One painting in particular, that of the Duchess of Milan, so delighted him that he 'has been in much better humour than ever he was, making musicians play on their instruments all day long . . . He cannot be one single moment without masques, which is a sign that he purposes to marry again.' Other portraits and reports confused the issue and Cromwell passed on the verdict without further comment, that Princess Anne of Cleves excelled the Duchess of Milan in beauty 'as the golden sun did the silvery moon'. Henry was delighted with the range of candidates, yet to choose by proxy was a dubious procedure, as well as invidious, and in the end his choice was determined on wider political grounds.

Cromwell had persuaded Henry of the importance of a foreign match, coupled with an alliance to end England's isolation, for once Charles v and Francis i agreed to a peace treaty, the long-heralded papal council would meet and in all probability require them to deal effectively with the English heretic. Undoubtedly a Hapsburg or a Valois bride would be the most advantageous. At first Henry was much taken with the idea of marrying Marie of Guise, now a widow, of whom he received excellent reports. Her physique was splendid and, as he put it, he 'had need of a big wife'. When he heard she was half promised to the King of Scots, his eagerness for her increased, yet before a portrait could be obtained Marie was formally betrothed to James v, whom she married in May 1538. By then Henry was deep in negotiations for the hand of the Duchess of Milan, a widow of sixteen, then living in Brussels. This Christina was the daughter of Christian II of Denmark, now deposed, and a niece of the Emperor Charles v. Since Henry could not inspect her, Hans Holbein was sent to Brussels to make a sketch, with which he hurried home to delight his master; as a result Henry declared himself to the Emperor and excitedly talked of affiancing all three of his children to Hapsburgs. He made one overriding condition: that the Emperor should include England in any peace he made with France. Yet there were other difficulties, for although dynastic marriages had always been the hallmark of the house of Hapsburg, Charles had no desire to give Henry a passport to intervene in the Milanese, the most sensitive area in the Imperialists' struggle with France. Another stumbling-block was Henry's affinity with Christina, who was a great niece of Catherine of Aragon, and he would never admit the validity of a papal dispensation on which the Emperor for his part insisted. The young widow of Francesco Sforza was herself alarmed at the prospect of sharing Henry's bed and board, for those about her suspected that 'her great aunt was poisoned, that the second wife was put to death and the third lost for lack of keeping her childbed.' All this augured ill.

Before these Hapsburg negotiations had ground to a halt Henry received various offers from France, where there was a glut of marriageable princesses and also one unattached prince – Charles, Francis's second son – who might do far worse than marry Mary Tudor, if only to trump a Hapsburg jack. Marie of Guise had two sisters, Louise and Renée, and if neither suited Henry there was Anne of Lorraine and two other nubile ladies. Once more Holbein crossed the Channel, but he only returned with sketches of two of the candidates, and to clear his own mind Henry suggested to Francis that the five princesses, with the Queen as chaperon, should all travel to Calais for a beauty parade at which he would select his bride. This was too much for Francis I and French propriety. Surely, Henry could trust another man's opinion? 'By God!' he retorted to the French ambassador, 'The thing touches me too near. I wish to see them and know them some time before deciding' and he blushed when the envoy suggested the knights of the Round Table had a more chivalrous code. Even if Henry had been able to choose a Valois princess, it is most unlikely Francis would have agreed to his insistence on being included in any treaty made with the Empire, and on taking his side in the event of a papal council.

While Henry dithered and demanded impossible terms he was overtaken by events, for on 18 June 1538 Charles and Francis agreed to a ten-year truce and next month met at Aigues Mortes to discuss repression of Protestant heresies. The worst had happened, for this *rapprochement* of Hapsburg and Valois left England truly isolated and before the year ended Pope Paul III at last promulgated the long prepared bull deposing Henry and absolving his subjects from their allegiance. The expatriate Reginald Pole immediately urged the Catholic powers to undertake a crusade against 'the most cruel and abominable tyrant' in Whitehall and provoked the fall of his family 'of the White Rose' left in England.

For the next three years, while the invasion scare lasted, Henry devoted very considerable resources to building an elaborate system of coastal defences at key points, along the Thames Estuary, on the Kent coast at Deal, Walmer, Dover and Sandgate, at Calshot and Hurst in Hampshire and in Cornwall. These were designed by a German engineer, Stefan van Haschenperg, who was appointed 'deviser of buildings'. His most notable works were the castles at St Mawes and Pendennis in Cornwall, whose remains indicate the foreign style of their construction, and the improvements he made to Dover Castle. In Essex and elsewhere there were palisades and bulwarks, thrown up by women and children working with shovels.

In casting about for an ally, as much as searching for a bride, Henry turned in desperation to the German princes and after many false starts settled on Cleves for a political alliance and a wife. Young Duke William, who had just come to rule in the duchies of Cleves, Juliers and Berg, was himself at odds with the Emperor over his inheritance of Gelderland and, like Henry, was Erastian and anti-papal without being Lutheran; though one of his sisters had married the Elector of Saxony, he had refused to join the German Princes' League. As an ally he had considerable merits, as Cleves was a barrier between Imperial Germany and the Hapsburg Netherlands. Besides its strategic position the duchy had become a recruiting ground for mercenaries, so Henry asked his ambassador to discover all he could about the Duke, 'earnestly to feel always the bottom of his stomach concerning' religion and politics. The Duke's two unmarried sisters, Anne and Amelia, had recently been painted by Lucas Cranach, but Henry wanted his envoys to see the ladies in person – or at least rather more of them than was visible in their 'monstrous habit' which hid their faces and concealed their figures. This request amazed the duchy chancellor: 'Why, would you see them naked?' he asked. In the end Master Holbein was sent out to paint both sisters and when Henry had inspected the portraits, pronounced himself satisfied with Anne. The question of her earlier precontract to the Duke of Lorraine's son seemed adequately answered to enable a marriage treaty to be signed with England on 6 October 1539.

Henry found this wooing by proxy a dispiriting business. Besides Holbein's portrait he had written reports which a series of ambassadors had sent to Cromwell. 'Every man praiseth the beauty of the same lady [Anne], as well for the face as for the whole body, above all ladies excellent', wrote Christopher Mont; another gave great weight to Duke William's words that his sister's looks 'would get her a good husband' whatever happened to Henry's negotiations. Nicholas Wotton had added a cautious note in underlining that Anne was a dull girl with few accomplishments; she was, he said, poorly educated, could at present speak only German and knew not a note of music, 'for they take it here in Germany for a rebuke and an occasion of lightness that great ladies should be learned or have any knowledge of music.' But for some reason, even if Henry saw this paper, he was not put off, finding no apparent signs of incompatibility. For a Princess of Cleves the King of England was certainly a great catch but, had her enquiries about him been as exhaustive as his about her, one wonders whether she would willingly have left the Rhineland.

After two and a quarter years there was once more to be a Queen's household, to fill a void at court and offer hope of preferment. When Catherine of Aragon had married Henry, her household had initially numbered one hundred and sixty, of whom eight had been Spaniards, and though Wolsey had succeeded in cutting down her establishment and replacing the Spanish ladies the number of persons attendant on the Queen had risen to nearly two hundred during Anne Boleyn's heyday, and Jane Seymour's household was not much smaller. Used to modest arrangements at her father's court, Anne of Cleves was not at all discouraged to find her personal staff numbered no more than 126, as a result of Cromwell's reforms, but was anxious to find places about her for all the men and women she had brought over from Cleves, little realising the vested interest of English courtiers in wanting to keep her compatriots to a minimum. In her entourage from Cleves had come Dr Cornelis, her physician, Schoulenburg the cook, Englebert the footman and three laundresses, all of whom might expect to be and were in fact, retained, but besides them were a number of gentlemen-in-waiting and fifteen ladies equally hopeful of posts about their mistress. Yet the signing of the marriage treaty had been the starting-gun for the race among the English nobility for the rich prizes of places in the new Queen's household for daughters, sisters and nieces. Norfolk had secured the appointment of his nieces Catherine Howard and Mary Norris as maids of honour, while Lady Lisle, wife of the Governor of Calais, had found a niche for one daughter and was hoping to be able to place a second. King Henry, when appealed to, said he had not finally decided on the number of the maids, or their names, but that all appointed must needs be 'fair . . . and meet for the room'. Other courtiers were just as tenacious as Lady Lisle so that Queen Anne found herself out-witted.

Even if Anne's household was smaller than her predecessor's, the very fact of there being a Queen's court again after the interregnum had a tremendous impact on Whitehall and the other palaces, so that it seemed to one eye-witness as if Anne had gathered round her 'a great court of noblemen and gentlemen as ever I think was seen in our master's day'. The Earl of Rutland, who had been Lord Chamberlain to Jane Seymour, now served Anne in the same office, while Sir Edward Baynton was again vice-Chamberlain and Sir John Dudley was master of the Horse. Her chaplains included Dr Owen Oglethorpe, friend of Peter Martyr and Coverdale, who would survive the vicissitudes of clerical life to crown Elizabeth in 1559. Heading the list of female attendants were six ladies-in-waiting, by now termed 'the great ladies of the household', whereas Catherine of Aragon had been served by eight. Two were indeed close to the Crown – Lady Margaret Douglas, daughter of Henry's sister, Margaret of Scotland, and Mary, Duchess of Richmond, widow of the King's natural son. They were joined by the Duchess of Suffolk, the Countess of Sussex and Ladies Howard and Clinton, all wives of leading councillors. These 'great ladies' had a ceremonial importance and were chiefly in evidence at special functions, whereas the ladies of the Bedchamber and of the Privy Chamber and the maids of honour were in daily contact with the Queen. The three surviving ladies from Cleves were naturally closest to Anne, but three Englishwomen, despite linguistic difficulties, became very much part of her domestic circle – Lady Rutland, wife of her Chamberlain, and two widows, Lady Rochford and Lady Edgecombe. Eleanor Rutland was by birth a Paston, whose family's fortunes were inevitably linked with the house of Howard; Lady Rochford, who had been dismissed from her post in Anne Boleyn's Bedchamber, had regained favour under Jane Seymour soon after her husband's execution; while Catherine Edgecombe had recently lost her second husband, the Devonshire Sir Piers Edgecombe. The last attendant of note was Mistress Lowe, from Cleves, mother of the maids of honour, a matronly confidante, whose influence extended throughout the Queen's apartments.

Anne had arrived at Calais by the overland route through Düsseldorf and Antwerp, as unnecessary travel by sea was reckoned a hazard for her complexion, as well as dangerous, and she waited at the English bridgehead for the weather to improve before embarking. Lord Lisle, the Governor, had arranged a joust and banquets, but the gale increased in force. Southampton, the Lord Admiral, who was to escort Anne to England was required by Henry to 'cheer my Lady and her train so they may think the time short', but he found entertaining her heavy going as they had no common language. One evening, through Dr Olisleger as interpreter, Anne asked Southampton to teach her a card game that Henry liked, so they played 'Sent', and Cromwell's son Gregory joined in. At last, after Christmas the weather improved and Anne made the crossing to Deal. By New Year's Eve she was at Rochester and although Henry was not due to meet his bride until 3 January near Greenwich, he could not keep away; he had been impatient ever since receiving Southampton's letter from Calais praising Anne and he wanted desperately to see her for himself. It was almost like court revels of thirty years back for he, with five of his Privy Chamber, disguised in marbled cloaks with hoods, came to Rochester Abbey in the afternoon of New Year's Day. Slipping into her room, he embraced her, pretending at first that he had come on the King's behalf with a gift. Anne was abashed and when she did realise he was her fiancé she could not speak to him, as he had expected, in English, but nervously looked out of the window watching a bull being baited. Henry who had come 'to nourish love', left as soon as he decently could, still clutching the present of furs that he thought she ill deserved. If this was beauty, what was ugliness? Holbein and the ambassadors had absolutely misled him, and in the barge on his way back to Greenwich he poured out his heart to Sir Anthony Browne, master of the Horse, saying 'I see nothing in this woman as men report of her and I marvel that wise men would make such reports as they have done'. When Cromwell asked him that evening how he liked Anne, he snapped, 'Nothing so well as she is spoken of. If I had known as much before as I know now, she should never have come into this realm.' He had thoroughly cold feet and while he could not escape acting his part at the official reception he prayed there might be some way of avoiding marriage.

At the foot of Shooters Hill on 3 January Anne was greeted by Rutland, her Chamberlain, and the English ladies assigned to her suite. Here she changed into robes of cloth of gold in a pavilion before riding to meet

Henry at Blackheath, accompanied by a great concourse of peers, bishops, city fathers and merchants from the German Steelyard, and to be escorted to Greenwich Palace. The French ambassador, Marillac, gave his first impressions of Anne to Francis I as being about thirty, 'tall and thin, of middling beauty, with determined and resolute countenance.' His report the same day to Montmorency was less restrained: those, he said, who saw Anne at close quarters find she is 'not so young as was at first thought, nor so handsome as people affirmed'; he detected a show of vivacity in her expression, but it was 'insufficient to counterbalance her want of beauty'. Nor did her dozen or so German maids of honour help to create a good impression, for each was dressed in clothes of identical material and colour, in a hideous style, looking downright dowdy as if they were members of some outlandish sisterhood.

Lady Browne, appointed to Anne's household, was quick to predict that Henry would never really love her, for she saw in the Queen 'such fashion and manner of bringing up so gross and far discrepant from the King's Highness' appetite.' In another room at Greenwich Cromwell was having an uncomfortable audience with his master, who reluctantly agreed that despite her looks Anne had a regal manner, yet Henry had found no sparkle. He postponed the marriage for two days while he clutched at the one straw – the question of Anne's pre-contract to Lorraine's son, but though the delegation from Cleves had not brought the documents, they satisfied the Privy Council with an instrument declaring that the Princess was free from all legal ties. When Cromwell reported this Henry told him he had been 'ill-handled' and had he not been afraid of 'making a ruffle in the world' and driving the Duke of Cleves into the Imperial camp, he would have sent Anne home. As things were he would have to go through with the ceremony, which would make it the most miserable Twelfth Night of his life. The evening before he sighed that it was 'a great yoke to enter into' and he made it quite clear to Cromwell just before going to the Queen's closet for the wedding, that 'If it were not to satisfy the world and my realm, I would not do that I must do this day for none earthly thing.' Acting with dignity would rescue him from becoming a laughing stock. After the ceremony he publicly kissed Anne and she went in procession wearing her hair long and on it a crown of diamonds and pearls set with rosemary.

Though for a few nights they shared the same great bed, theirs was a marriage in name only. Cromwell, hoping that by some miracle Anne might summon some undisclosed reserves of feminine wiles to arouse her husband, unwisely asked Henry how he found her and was told his distaste was greater than ever, 'for by her breasts and belly she should be no maid; which when I felt them struck me so to the heart that I had neither will nor courage to the rest'. Over the next few weeks the gentlemen of the Privy Chamber heard from their master intimate details of why he never succeeded in achieving intercourse. Anne was plain, timid, frigid and scared of the colossus beside her, and as she had no appeal for him he could never 'be provoked and steered to know her carnally'. His doctors, Butts and Chamber, were convinced their master was not impotent; the reason the marriage was never consummated was 'he had found her body disordered and indisposed to excite and provoke any lust in him'. It was not for lack of interest on his part that she remained a virgin. By April he was sure he

Holbein's drawings of brooches, pendants and necklaces, worn by the ladies of the court.

would 'never have any more children if he so continued, declaring that before God he thought she was not his lawful wife.' As the master of the Horse could testify, the best brood mares in his stables came from Flanders, so if Henry dubbed Anne 'the Flanders Mare', as tradition has it, it was done with devastating irony.

In the Queen's apartments the ladies of the Bedchamber discussed the problem in their own way and, as her English improved, even questioned Anne herself. They hoped she was pregnant, and when she said she was certainly not, Lady Edgecombe asked 'How is it possible for your Grace to know that and lie every night with the King?' while Lady Rochford said 'By Our Lady, Madam, I think your Grace is a maid still?' 'Why', replied Anne, 'when he comes to bed he kisses me and taketh me by the hand and biddeth me "Good night, Sweet Heart"; and in the morning kisses me and biddeth me "Farewell, Darling". Is not this enough?' Lady Rochford burst out 'Madam, there must be more than this or it will be long or we have a Duke of York, which all this realm most desireth.' 'Nay', said Anne, 'is not this enough? I am contented with this, for I know no more'.

Anne had her own diversions, with a tumbler performing his feats to enliven a winter evening, and gambling at cards, as Southampton had taught her, or at 'blank dice' in her Chamber at Baynards Castle and Whitehall, when her gentlewomen generally won modest sums from her. Her English improved rapidly. Though she could not play any instrument herself, it is clear from the entries in her private accounts how important she regarded music; no doubt this was Henry's influence, and besides her own musicians she would also engage the minstrels attached to Prince Edward's household to play the music she fancied. The excitement of the chase and the roughness of outdoor life were not for Anne, though she enjoyed strolling through the gardens, finding out the English names of plants and shrubs and she tipped palace gardeners more frequently and more generously than bargemen. Her only pet was a parrot. Mr Locke made her plain black dresses of damask and satin, which served as a backcloth for her jewellery, of which she was fond, and one of her few personal extravagances as Queen was to buy a brooch depicting the tale of Sampson, garnished with diamonds.

By Easter Henry's interest in one of Anne's maids of honour was no longer a secret at court. Few thought that Catherine Howard would ever become more than a mistress, yet the King was already thinking in terms of a divorce from Anne. His conscience had continued to nag him and the more he dwelt on his affairs the more certain he was that his marriage was invalid. God had withheld his blessing from his relations with Anne because they were unlawful, and he now realised that her pre-contract with Francis, Marquis de Pont à Mousson, Lorraine's son, must be as great a stumbling-block to connubial bliss as Catherine of Aragon's marriage with Prince Arthur had been. It was bound to be a fruitless marriage, devoid of happiness, as it was against canon and civil law, and as an expert in these matters himself through wretched personal experience he would not be shouted down by councillors and lawyers, whose task would merely be to find the means to untie the knot with Anne, whether or not he married Mistress Howard. This time at least he would not be at the mercy of a partial, captive pope. The personal affairs of a monarch, however, could not remain private – he knew they were already being caught up in wider questions of politics and that however understanding Anne of Cleves might prove, the palace revolution would require scapegoats and produce traitors. It was not only his wife that troubled him; his alliance with the German Protestant princes was also a marriage of convenience from which he wanted a divorce. The Hapsburg-Valois Ten Year Truce was crumbling, for Charles V had invested Philip of Spain with the Duchy of Milan, and another round of Continental warfare would free Henry from the need of an alliance with Cleves.

Some six months before Anne had landed, Cromwell had lost his outright ascendancy with the King and many at court reckoned his work as architect of the Reformation Monarchy was finished. As the driving force behind the royal supremacy, the Dissolution of the Monasteries, and the re-organisation of government he had inevitably made enemies who would not hesitate to exploit any failures that could be pinned on the Lord Privy Seal. He was all the more vulnerable because of the offices he had amassed, so that he could be called to answer to the King for many areas of administration and policy, while men coveting his posts dogged his steps.

Cromwell's achievement in secular affairs was no less striking than his ecclesiastical policy, and a thorough overhaul of the machinery of government was a necessary counterpart to the royal supremacy in the development of the modern state. His earliest offices in the King's service had all been concerned with finance – as master of the Jewels in the Chamber, then the chief financial department, as clerk of the Hanaper in Chancery and, from 1533, as Chancellor of the Exchequer, and he retained these posts despite the rapid promotion that followed. His experience enabled him to become what amounted to a 'minister of finance' and he had a far wider appreciation of problems than the Lord Treasurer, often away on diplomatic or military duties, whose knowledge of finance did not range beyond the Exchequer. Cromwell's next three posts, principal Secretary (1534–40), master of the Rolls (1534–6) and Lord Privy Seal (1536–40), brought under his control the major government secretariats – the clerks respectively of the Signet, of Chancery and of the Privy Seal. These offices gave him a unique position at the centre of the administration, and he could see the existing system as a whole, compare anomalies, understand procedures and reach sensible conclusions about needed reforms. No one without this detailed knowledge of specialised departments could have prepared reforms that were feasible and made a comprehensive plan for efficient government.

We need not pursue the details of the 'revolution in government' that Cromwell accomplished, for he has found his own remembrancer in Professor Geoffrey Elton. Basically, he transformed the medieval system, which had sufficed for Wolsey, into an administrative machine suited to the modern, national state. 'Household' government had depended on the King's personal actions and Cromwell had to devise a system in which departments could function independently of the sovereign's own intervention. He left behind him a system of household officers as political heads of specialist departments, all of them privy councillors, who were the equivalent of cabinet ministers of a later age, and these were fully supported by professional civil servants. Thus a thoroughly bureaucratic organisation replaced the personal control by kings of old. Antiquated methods of procedure were abandoned and paperwork supplanted orders by word of

A signet warrant under the King's signature made by a wooden stamp in 1544.

mouth. In the financial sphere there were now specialist departments, such as the Court of Augmentations under its Chancellor, Sir Richard Rich, created to administer the revenues of former monastic property, while the officials of the Chamber no longer accounted to the King himself, but became an integral part of the 'national' financial machinery. Gone for ever were the days when a king like Henry VII checked accounts himself, and when an audit could be postponed indefinitely if he could not find the time for it. Men now talked about 'the national revenue', not about 'the King's finances', for of a truth all the Sovereign's private concerns had become 'nationalised'. Another remarkable feature was the development of the office of principal Secretary of State, for as a result of Cromwell's extraordinary position there was literally no area of government which lay outside its purview.

An essential part of these reforms was the remodelling of the royal household on the lines begun by Wolsey, but not resumed for another fourteen years. When he had first come to live at court Cromwell's eagle eye had caught many things amiss and men began to talk about his plans for 'abridging the King's house', yet his earliest schemes failed. Surmounting the crisis of the Pilgrimage of Grace had been costly and special measures for the defence of the country in the next two years added to Henry's liabilities, pointing to the need for economy at the centre, to be achieved in part an onslaught on extravagance and waste, in part by administrative reforms that would curb numbers. At last, on Christmas Eve 1539, as Henry waited at Greenwich for news of Anne's crossing, he inaugurated Cromwell's household ordinances, and the new system survived until the days of the Prince Consort.

Henry was prepared to endorse reforms that would make for economies in the 'below stairs' departments, provided his own Chamber was given an establishment more appropriate to his idea of majesty, and that he could revive his personal bodyguard, the company of 'Spears' or Gentlemen Pensioners, founded at his accession but subsequently disbanded. He had

An elaborately enamelled bowl from the Tudor collection. This piece is one of three named in the Tudor inventory of plate, which can be identified today.

been pressing for a revival of the Spears since early in 1537 and had thought in terms of one hundred men, though Cromwell managed to beat him down to fifty. The King had been envious of the bodyguard of Francis I, the famed Becs de Corbin, and wanted a similar corps of young men from good families, with splendid physiques, like Wolsey's tall chaplains, who would be an ornament to his court, with a full ceremonial role, and at the same time would form an élite of highly-trained soldiers in time of war – which indeed loomed near. In his orders re-establishing the Gentlemen Pensioners at Christmas 1539, the King declared that there were 'many young gentlemen of noble blood which have no exercise in the feats of arms in handling and reining the spear and other feats of war on horseback', but though the spear was to be their weapon in war, at court they would serve on foot with pole-axes, to distinguish them from the ninety strong Yeomen of the Guard, armed with halberds. Their duties were defined thoroughly and there were fines for absence and irresponsibility. Sir Anthony Browne, a gentleman of the Privy Chamber, was appointed the first Captain. At a stroke, then, there were to be fifty new places at court; there was a rush of applicants and the first list of appointments is a roll call of the families who would leave their mark on Tudor history – Carew and Zouche, Ashley and Wingfield, Herbert, Ferrers and the rest.

Since the Eltham Ordinance there had been fresh orders for the gentlemen of the Privy Chamber, who from 1533 had been required to attend in two groups of seven for a six weeks' tour of duty, yet even this arrangement had proved insufficient. Now Cromwell considered the Chamber as a whole and assigned the Privy Chamber sixteen gentlemen, two gentlemen ushers, four gentlemen ushers daily waiters, three grooms and two barbers. The outer Chamber was now to be staffed by three cup-bearers, three carvers and three sewers, four squires for the Body – a reduction – and two surveyors. A yeoman and a groom sufficed for the King's Robes and three officers and two pages for the Beds, while there was now a single groom porter. As a reserve of servants, there were to be eight gentlemen ushers as quarter waiters, four sewers, four pages and fourteen grooms, all without livery and basic allowances at court. Taken together this represents a considerable increase in the establishment since 1526 and shows how successful Henry was in opposing Cromwell's plan of economies for the Chamber.

Twelve peers and senior officials were entitled, when at court, to feed at the King's board, from the Lord Chancellor downwards, but of those named in Cromwell's list only the vice-Chamberlain, Sir Anthony Wingfield, and the Captain and Lieutenant of the Gentlemen Pensioners were invariably present. The officials of other departments 'on the King's side' – Counting House, Chapel and Jewel House – and the King's doctors and minstrels were given clear instructions about where to take their meals, while similar arrangements were made for the Queen's Chamber and its sub-departments.

A notable absentee from Cromwell's list was Will Somers, the King's fool, who not only regarded himself as a servant of the Chamber but was always paid as such. Perhaps the omission of his name was itself the prank of a clerk, for besides being a man whose company Henry would no more forego than that of James Hill, his chief singer, Somers got on very well with Cromwell. The minister had indeed to be thankful for Somers' jokes to

Henry about the ways in which he was being cheated by the household system as it was. Tradition has it that Richard Fermour, a merchant of the Staple of Calais, had introduced Somers, then his servant, to the King at Greenwich in 1525 and that Henry had been so delighted with his mock-serious repartee that he gave him a place as a fool. In physique he was the very antithesis of Henry – short, lean and stooping, almost like a hunchback; and to laugh at royal pomp the more readily he would often carry a monkey. A curious friendship developed between the two men and when Henry was in pain with his leg, Somers was the only person who could cheer him. Foreign ambassadors' reports tell us nothing about his antics or saws, for he was not paraded as a pet and instead Somers kept behind the scenes, serving his master with adroit circumspection, becoming almost a confessor. Wives changed, ministers fell, palace officials incurred the royal displeasure, but Will Somers went on for ever. In the last ten years of the reign he was perhaps the man nearest Henry's thoughts and he never wittingly allowed himself to be exploited by factions at court.

Although Cromwell had to acquiesce in Henry's demands for staffing the

Henry with Princess Mary and his jester, Will Somers.

Chamber he did succeed in controlling its expenditure by making it, and every other department of the household above and below stairs, subject to the Counting House, or Board of Green Cloth, over which a new official, the Lord Great Master of the Household, was to preside. Until now, as we have seen, the traditional separation of the King's and the Queen's Chambers both from each other and, more significantly, from the household below stairs, had been maintained, hallowed by the complementary if not outright rival rule of the Lord Chamberlain and the Lord Steward. What was needed was a powerful administrative body that could regulate the entire court, and Cromwell placed his faith in the Board of Green Cloth under the Great Master, on the lines of the 'grand maître' of the French court. The time was propitious for a change, since George, Earl of Shrewsbury, Lord Steward since the opening of the reign, had just died and his post had been left unfilled, although Suffolk had been granted the reversion of it. Suffolk was a man of the right seniority and weight to impose his will on the court, and himself introduced the bill in Parliament establishing the office of Lord Great Master and confirming his appointment to it. The title mattered far less than the calibre of the man bearing it and though Queen Mary abandoned the new name to revive the old in 1554, the supremacy of the office was by then undisputed. Significantly Suffolk's successor as Great Master in 1545 was the reigning Lord Chamberlain, Lord St John, who recognised that his new appointment was very much a promotion.

At the new style Board of Green Cloth with the Lord Great Master sat the treasurer and controller of the Household, and at least one of these had to attend a meeting in the Counting House at 8 o'clock every morning with the cofferer, the two clerks of the Green Cloth and the two clerks controller. This arrangement ensured thorough supervision of the domestic expenditure of every department of the palace, as all purchases had to be made through the cofferer, who scrutinised the purveyor's accounts. The complicated financial checks and counterchecks now introduced were foolproof, collusion and fraudulent accounting became impossible, and if the paperwork increased, at least accounts were regularly balanced and audited,

A grotesque jousting helmet, presented to Henry by the Emperor Charles V.

budgets prepared and a formidable campaign in business efficiency mounted. The Board was not merely concerned with tallies, journals and counter rolls, for it planned the daily menus for 10 a.m. dinner and 4 p.m. supper and was charged with keeping discipline among the army of royal retainers. The Great Master and treasurer, with other commitments as privy councillors, could not expect to give much time to the affairs of the Counting House, but the controller and particularly the cofferer were very much concerned with the intimate details of running a vast establishment. The clerks were required to go the rounds at mealtimes seeing that no interlopers were feeding at the King's expense in the various household departments and that no meals were being sent to 'private chambers'. They checked all stores in every department and they alone authorised the payment of wages and allowances, even those of the Chamber officials.

To stop petty pilfering the perks of every office were laid down precisely. The groom of the Scalding House, for instance, was allowed the feathers of all poultry plucked, the clerk of the Acatary kept the heads and skins of all calves slaughtered, and the yeoman of the Bake House could do what he liked with the cinders drawn from the oven fires. The serjeant porters at the palace gates were on pain of fine to keep a strict watch on people leaving and if they suspected goods were being smuggled out, whether firewood or silver cups, they were to summon the Knight Marshal. There were strict rules about the keeping of servants, pets and vagabonds, and one of the porters was to tour the buildings four times a day ejecting intruders – this was especially important at Whitehall where the public had a right of way through the palace. When the court moved on to another residence or went on progress the Knight Harbinger had undisputed authority to assign billets.

Everyone's duties and the standard of their performance were set down, often within a timetable, to ensure that tasks were no longer skimped or unnecessarily prolonged and to achieve the maximum degree of supervision as a war on waste. Two clerks of the Green Cloth had to inspect the food in the Larder provided for the King's table and witness its delivery to the master cook. Extra locks were put on the cellar and buttery doors that could only be opened by an official from the Counting House. No household officer could leave court without the express permission of the Lord Great Master, treasurer or controller. Altogether the standard of service in the palace was elevated to a new level, and if the emphasis in Cromwell's Ordinance was on fines and discipline it is worth remembering how highly he valued professional service, whether it was in the spicery or the cellar, and envisaged every department being able to provide a satisfactory career structure. Indeed, he wanted the head of each department not to take on any servant who seemed unlikely to qualify for promotion.

The bureaucratic system swiftly took root. Any departure from the duties, numbers of staff or allowances provided in the Ordinance required specific authority and so we find Suffolk as Lord Great Master allowing the Queen's maids of honour to have every day for breakfast a chine of beef and for the gentlemen singers to receive a larger meat ration. Anne Harris had contracted to wash the royal table linen for £10 a year and had subsequently succeeded in having this raised to £16 13s. 4d., but when in 1543 she asked for a further rise, to bring it to a round £20, her claim went right up to the

Henry dining in the Privy Chamber, a pen and ink sketch by Holbein.

An ale mug of German stoneware, with English gilt mounts. The centre of the lid bears an enamelled design and the inscription 'The tongue that lieth killeth the soul'.

Board of Green Cloth, which ruled after due consideration that she could receive her claim, but reduced her allowances for fuel, soap and sweet powder. Sir John Gaze, the controller, was at pains to make a detailed list of Anne's duties, requiring her to wash every week seven long breakfast cloths, seven short ones, eight hand towels and three dozen napkins.

The court ate its way through an enormous amount of food. An example of a full menu for dinner is the fare provided for Henry and his entourage when they visited the Marquess of Exeter at Horsley in Surrey, during the 1533 summer progress. The first course consisted of salads of damsons, artichokes, cabbage lettuces, purslane and cucumbers, with which were served cold dishes of stewed sparrows, carp, capons in lemon, larded pheasants, duck, gulls, brews, forced rabbit, pasty of venison from fallow deer and pear pasty. This was followed by a hot course of stork, gannet, heron, pullets, quail, partridge, fresh sturgeon, pasty of venison from red deer, chickens baked in caudle and fritters. Once these dishes were removed the third and last course was served, consisting of jelly, blancmange, apples with pistachios, pears with carraway, filberts, scraped cheese with sugar, clotted cream with sugar, quince pie, marchpane and rounded off with the customary wafers and hippocras, the cordial of spiced wine that was the Tudor equivalent of a glass of port. This was by no means a lavish repast compared with some of the banquets given at Whitehall for special embassies and it was not surprising that the English were acquiring a reputation abroad for gluttony. Cooked vegetables were rare and bread was eaten with meat and fish. There was a great range of game available – larks, teal, cranes, snipe, bustard, godwits and pipers often feature – and these, like the meat and fish, were generally cooked in herbs and heavily spiced to conceal the unpalatable fact that they were not as fresh as might be. Judging from the menus, Henry was fond of galantines and game pies, baked with oranges, and regarded haggis as very much an English dish.

For all his patronage at court and his sponsorship of parliamentary candidates, Cromwell never built up a party of followers. He sought to dominate the whole council, not to lead a party on it, until it was too late, for only when his days were running out did he hand over the principal Secretaryship to Sadler and Wriothesley in the hope that he could command two firm votes in council. The privy council spoke with one voice and though there was debate there was, in theory, no acknowledged faction. The title 'Lord President' was borne by Suffolk out of deference to his seniority, yet of them all Cromwell was reckoned *primus inter pares*. Southampton, the Lord Admiral, had like Suffolk been close to Henry from his youth, and while Audley, More's successor as Lord Chancellor, had once shared Cromwell's outlook he was essentially a man who followed the King. Grants of monastic lands had enabled him to embark on building his fine house at Audley End, near Saffron Walden, which spurred young Russell, another careerist, to begin Chenies. The remaining lay members of the 'inner council' of the later 1530s (not so different in size and composition from a modern cabinet) were with one exception men epitomised by Sir William Paulet, the controller of the Household, who was, in his own words, made of the willow, not the oak, and would change course as expediency dictated. The exception was Norfolk.

Thomas Howard, the third Duke, seeing himself as the embodiment of the ruling caste, had always thought Cromwell an upstart and his son, Surrey, called him 'that foul churl'. Norfolk had expected to profit from Wolsey's fall, but as the years went by found he had been out-manoeuvred. Holbein's portrait, painted in 1539, with the expression giving nothing away except his concern for his health – he was a martyr to both rheumatism and indigestion – shows him clutching the Lord Treasurer's white staff, which he had still clung to despite his niece's execution. He had stayed in semi-retirement from court at his palace at Kenninghall until Henry summoned him to command the army against the rebels. Though he had rigorously suppressed the Pilgrimage of Grace, scoffed at the priests' 'old *mumpsimus* and superstitions' and shared in the scramble for monastic lands, he was essentially a conservative. When he discovered an Exchequer clerk had married an ex-nun, he upbraided the man, who unwisely quoted Scripture at him, to justify himself, but the Lord Treasurer replied, 'I have never read the Scripture, nor never will read it. It was merry in England afore the New Learning came up; yea, I would all things were as hath been in times past.' So long as Cromwell could keep him from court, isolated at Kenninghall, there was no danger from Norfolk. He pleaded with the Lord Privy Seal to be allowed to return to the council chamber and serve his

Will Somers, Henry's fool, listens to his master playing on the harp; another illustration from the King's own psalter, about 1540.

onfitebor tibi in feculum quia

& expectabo nomen tuum quoniam b

in confpectu fanctorum tuorum G

patri Sicut erat.

in

in

li

e.

r

Stephen Gardiner, Bishop of Winchester, from a portrait at Hardwick Hall.

A cameo of Henry VIII and Prince Edward, showing the King's warm affection for his son and heir.

sovereign, trying to build up a degree of friendship by asking Cromwell to stand godfather for his grandson and to be executor of his will, but the more amicable he showed himself, the more suspicious Cromwell became; as Norfolk's wife had warned him, 'the duke can speak [as] fair to his enemy as to his friend', but he needed no warning.

On the 'inner council' there were only four clerics, where the Reformist Archbishop Cranmer was outnumbered by three conservative churchmen, the bishops of Durham, Chichester and Winchester. Cuthbert Tunstall, Bishop of Durham since 1530, had earlier on held at different times two of Cromwell's offices (master of the Rolls and Lord Privy Seal), but there was no *rapport* between the two men. After the Pilgrimage of Grace he became President of the council in the North and he was not often present at privy council meetings. But Parliament was another matter and the Prince

Bishop, faithful to Catholic dogma, took a leading role in opposing Cranmer in the debate on doctrine in the Lords that led to the Act of Six Articles. Richard Sampson, now Bishop of Chichester, had been nurtured in Wolsey's secretariat and, before the Cardinal fell, had been singled out by Henry to become Dean of the Chapel Royal. He was a most regular attendant in council.

But the effective clerical leader of the conservatives was Stephen Gardiner, who had never forgiven Cromwell for ousting him from the Secretaryship in April 1534. His arrogance, which had been noted even in his young days when he taught canon and civil law at Trinity Hall, Cambridge, always made him a difficult colleague and more than any bishop he disliked Cromwell's powers as vice-regent in spiritual affairs and his holding as a layman the prebend of Sarum and the deanery of Wells. Their correspondence became acrimonious and Gardiner's opposition to Cromwell's was all the more vehement for having a personal edge. The Bishop had made his peace with the King by writing a tract on Obedience which lauded the royal supremacy in terms that Cromwell surely approved, and this had brought him the post of ambassador to France in September 1535, which he held for three years. As with Norfolk, Cromwell was anxious to keep Gardiner from court and council, but when Parliament met in 1539 the Bishop, in alliance with Norfolk, was able to challenge the minister's rule.

The parliamentary session of 1539, which gave royal proclamations the force of law and savagely attainted the Countess of Salisbury for the polemical attacks on Henry by her emigré son, Reginald Pole, is memorable for the first authoritative statement of the doctrine of the English Church, the Act of Six Articles, which was intended as an Act of Unity, but in the event only served to intensify the divisions that had been hardening for a decade. The Ten Articles drawn up by Convocation in 1536 and the statement of faith in the Bishop's Book the following year, largely the work of Cranmer, had shown how far Henry and his bishops were progressing on the road to Wittenberg, while Cromwell's Injunctions as Vicar-General, requiring a copy of the Bible in English to be placed in every parish church, stressed the Scriptural basis of a Reformed Church. Pilgrimages to holy shrines, the veneration of relics and the monastic life were over. To the Reformist clergy like Hugh Latimer, Bishop of Worcester, who had preached Jane Seymour's funeral sermon, Henry had called his people out of darkness into the marvellous light of Christ and the comings and goings of envoys from the Lutheran princes of Germany suggested further reforms in the direction of Continental Protestantism. Cranmer, Latimer and Shaxton of Salisbury placed their faith in Cromwell being able to pilot further measures through Parliament and council for the salvation of England.

King Henry, as befitted the Supreme Head of the Church, was himself searching for a doctrinal formula no less diligently than his bishops, as the marginal jottings in his theological tracts show. A new book, hot from the press would be tossed in turn to two gentlemen of the Chamber of different outlook, and then Henry would chair a discussion between them on the book's merits. The breach with Rome had launched him on a theological voyage with no clear destination in mind, whereas the Reformers knew precisely where they wanted him to go to achieve a renewal of the Christian

Title-page of Cranmer's great Bible, 1540, printed by Richard Grafton, showing Henry, the Supreme Head of the Church, in the image of God.

191

life and the conservatives wanted a Catholic Church without the Pope. The King could not expect to 'throw a man headlong from the top of a high tower and bid him stay when he was half-way down', and his own inclinations were a strange mixture, keeping him far from the Lutheran position and regarding the 'perfect School of Christ', just established by Calvin in Geneva, a fount of abominable heresies. He held most firmly to the Catholic doctrine of transubstantiation, clung to the idea of Purgatory and delighted in ceremonial and the customary observances which, as much as the music, enhanced the beauty of a solemn mass in the Chapel Royal. On the other hand he was against extreme unction, regarded auricular confession as unimportant and took what a later age would deem a rather 'Low Church' view of ordination to the priesthood, even though he insisted on clerical celibacy and denied the cup to the laity. Court preachers who were expected to take the pulpit for at least an hour, though not more than ninety minutes, had to steer a difficult course. Henry was himself present in the Lords in the spring of 1539 for the great debate. Gardiner, back at court for the sessions, now had the opportunity of discussions with the King, and

Giralmo da Treviso's painting of the four Evangelists stoning the Pope. Such anti-papal paintings found favour at court at this period.

succeeded with the aid of Tunstall, Sampson, Archbishop Lee of York and Stokesley of London in worsting the Reformists led by Cranmer, Latimer and Shaxton. The conservatives did not win all their points, for Henry refused to countenance compulsory confession, but the Six Articles effectively put back the clock. Though Latimer and Shaxton resigned their sees, Cromwell survived the onslaught of Gardiner and Norfolk, to the surprise of not a few, and would endeavour to keep in step with his monarch, who undoubtedly achieved popularity from the Act, shrewdly sensing that his subjects were by and large 'more inclined to the old religion than the new opinions'.

While the negotiations for the Cleves marriage proceeded, assurances were given to Anne by Dr Robert Barnes, Henry's accredited envoy to Denmark and the Duchy, that despite the 'Whip with Six Strings' there was no persecution of Lutherans in England, but rather a complete 'freedom of the Gospel'. Barnes, like Luther an ex-Augustinian friar, had experienced the truth of the Gospel with Hugh Latimer in Cambridge in the year before Anne Boleyn had come to court; and although Henry did not care for a man whom Luther was affectionately to dub 'Saint Robert', he used him for various diplomatic missions to Germany and Scandinavia where his avowed Protestant sympathies would be an asset. He was reputedly the first cleric in England to say divine service entirely in the vernacular. Feeling secure with Anne of Cleves in Whitehall as patron and Gardiner out of the council, he decided to fly a dangerous theological kite. The Lenten sermons at Paul's Cross were in Tudor days akin to the 'Bishop of London's Lent Book', except that their influence in an age of theological controversy was far, far greater. When Gardiner found that Barnes was to preach on the first Sunday in Lent 1540 he insisted on substituting his own name and went out of his way to make a forceful attack on him in his sermon. 'The devil is not yet gone', he said, 'for men who no longer wear friars' habit offer heaven without works', – yea, a man 'might live in his pleasure and yet have heaven at the last!' A fortnight later Dr Barnes made a virulent reply to Gardiner at Paul's Cross and the Bishop complained to the King, who summoned the two disputants to court to reach 'concord in truth'. In the King's Chamber Barnes offered his submission but Henry would have none of it, and leaving his seat walked across to the altar that always stood in his room, to genuflect before the reserved host and said to the doctor: 'Submit not to me; I am a mortal man, but yonder is the Maker of us all, the author of truth.' He required Gardiner and Barnes to confer together with witnesses present and after two days Barnes on his knees declared himself convinced of his errors and begged the Bishop to take him as a pupil. Alas, after a brief spell Barnes could not bear my Lord of Winchester's company any longer, so Henry again called him in and ordered Barnes and two of his chief supporters to recant their outlandish beliefs publicly in Easter week; when they subsequently annulled their recantations they were sent to the Tower.

When Parliament re-assembled a few days later Cromwell made a notable speech pointing to religious disunity, for 'there were many incendiaries and much cockle among the wheat', and he reported that the King 'leaned neither to the right nor the left hand', but wanted pure doctrine set forth so that disputes about the Scriptures and ceremonies might cease.

On 17 April, as abundant confirmation of his position as chief minister, Cromwell was created Earl of Essex and appointed to the high office of Lord Great Chamberlain of England, so that power seemed as much out of Norfolk's grasp as ever. Ironically, however, parliamentary business kept Cromwell in London while Norfolk and Gardiner were much with the King at Greenwich, ensuring that Catherine Howard was frequently in his company. Cromwell had indeed attempted once again to keep the Duke away from court since his return from an embassy to France, arguing that a case of sweating sickness at Kenninghall made him a liability at court, but Norfolk denied there was any danger and demanded to know the King's own views. Both men knew that to be exiled from the Privy Chamber was to be undone.

Once Henry had determined on a divorce from Anne of Cleves he naturally turned to Cromwell to effect it. Since he had promoted the match, he would find the means of undoing it, as he had with Catherine of Aragon and Anne Boleyn, though since Henry had never consummated this marriage there should be little difficulty. Yet Cromwell knew the ruthless logic of the situation, for once free from Anne, Henry would marry the beautiful and orthodox Catherine Howard, niece of his enemy Norfolk, who would not hesitate to wreak the utmost vengeance on him. Much more than Howard dynastic ambition and the prize of power was involved, for Catherine would be the saviour of conservative theology just as Anne Boleyn had been the handmaiden of Protestantism. In 1540 as in 1532 religion and politics were inextricably entangled in Henry's marital affairs. Cromwell, like a cornered animal, attacked wildly in all directions. Lord Lisle was brought home from Calais on a charge of treason, Bishop Sampson of Chichester with lesser conservative churchmen was arrested, and Cromwell was said to be about to pounce on five other bishops, while there were rumours of the release of Barnes from the Tower and also of Latimer, who was under house arrest.

Twice early in June, Wriothesley spoke secretly with Cromwell at Bermondsey, urging him to devise a divorce, 'But what and how?' asked Essex in desperation; it was, he lamented, 'a great matter'. Within the week he was arrested at the council table by the Captain of the Guard, was stripped of his decorations and seal by Norfolk and Southampton, and taken by river to the Tower.

To add to the irony, the Act of Attainder against Cromwell opened with a fulsome statement of that royal supremacy which he had erected, and then deplored the fact that a man of 'very base and low degree', promoted to be the King's most trusty counsellor had proved a false traitor; the allusions to his humble origins with which the document is peppered, smacked of Norfolk. The charges of maladministration and abuse of power were nothing but generalities: 'Full of pride' he had dealt in 'weighty causes' without the King's knowledge and pretended to great power over him, saying he was sure of him, a thing which no subject should say of his sovereign. Was it unusual that Cromwell who had been at the hub of affairs for eight years should admit he was vulnerable? 'I have meddled in so many matters under your Highness', he wrote from the Tower, 'that I am not able to answer them all.' Two items only in the list of charges, if they were true, would be sufficient under Cromwell's own Treasons Act of

A design for a dagger by Holbein.

1534. These were words allegedly spoken on 31 March 1539 declaring that the teaching of Robert Barnes and others accused of heresy was good and that 'if the King would turn from it, yet I would not turn; and if the King did turn I would fight in the field in mine own person.' Secondly, there were the words he allegedly spoke nine months later when, taunted about his lowly birth, that 'if the Lords would handle him so, he would give them such a breakfast as never was made in England and that the proudest should know.' These incriminating 'proofs' of treason were supplied by Sir George Throckmorton, a clear enemy of Cromwell's, and Sir Richard Rich, who had happily perjured himself at Sir Thomas More's trial. Fabrications though they were, Henry believed them and there was circumstantial evidence that fitted; Cromwell's abhorrence of the full vigour of the Six Articles, his search for an alliance with the Lutheran princes, the Cleves marriage itself, the reports that the heretic Barnes was often with the Queen, the fact that Gerrard, one of Barnes's allies in the Tower, was a friend and that Jerome, the other, was vicar of Stepney, the Earl's London parish. He had once told a group of Lutheran envoys that 'as the world stood he would believe even as his master the King believed', and yet in the search for doctrine Cromwell had found himself ahead of his master. Once he had supplied statements about the Cleves marriage needed for its annulment, he was executed, professing at the last the Catholic faith, though his enemies had clearly manoeuvred Henry into believing that he was, like Barnes 'a sacramentary', or Anabaptist. Two days afterwards Barnes, Gerrard and Jerome were burnt as heretics at Smithfield.

Henry had been so stunned by the accusation of treasonable heresy that he did not attempt to save Cromwell. Archibishop Cranmer had courageously intervened, for he had loved him as a friend and for the devotion he bore to the King, a servant 'in my judgment, in wisdom, diligence, faithfulness and experience as no prince in this realm ever had . . . I am very sorrowful; for who shall your Grace trust hereafter, if you may not trust him?' Before long Henry became convinced that he had been condemned 'on light pretexts' and looked back on him as 'the best servant he ever had', and the words of his last letter rang true: 'As for the Commonwealth I have done my best and no one can justly accuse me of having done wrong wilfully.' For the moment Henry's popularity increased as the most hated man in England was thrown to the wolves, as Empson and Dudley had been, and his fall eased the divorce from Anne by helping Henry to save his face with Charles v and Francis I. Six months later, incredibly, Gregory Cromwell, the son of the fallen minister, was created a baron, though the fact that his wife was a sister of Jane Seymour and was back at court under Catherine Howard clearly tempered the winds. Almost singlehanded, the late Lord Privy Seal had reformed the administrative machinery of court and kingdom to make Henry more powerful and better served than any predecessor and paid the penalty that stage-managing a revolution in government involved. He had proved himself Henry's ablest servant, a man far more attuned to the King's own interests than his old master, the Cardinal, had been and he would have no successor, for while Norfolk and Gardiner had triumphed, distributed Cromwell's offices and took over much of the patronage he had exercised, neither individually nor jointly did they achieve his power. Henceforth Henry would be his own chief minister.

When Lords and Commons humbly petitioned the King that they doubted the validity of his marriage, Henry himself, his chief ministers and household officials made their declarations to serve as irrefutable evidence, while Wriothesley and Suffolk went on a delicate mission to Anne, sent out of the way to Richmond 'for her health', to obtain her consent to a divorce, as canon law prescribed. Eminently sensible, she agreed without any argument and, as a result, on 9 July Convocation annulled the marriage on the grounds of Henry's lack of consent to it (proved by the fact that it had never been consummated), and of Anne's alleged pre-contract to young Lorraine. Henry's doubtful conscience had been eased by the determination of two archbishops, sixteen bishops and 139 other learned clerics. All had been accomplished within a week. It remained for the Council under Gardiner to petition Henry 'to frame his most noble love' to a noble lady 'by whom His Majesty might have more store of fruit and succession' and on the day that Cromwell was executed, he married Catherine Howard.

The arrangements were speedily completed to their mutual satisfaction. Having lost a wife, Henry had gained a 'sister' and he decreed that the Princess Anne of Cleves was to have precedence over all ladies in England after the new Queen and the King's daughters. She was to be granted an income of £500, assigned Richmond and the manor of Bletchingley as her residences, and allowed to retain her jewels, plate and tapestry hangings. It mattered little to her that her establishment had been reduced overnight from one hundred and twenty-six to fifteen, or that her Chamberlain was now Sir William Goring instead of the Earl of Rutland, for most of her staff were German compatriots, including Dr Cornelis, Mistress Gertrude and Schoulenburg the cook, who would form a close family circle, transforming Richmond into a minute Rhenish principality. Had she really wanted, Anne could have returned to Cleves, but sensibly she preferred the comfort and the assured position of an expatriate princess to an anomalous niche in her brother's court where she would have been a liability to the duchy revenues and, wretched thought, might have to endure a second dynastic marriage. It was a relief to have finished with matrimony.

In informing his ambassadors of the palace revolution, Henry underlined the fact that Anne was most cheerful and had agreed to their divorce without 'lamentation, thought or pensiveness'. She herself had written to her brother in Cleves assuring him that Henry was treating his 'adopted sister' with more liberality than she could possibly have deserved and making plain that 'my body remaineth in the integrity which I brought into this realm'. Ironically, now that she was free to do as she liked, she cast aside her dowdiness and each day seemed to be clad 'in a new dress of some strange fashion or other'. She lived on for another seventeen years, almost forgotten, thankful that her plainness and lack of vivacity had proved such a rich investment. Of course the Duke of Cleves could never admit the invalidity of Anne's marriage to Henry, but any attempt to restore the reputation of his repudiated sister was a waste of breath and, as time went by, men appreciated the aptness of his laconic comment that he was 'glad his sister had fared no worse'.

Above Henry's scissors, decorated with his arms.

Right Holbein's painting of *The Ambassadors*, 1533: one of the first commissions he received on settling permanently in England that led to his employment at court.

Overleaf left The Henry Grace à Dieu, the pride of Henry's navy. The 1500 ton galley, laid down in 1514 with 186 guns, was rebuilt in 1540 as a 100 ton vessel of 122 guns; a drawing from Anthony Anthony's roll of the navy, 1546.

6 The Cankered Rose

'The King is so amorous of Catherine Howard that he cannot treat her well enough and caresses her more than he did the others.'

Charles de Marillac, French ambassador in London to Anne de Montmorency (Sept. 1540)

'The King . . . being solicited by his Council to marry again took to wife Catherine, daughter of the late Lord Edmund Howard, thinking now in his old age to have obtained a jewel for womanhood, but this joy is turned to extreme sorrow; . . . having heard that she was not a woman of such purity as was esteemed.'

The Privy Council to Sir William Paget, Henry's ambassador to France (Nov. 1541)

In the aftermath of the *coup d'état* and the divorce, it was necessarily a quiet wedding, though Catherine was promised a coronation in due course. She was no more than twenty, the youngest and most beautiful of all Henry's brides and a complete contrast in every respect from her immediate predecessor. Instead of having to rely on artists' impressions Henry had trusted his own eyes and been enraptured by the young lady that Norfolk had paraded before him. When casting around for a successor to Jane, he had specified a tall princess, to match his own height, but now he had chosen someone of 'very diminutive stature', though she was fashionably plump. Not just her eyes sparkled, but her whole face, with a natural vivacity, and if she had the Howard nose, Catherine boasted her own sensual lips that, with her auburn hair, gave her some resemblance to Anne Boleyn. Gay, frivolous and quick-tempered, her family had found schooling her in courtly behaviour a difficult task, yet now she moved with 'superlative grace' as Queen. 'Her countenance is very delightful,' wrote the French ambassador, 'of which the King is so greatly enamoured that he knows not how to make sufficient demonstrations of his affections for her.' The inscription on the new coins proclaimed what Henry thought of her – 'a blushing rose without a thorn'.

To those that remembered Catherine's parentage, her royal marriage seemed like a fairy-tale. Her father Lord Edmund Howard, born in the same year as the King, had been very much a younger son, with all the dis-

Henry's field and tilt armour, made at the Greenwich armoury in 1540. The contrast with his armour as a young man is striking, showing the swollen size of Henry's body in later life, (not to scale).

Above Holbein's sketches of dress worn at Henry's court in about 1540.

Below Henry in old age.

advantages it implied, seeing position and wealth go to his elder brother, heir to the dukedom, while he remained undervalued and perenially short of money. Lord Edmund disliked the life of a courtier and, whether this was cause or effect is uncertain, Henry had no regard for him. After angling for a suitable appointment for years he had become Controller of Calais in 1531, relieved to have an assured, if small, income and delighted that this post was away from court; a few months before his death in 1539 he was removed from office. Like many younger sons he had married a widow, to help his finances, and Joyce Leigh, with landed property in Kent, brought with her four children by her first marriage and provided him with three sons and five daughters (of whom Catherine was perhaps the third). On Joyce's death Lord Edmund married in turn two other widows, Dorothy Troyes, mother of eight, and Margaret Jennings, though there were no Howard children of these marriages. At a tender age, like her brothers and sisters, Catherine was sent away from home to Horsham, to live in the house of her step-grandmother, the Dowager Duchess of Norfolk, who saw to the upbringing of a great many Howard children; with Lord Edmund away in Calais and the fact that their own mother had died there was especial value in the customary arrangements. When they had reached their mid-teens most of the children graduated from Horsham to Lambeth House as a preparation for court, a career or marriage, a springboard for making one's way in the world, so long as the Duke was Lord Treasurer of England. In due course, thanks to her uncle's influence, as we have seen, Catherine succeeded in becoming a maid of honour to Anne of Cleves and now, eight months later, was her successor as Queen.

The bridegroom was not the realisation of a young girl's dream of Adonis, but a colossus of forty-nine, with swollen features, sagging jaws, eyes that were never fully opened but never quite closed, pained by an ulcerous leg and engrossed with an invalid's concern for his health; yet he was King and was passionately in love with Catherine, treating her as an indulgent father treats a favourite daughter. He showed her off at state banquets and on progress and continued to lavish jewels and other costly presents on her each month, such as a gold brooch, studded with diamonds and rubies, depicting the tale of Noah or the collar with her personal cipher set in diamonds. A contemporary's view that 'the King had no wife who made him spend so much money in dresses and jewels as she did, and every day some fresh caprice' was a pardonable exaggeration. After five months of marriage Catherine received an enormous grant of lands in full satisfaction of her jointure and these included properties once given to Jane Seymour, but also lands that had belonged to Thomas Cromwell and to the Marquess of Exeter. Many of her household had served Anne of Cleves and Jane before her; yet in finding family places at court the Howards far outdid the Boleyns and Seymours. Under her grandmother of Norfolk's rule at court were serving two aunts, Lady Bridgewater and Lady Margaret Howard, and two of Catherine's sisters, Margaret, married to Sir Thomas Arundel, and Isabella, wife of Sir Edward Baynton who had spent his entire career in the service of Henry's queens, and Elizabeth Cromwell, who had been a sister of Queen Jane; one wonders what Lady Cromwell made of the doggerel verses lampooning her late father-in-law, written by Thomas Smyth, clerk to the Queen's council, and sold as broadsheets. Gone was the

Instrument case which belonged to Henry's barber surgeon.

Carved ivory head of a lady's hair-pin, showing the peaked head-dress worn by ladies at court at this period. Excavated from the Palace of Whitehall.

Henry's sword and scabbard.

dowdiness of the 'Dutch ladies', for Catherine dressed herself and her women 'after the French fashion', with her peaked head-dress making her look the image of the Queen of Hearts in a pack of cards, just as Henry liked to think himself as depicted in the King of Hearts. Catherine took as her device 'Non autre volonté que le sienne', to testify somewhat unnecessarily that Henry was the only man in her life.

She had ridden from London, and he from Hampton Court, to meet at Oatlands, the manor house near Weybridge in Surrey which he had bought three years before, because he wanted to add the estate that went with it to his honour of Hampton, and here they were married on 28 July, while Cromwell was being executed on Tower Green. Not for another fortnight was Catherine prayed for as Queen at mass in the Chapel Royal and when the news reached Germany the Protestant Melanchthon was rather disgusted: 'Let us cease to sing the praises of the English Nero', he wrote, vowing to revise the preface to his book of *Commonplaces* in which he had lauded Henry. The King seemed rejuvenated and prolonged his honeymoon with a lengthy hunting progress through Surrey and Berkshire to Grafton in Northamptonshire and back through Catherine of Aragon's house at Dunstable and Wolsey's manor of the More to Windsor. He was anxious to avoid London in that hot summer, in which not a shower of rain fell between June and early October, for with the heat as always came the plague. He 'has taken a new mode of living, to rise between 5 and 6 a.m., hear mass at 7 and then ride until dinner time, which is 10 a.m. He says he feels much better thus in the country than when he resides all winter in London,' reported Marillac, the French ambassador. The international scene was no longer threatening and he could take time off from politics. By then, after so extended a holiday together, people were already assuming that Catherine was with child, but Henry seemed anxious to slip away with her from Windsor to Oatlands again, with a handful of servants in mid-December for a few further days of quiet before the Christmas festivities at Hampton Court. The new Queen had certainly upset the staid routine of the court calendar.

Princess Mary, three years older than the Queen, was in poor health and depressed at the renewed search for a husband for her, with negotiations see-sawing between the Emperor and the third son of Francis I, Charles, Duke of Orléans. She still kept away from court, reluctant at having to pay homage to Catherine, who had been quick to take offence and saw that she was deprived of two of her maids as a punishment for not treating her with as much respect as she had paid to Queens Jane and Anne. New Year's gifts were exchanged by proxy, and the feud between the two rumbled on for several months. By contrast Princess Anne of Cleves was the soul of tact. She rode over from Richmond, where she now lived, with a gift for Henry of two horses with violet velvet trappings; it was the anniversary of their first meeting. Anne insisted on addressing Catherine on her knees and in consequence had a kindly reception, and before she left had passed over to her a ring and two lap dogs that Henry had given her. When the King entered the room he gave her a brotherly kiss and they sat down to supper *à trois*, and after Henry had retired to bed Catherine and Anne danced together into the night. Among the seasonal fare were three pies made from the largest wild boar ever killed in France, a gift from Francis I.

With the worst of the winter over Henry was restless to leave court, for he was disappointed that after seven months of marriage Catherine showed no signs of presenting him with another heir and, hoping a change of scene and air would do them both good, he made plans to visit the new fortifications at Dover. At the end of February, however, he fell ill, perhaps of a tertian fever which led to complications with his ulcerous leg. By keeping the fluid drained the surgeons put him out of danger, but he remained in pain and was unusually quick-tempered during his convalescence. Few escaped the cutting edge of his tongue and he lamented that most of his council were time-servers, looking to their own profit, though he could still tell the good servants from the flatterers. Catherine, who had since marriage done 'nothing but dance and rejoice', found life miserably dull; Shrove Tuesday passed without a play or even music and the gloom of Henry's *mal d'esprit* enveloped the reduced court at Hampton. The bustle of visitors ceased so that the 'court resembled more a private family than a King's train'. Catherine had not bargained on life in an invalid's household, with little to distinguish one day from another, and began to seek distraction in the company of Thomas Culpeper, a gentleman of the Privy Chamber. Henry promised her that once he was fit they would undertake an extended progress as far as York.

Henry's prolonged journey through the Midlands and North Country in 1541 was no ordinary progress, for while he diverted himself *en route* with hunting, its purpose was entirely political. This was to be a state visit of maximum splendour to impress the survivors of the Pilgrimage of Grace with the King's power and majesty, and so numerous were his armed followers that it seemed 'more like a military camp' than a court. To show the citizens of York that his strong arm could reach even through their gates great pieces of artillery were sent by sea from London and up the Ouse. The men planning the expedition studied the arrangements for the Field of Cloth of Gold, for there had been nothing on quite so grandiose a scale since 1520. Some five thousand horses were needed and two hundred tents and pavilions as supplementary accommodation, while to dazzle the beholder the richest tapestries, plate and robes were brought from Whitehall. Next to Henry himself all eyes were on his young Queen, as the great entourage made its stately, colourful way through the countryside, halting at towns and cities, where every street was decorated, for receptions and banquets. The only ministers left in London were Archbishop Cranmer, Lord Chancellor Audley, the Earl of Hertford (as Edward Seymour had become) and Sadler, to continue administration, referring every matter of importance to the council with the King; indeed various diplomats such as Marillac stayed the entire four months with Henry. Princess Mary went with the itinerant court to show the northerners that the child of Catherine of Aragon was Henry's most dutiful daughter, but to take Prince Edward involved too many risks.

Heralds, henchmen and archers all had their part in creating the setting for the sovereign. It was half a century since York and the lands north of the River Trent had seen their monarch and Henry would leave them with the visual memory of the Prince personified in the illustration to the Great Bible of 'one descended from heaven'. People indeed were awestruck by the pageantry. At Lincoln, where the troubles of 1537 had begun, Henry arrived at the outskirts on 9 August wearing Lincoln green and then changed in a tent into ceremonial cloth of gold for the state entry to the city, with a long procession including 'children of honour' wending its way to the Minster for a solemn *Te Deum*. The banquets offered by mayors and sheriffs relieved the strain on the royal commissariat, but for most of the four months the usual number of meals had to be served as at Whitehall or Hampton, but provided from field kitchens. At Hatfield Chase in Yorkshire the King's party slew two hundred deer one day and nearly as many the next, while the marshes produced a rich harvest of fish and waterfowl.

It was a notable achievement that the time-table was faithfully kept until Doncaster was reached, and Henry finally reached York on 16 September, seventy-eight days after leaving London. Those who had remained loyal to the Crown in the rebellion were assembled quite separately from the rest who, long punished for their offences, now knelt before the King to make further pleas for clemency, accompanied by gifts of fat purses. Outside the city men worked night and day to refurbish in resplendent style an old abbey, in the grounds of which the royal pavilions had been erected. Henry had hoped he might persuade his nephew, James V of Scotland, to come to him at York, and the abbey was to have been the scene of their conference. James never ventured south, and some imagined the preparations heralded a York coronation for Queen Catherine. From her wedding day it had been tacitly assumed that she would earn a coronation when she became pregnant, and the citizens of York were in some hope of having a new Duke of York.

Although Henry's hopes of another child remained unfulfilled he returned

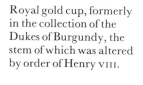

Royal gold cup, formerly in the collection of the Dukes of Burgundy, the stem of which was altered by order of Henry VIII.

from the north to Hampton Court in good heart, delighted with his expedition and gave out that special prayers were to be offered on All Saints' Day in thanksgiving for his safe return and 'for the good life he led and trusted to lead' with his jewel of a wife, whose Catholic orthodoxy was above reproach, whose morals above suspicion. Next day Cranmer at last set down a resumé of the sordid details of Catherine's past, which John Lassels had communicated to him, and slipped the paper into Henry's hand during a mass for the Dead on All Souls' Day, bidding him read it in private.

John Lassels had revealed to Cranmer the information his sister, Mary, who had been chamberer to the Dowager Duchess of Norfolk, had told him about acts of impropriety which Catherine had committed with Henry Mannox, a lutanist who had come to teach music at her step-grandmother's home at Horsham, and with Francis Dereham, a young gentleman pensioner in the Duke of Norfolk's livery, who had spent many illicit nights in the maidens' dormitory at Lambeth House. Though all this had happened before Catherine's marriage to Henry it was not a pretty story and, mindful of the fate of Anne Boleyn, Lassels was aware of the danger of keeping this information to himself, yet from what we know of the man's past and future he was a convinced Reformer and hoped that the downfall of Catherine and her family might advance the Protestant cause. Perhaps, too, Mary Lassels, the confidante of Catherine as a girl, but now herself married, was jealous that others who had known her in her days under the Dowager Duchess's roof had been found places at court, while she had been neglected. Indeed, there is the hint of blackmail in the pressures exerted by the others who had known Catherine's past to gain appointments; Joan Bulmer, Catherine Tylney, Alice Restwold and Margaret Morton all became chamberers to the Queen and, as late as August 1541, Francis Dereham was appointed her private secretary.

When he was examined Dereham did not deny intimacy with Catherine at Lambeth, but pleaded that he and she had been betrothed and so in the eyes of the Church were innocent of adultery. There seemed a good chance that Henry would accept this notion of a pre-contract with Dereham as grounds for a divorce and subsequently return her to her family, yet the Queen steadfastly denied there had been any understanding between them to marry. At this point the council's interrogations brought to view Thomas Culpeper, for to show his own innocence since the royal marriage Dereham said that Culpeper 'had succeeded him in the Queen's affections', and people remembered Culpeper boasting that were the King dead 'I am sure I might marry her'. Evidence of a kind was pieced together and the Queen admitted that she had met him by the backstairs, called him her 'little sweet fool' and given him presents, but she absolutely denied any relationship with him and said these rumours stemmed from the wicked imagination of Lady Rochford. When the Bedchamber women were again cross-examined Margaret Morton said she never suspected the Queen until at Hatfield she saw her look out of her window on Culpeper 'after such sort that she thought there was love between them'; at Lincoln, said Catherine Tylney, the Queen went to Lady Rochford's chamber up a pair of stairs from her own, but she could not tell who came in. It appeared that at every residence they reached on the progress north the Queen would 'seek for the back doors and backstairs herself' and that at Pontefract all the women feared the King had set a guard to watch her. Culpeper admitted many secret meetings with Catherine since the previous spring and though even on the rack he denied adultery had ever taken place he confessed 'he intended and meant to do with the Queen and that in likewise the Queen so would to do with him.' Lady Rochford, he said, had provoked him into loving Catherine and, indeed, that lady emerged even in her muddled evidence as the *agent provocateur*. She had been born plain Jane Parker in the days when her father was a mere usher-in-ordinary to the King, until his long service earned him a barony as Lord Morley, and had spent the greater part of her life at court. She had married George Boleyn in the year in which Henry began his affair with Anne, but we know nothing of this relationship. If it was just to avenge herself on Henry for George's execution that she encouraged Catherine Howard's infidelities, she must have known the danger she was running. Yet it was the Queen herself who was revealed as being most active in promoting the affair and there was the damaging letter she sent to Culpeper signed 'Yours as long as life endures.' Sickened by an aged husband for whom she had no love, Catherine had tried desperately to find consolation in a lover. In times past Henry had done just that, when he had tired of Catherine of Aragon. Catherine Howard may even have hoped that Culpeper might have fathered a child that she could pass off as Henry's own offspring, for she could never feel safe as Queen until she had produced a baby prince.

The testimony of the witnesses, however conflicting and partial, leaves little to the imagination. 'Courtly love' was one thing, but the indiscreet behaviour of the Queen's household was in another category. Too many maids of honour, who were expected to be above reproach like vestal virgins, were having affairs of their own, while Catherine's brother Charles was daring to flirt with Lady Margaret Douglas, the King's niece. If it was hard on the Howards that their Dowager Duchess appeared as little better than keeper of a high-class bawdy house for young gallants at Lambeth, it was monstrous for the King to appear to being cuckolded under his very nose. The presumptive guilt was the presumptive guilt of high treason.

At first Henry had found it impossible to believe the allegations made in Cranmer's paper that Catherine had been unchaste before her marriage and he even thought Dereham's original confession a pack of lies. But later, at a council meeting at the Bishop of Winchester's house in Southwark, it became impossible for him to reject the overriding presumption of guilt, and his fury at being deceived by one he had loved so tenderly knew no bounds; what he had mistaken for a blushing rose without a thorn had been a fading bloom of a cankered bush, shrivelled and deformed despite its age. Like a madman he called for a sword and said the wicked woman had 'never such delight in her incontinency as she should have torture in her death'. Then weeping, self-pity overcame rage, and he 'regretted his ill luck in meeting with such ill-conditioned wives' and blamed the council for ensnaring him with Catherine. Never had his self esteem been wounded so seriously and to put her out of his mind he went hunting by day and spent the evenings with his musicians.

Catherine remained under guard at Hampton expecting to be sent to the Tower, but Henry, still uncertain at that stage whether he would save her from the executioner, behaved with undue leniency and sent her instead to

Syon House, where until recently a convent of Bridgettines had kept their austere rule. For a few days longer she was still Queen, though her attendants were reduced to a handful. Her two rooms were to be 'furnished moderately as her life and condition hath deserved' and the hangings were to be of 'mean stuff, without any cloth of estate'. She could take with her four ladies-in-waiting and two chamberers of her own choice, provided Lady Baynton was one, whose husband Sir Edward. as vice-Chamberlain. was to take charge of the little household. To assure her that she was not a close prisoner, Catherine was allowed her 'privy keys'. All her jewels were taken from her and inventoried – the gold pomander chains, purses and brooches, the rich habiliments, carcanes and partletts which Henry had showered on her since before marriage, and no item among the six changes of clothes delivered from her wardrobe for use at Syon House bore any precious stones.

Despite her weeping and refusal to eat Catherine was thought sufficiently recovered to be taken to Syon on 14 November and once installed there she regained something of her composure, 'making good cheer, fatter and handsomer than ever', concerned to present a good appearance, 'more imperious and commanding, and more difficult to please than she ever was when living with the King'. Those two rooms at Syon House were her little kingdom for two months until she was taken to the Tower for three days right at the end. All the ladies and gentlemen of the Queen's household had assembled on 13 November before the Lord Chancellor to be warned of the danger of concealing information and reminded of the King's goodness. Those of them who were not accompanying Catherine to Syon House were to pack their bags. A few servants were sent with Princess Mary to join her brother Edward's household, while Lady Margaret Douglas and the Duchess of Richmond were to go to Kenninghall; for the others arrangements were speedily made for returning to their families and friends. One maid of honour, Anne Basset, daughter of Lady Lisle, who had originally come from Calais to serve Anne of Cleves, was now specially favoured, because of the calamity of her step-father, Lord Lisle, being in the Tower.

The house of Howard was indeed in the dock, though its Duke contrived to laugh nervously while Culpeper and Dereham were being tried and then he made straight for Kenninghall to be miles away from Henry's wrath. Before the trial of his relatives he wrote a grovelling letter to the King, disowning Catherine, and he feared that the abominable deeds of his nieces and the reputed treasons of many of his family would make Henry 'conceive a displeasure against him', so he begged for some assurance of his favour. A week later in Westminster Hall Lord William Howard and his wife Margaret, Catherine, Lady Bridgewater, the Queen's aunt, Anne Howard the wife of her brother Henry, and her step-grandmother, the Dowager Duchess, with various of their servants were found guilty of misprision of treason in concealing Catherine's unchastity and were sentenced to forfeit all their possessions and to suffer perpetual imprisonment, though subsequently all of these were pardoned and released, but there was no reprieve for Lady Rochford. To guard against further matrimonial perils the Act of Attainder against Catherine also made it treason for any unchaste woman to marry the King or for any person to conceal her past. As a pawn in Howard dynastic ambitions Catherine could still make one further move to

Henry's writing desk.

save their game, and before she left for the Tower she begged the lords of the council to implore the King 'not to impute her crime to her whole kindred and family'. She was executed on 13 February 1542. By siding with Catherine's accusers Norfolk indeed still held onto the treasurership, but he never recovered his prestige and remained under the cloud of Henry's displeasure.

A monarchy had always implied a hierarchical society, with titles of honour, and it is a platitude that during the Wars of the Roses the peerage had been decimated so that in 1485 there were only fifty-seven noble survivors. By 1509 there were as few as forty-five peers, comprising one duke (Buckingham), one marquess (Dorset), twelve earls and thirty-one barons. Henry set out to attract these formidable potentates from distant shires to his service at court, weaned them from their inveterate feuding and reduced their chances of causing him trouble by redirecting their energies towards tasks in the administration and the armed forces; and his court, as it developed, became a powerful magnet that few dared resist. Social position had hitherto always depended on landed property, but King Henry made personal service to him the fundamental requisite for acquiring or retaining estates, just as in the early feudal state military service had been the overriding obligation for tenants-in-chief.

To take the places of those attainted, or the lines that had lapsed for lack of heirs, Henry made various new creations on a modest scale, but had no intention of inflating the system of honours. In his entire reign he restored two dukedoms, that of Norfolk for the Howards and of Cornwall for his son,

Prince Edward, and created two new dukedoms, Suffolk for his sister Mary's husband and Richmond for his natural son, Fitzroy. Only two subjects were elevated to the marquisate, Henry Courtenay, Earl of Devon, as Marquess of Exeter, which he enjoyed for thirteen years, and Anne Boleyn as Marquess of Pembroke. Henry revived or created a total of fifteen earldoms in thirty-seven years: of these all except the revived earldom of Salisbury, now held by Lady Margaret Pole, took the names of English counties. Two went to his son Fitzroy – the earldoms of Nottingham and Somerset, held in conjunction with his duchy of Richmond – while a third, Lincoln, went to his nephew Henry Brandon. Apart from the restoration of William Courtenay to the family earldom of Devon, the other earls had all been born commoners – Boleyn, Clifford, Cromwell, Fitzwilliam, Hastings, Manners, Radcliffe, Seymour and Somerset. In addition Henry created twenty-six baronies. Though he left the peerage numerically stronger than he found it, it remained compact and inter-related. Men from older lines, or who became linked by marriage with families boasting an ancient title, looked with askance at 'the new men' ennobled by Henry, but Buckingham, Exeter and Norfolk, who were the most outspoken, all came to realise very forcibly how much even their own titles and positions depended on the King.

The Garter, the most distinguished of the orders of chivalry, had been limited to the sovereign and twenty-five knights by its original constitution under Edward III. Excluding foreign princes, who were customarily elected to the order, there were forty-five subjects who became knights of the Garter in the reign and there was never much haste to fill vacancies caused by death or disgrace. Appointments to the Order of the Bath were limited to coronations, or technically to the eve of coronation day, when the new knights kept vigil in St John's Chapel in the Tower. At Henry's crowning twenty-seven had been created and at Anne Boleyn's eighteen. During the reign 740 knights bachelors were made, though over half of these were dubbed on the field during the wars with France and Scotland in 1513, 1523 and 1544–5. Henry clearly regarded knighthood as inseparable from military prowess and in the year of Flodden and the Spurs no fewer than 203 knights were made, whereas in 1514 there were none and in 1515 only two. The only notable peace-time creations of knights bachelors were 40 in 1529, after Wolsey's fall, 28 in 1533 at Anne Boleyn's coronation (in addition to the knights of the Bath) and 48 in 1538 after the suppression of the Pilgrimage of Grace. Below the knights in the social ladder came the gentry, and from 1530 the heralds began making their series of visitations in the counties registering pedigrees and issuing coats of arms which the new gentry regarded as their certificates of gentility.

The problem of rival claimants to the throne had been greatly eased by the early deaths or infertility of those descended from the Yorkists. Compared with France, where there were prolific lines of princes and princesses of the royal blood who survived infancy, the families of Henry VII and his son were indeed tiny. Yet there were in the event three grandchildren of Elizabeth of York, whereas only one of her six sisters, Catherine Plantaganet, who married Lord William Courtenay, produced a son, the future Earl of Devon and Marquess of Exeter, and on being widowed she took a vow of perpetual chastity. Of the other five daughters of Edward IV, two died young; Cecily, who married Lord Wells, and Anne, who became the first wife of the Earl of Surrey, victor of Flodden, both died without heirs; while the last, Bridget, entered the Dominican convent at Dartford. But for a remarkable series of accidents these five sisters-in-law of Henry Tudor might have given birth to a considerable cousinage for Henry VIII, instead of a single peer – Exeter.

From Edward IV's second brother, George, the Duke of Clarence, who had ended his days in a butt of malmsey, sprang Margaret Plantaganet who had married Sir Richard Pole to produce three sons, Henry, Lord Montague, Cardinal Reginald Pole and Sir Geoffrey Pole. Another Yorkist claim stemmed from Elizabeth Plantaganet, Edward IV's sister, who had married John de la Pole, Duke of Suffolk – quite a different family from the Poles. The strength of their son Edmund's claim to the throne had been such that Henry VII had confined him to the Tower in 1506 and, when there were rumours that the King of France was about to acknowledge him as rightful king, Henry VIII ordered his execution on the eve of leaving for his French campaign in 1513. Edmund's brother, Richard, known to supporters as 'the White Rose', though he styled himself 'Duke of Suffolk', ended his exile by being killed by the side of Francis I at the battle of Pavia in 1525. When news of his death reached Henry he exclaimed, somewhat prematurely, 'All the enemies of England are gone!' and ordered the messenger to be given more wine.

There were still, indeed, other potential claimants, deriving from the marriages of the sisters of Elizabeth Woodville, Edward IV's consort; yet the only branch to have caused trouble was the youngest, the Stafford line, from Catherine Woodville's marriage with Henry Stafford, whose son, Edward, Duke of Buckingham had been executed for treason in 1521. Buckingham, so closely allied by marriage and descent to the older nobility, was too formidable a potentate for royal comfort, and embodied opposition, as we have noticed, to Wolsey. He was essentially the one survivor from an older feudalism, with his extensive lands in a dozen counties, his liveried retainers at Penshurst and his newly built castle at Thornbury in Gloucestershire, commanding the Welsh borders, where on red letter days he entertained to dinner one hundred and thirty local gentry. A bluff character, it was only to be expected that he would find himself trapped by indiscreet murmurings that one day he would be King. This one man's lands were parcelled out to nine different peers. Charles V was convinced that Wolsey was to blame for Buckingham's death and declared 'A butcher's dog has killed the finest buck in England.' Once his, and the de la Pole lines had been cut off, the mantle of disaffection fell on the Courtenays and Poles.

Henry Courtenay, Earl of Devon, had married the daughter of Erasmus's friend, Lord Mountjoy, and she, like Lady Margaret Pole, had been very close to Catherine of Aragon; both ladies had been implicated in the affair of the Nun of Kent and remained devout followers of Romanism. Courtenay himself had been singled out by Henry for advancement so that in 1525 he had been created Marquess of Exeter and appointed constable of Windsor Castle and high steward of the Duchy of Cornwall. Though he spent much of the year at Horsley, Surrey, his lands, augmented by large tracts of former monastic properties, and his strength lay in the West Country where

Thornbury Castle,
Gloucestershire, built by
Edward, Duke of
Buckingham.

Edward, Duke of Bucking-
ham, executed in 1521 for
his proximity to the blood
royal; an implacable
enemy of Wolsey.

members of a near-feudal tenantry saw that now 'the White Rose' was gone, their lord and master of Exeter would 'wear the garland at last' himself. Where Buckingham could not abide the Cardinal, Exeter could not stomach Cromwell and in the aftermath of the Pilgrimage of Grace he drifted into conspiracy with the Poles, while his wife quite independently maintained a treasonable correspondence with the Imperial ambassador.

The activities of Cardinal Reginald Pole on the Continent had made his mother and brothers vulnerable. When he was intriguing at Cambrai in 1537 Henry would dearly have had him 'trussed up and delivered to Calais', and the publication of his manifesto on church unity compromised the entire White Rose party in England; 'the King, to be avenged of Reynold, will kill us all.' His elder brother, Lord Montague, a man of taste and wit who enjoyed reading Thomas More's books, bemoaned the mismanagement of the Pilgrimage of Grace, yet his subsequent armchair plotting did not amount to more than pungent comments about the King and his courtiers, who did not care an iota for the nobility provided they could live at their pleasure. 'They were flatterers who followed the court and none served the King but knaves'; the Supreme Head of the Church 'had a sore leg that no poor man would be glad of, and . . . should not live long for all his authority next God's'; again, 'his whole issue stands accursed'. His younger brother Sir Geoffrey Pole, had been to court in October 1537, 'but the King would not suffer him to come in', so he removed himself to Bockmore, Montague's Buckinghamshire house, relieved to be no more among knaves. Montague related to Geoffrey his dream that the King had died, commenting that though he was still alive 'he will one day die suddenly; his leg will kill him and then we shall have jolly stirring'.

The haze of uncertainty was cleared towards the end of 1538 when Henry moved piecemeal against the Poles, beginning with Sir Geoffrey, who in a frenzy remembered too many idle remarks. In early November Montague and Exeter were sent to the Tower and were joined later in the month by the Marchioness of Exeter, her little son, Edward Courtenay, and later on Montague's heir, Henry Pole. In the event only Montague and Exeter were executed, for though they had not 'compassed the death of the sovereign' they had made it quite plain they would not be sorry when he died, and this was sufficient crime under the Treasons Act. The Countess of Salisbury had been closely questioned at her home at Warblington, 'by traitoring her to the ninth degree, yet will she nothing utter, but maketh herself clean' in an earnest, manly voice. Only after Montague's execution and the subsequent general Act of Attainder was she brought to the Tower where she remained in some state for two years until, on the eve of his great progress north, Henry ordered her, and other traitors in custody, to be executed. Thus perished the last of the Plantaganets, 'a lady of virtue and honour, if there be one in England'. Her youngest son, Geoffrey, had been pardoned, so too had the Marchioness of Exeter and Lady Courtenay. 'I do not hear that any of the royal race are left', wrote a Londoner to a friend in Germany in 1541, 'except a nephew of the Cardinal [Henry Pole] and another boy, the son of the Marquess of Exeter [Edward Courtenay]. They are both children and in prison and condemned.' Henry was taking no further chances on the revival of the White Rose.

Two courtiers of long standing who found themselves caught up in the

Exeter Conspiracy were Sir Nicholas Carew and Sir Edward Neville, who were both executed. Carew had crowned a career in the King's service by becoming master of the Horse and was accused of knowing Exeter to be a traitor and failing to reveal this to the King. The evidence is flimsy, but he was known to be a warm friend of Princess Mary and to have frequented Exeter's house at Horsley, with Montague and Sir Edward Neville, where sometimes he would sing political songs in the garden. Neville, who had been knighted by Henry long ago at Tournai, in due course became standard bearer and master of the Buckhounds. Though prominent at Prince Edward's baptism, the court had become anathema to him, largely because he disliked Cromwell, and he could never bridle his tongue. 'God's Blood!' he said, 'I am made a fool amongst them, but I laugh and make merry to drive forth the time. The King keepeth a sort of knaves here, that we dare neither look nor speak; and if I were able to live I would rather live any life in the world than tarry in the Privy Chamber!' – which had been his home for over twenty years. Henry saw the danger to his old companion of the tilt-yard and warned him to avoid his brother-in-law of Montague's company, yet Neville's indiscreet remarks snared him in the Treasons Act.

Henry VIII did not for motives of self-preservation deliberately seek to destroy subjects with royal blood in their veins, or else the imprisonments and executions would have been far more extensive. His early elevation of Lady Margaret Pole to become Countess of Salisbury was an open-handed gesture, and those like the Bourchier peers, Lords Berners and Essex, who gave no rise to suspicion were left undisturbed, given tasks to do and rewarded with lands. Similarly the earls of Rutland, who were descended from Edward IV's sister Ann, and the earls of Bath, who traced their princely connexion to Thomas of Woodstock, died in their beds, full of honours after loyal service. Nor did the King object in principle to marriages between princesses and subjects, provided his permission was obtained, and he placed no obstacles in the way of the marriages of his sister Mary's daughters by Suffolk (whose own wedding had so displeased him), the one to the Marquess of Dorset which led to the birth of Lady Jane Grey, and the other to the Earl of Cumberland. Though he acted severely when he heard of the betrothal of Lady Margaret Douglas to Lord Thomas Howard and sent both to the Tower, this was largely because of Lady Margaret's dual claims – in Scotland as well as in England – and their affair provoked an Act forbidding male subjects marrying into the royal family without his consent. Effectively Henry was independent from the old reliance upon royal relatives which had dominated the courts of the fourteenth and fifteenth centuries, yet his own four marriages with English subjects forced him to lean in turn on the families of Boleyn, Seymour, Howard and finally Parr, with their considerable cousinages. These families had replaced the Plantaganets, Nevilles and Woodvilles of an earlier age and, as a result, the court was still able to remain very much a family affair.

Bishop Gardiner, to whose house Henry had come across the river to meet Catherine before their marriage, was not compromised by her fall. A lawyer by training, he fervently believed in authority and the omnipotence of the King's supremacy and met the challenge of doctrinal novelties by clinging to the Church as he knew it – Catholicism without the Pope. Henry

Right Holbein's painting commemorating Henry's grant of a charter to the Company of Barber Surgeons of London, 1541.

Overleaf left Holbein's last portrait of Henry, 1542.

Overleaf right Princess Mary at the age of twenty-eight, in 1544; portrait by an unknown artist.

ANNO DNI   1544

...AD MARI   DOVGHTER TO
...THE MOST   VERTVOVS PRINC...
...ING HENRI   THE EIGHT

THE AGE OF   XXVIII YERES

saw there was a place for Gardiner as well as for Cranmer and in 1542, even more than in 1540, was concerned to maintain a balance between the parties which each led, both in his administration and in the Church. Yet for Cranmer the King had an affection which he denied to Gardiner. He admired his great learning, which made his own knowledge of the Early Fathers seem superficial, and he sensed how much the Archbishop would have preferred a life of study as a Cambridge don, patiently seeking the truth. When Gardiner argued with the King about the validity of the Apostolic Canons, the latter shook his head with a smile, 'My Lord of Canterbury is too old a truant for us twain.' He respected Cranmer's other-worldliness, his lack of ambition and the way he discounted pomp and wealth in an age when so many ecclesiastics were on the make. He knew how vulnerable the Archbishop was from attacks from Gardiner and others on the scores of his absence from council meetings, his correspondence with German Lutherans and his secret marriage; here was a mortal man like himself, who had fallen in love and married. Above all he appreciated Cranmer's devoted service, from the days when he had suggested canvassing university opinion on the divorce, through all the twists of policy that only a man with a truly open mind could have achieved, and he envied his charitable nature.

When the canons of Canterbury, no doubt spurred on by Gardiner, who coveted the archbishopric, charged Cranmer with heresy in the spring of 1543, Henry intervened. He called at Lambeth in his barge and invited Cranmer to join him on the river, saying 'Ah, my chaplain, I have news for you. I know now who is the greatest heretic in Kent!' When shown the canons' charges Cranmer merely asked that a commission be appointed to investigate them, but Henry insisted that Cranmer take charge of the enquiry against himself. It was perhaps on this occasion that Henry asked him whether he thought that his bedchamber was exempt from the Six Articles, meaning that in defiance of the law he had a wife. The Archbishop apparently confessed that he was indeed married, though he had sent Margaret home to Germany in 1540 when clerical celibacy was again enforced, and as a result of the King's understanding attitude, with hints that he would stand by him, Cranmer's wife returned to England before the end of that year. Two years later when he was in danger of being arrested at the council table, as Cromwell had been, Henry alerted him, giving him his ring which he needed only to show to his accusers to be given the right of personal appeal to the sovereign. Next morning, Norfolk, Russell and the others kept him waiting in the ante-room to try and unnerve him and then called him in to the council chamber; seated and wearing their caps they told him he was being sent to the Tower for heresy. When he produced the royal ring they were astonished and by the time Henry had finished up-braiding them, they felt very small. 'Whoso loveth me will so regard him' came the command; 'I pray you use not my friends so'. It was the same when Sir John Gostwick questioned Cranmer's orthodoxy in the House of Commons. 'Tell that varlet Gostwick', stormed Henry when he heard of it, 'that I will surely make of him a poor Gostwick and otherwise punish him if he do not acknowledge his fault unto my Lord of Canterbury.' Cranmer endeavoured to live up to the Biblical exhortation to 'strive for the truth unto death, and the Lord shall fight for thee' and secure, while Henry lived,

Left The Parr Pot, made of milk glass, possibly of English manufacture. The silver mounts are marked 1546–7, and the coat of arms shows the pot to have belonged to Sir William Parr, Catherine Parr's uncle and chamberlain.

he pursued his moderate reforms, including much work on a liturgy in English, and carried the King with him.

William Fitzwilliam, Earl of Southampton, had justifiably shifted Henry's displeasure over the Cleves marriage to Cromwell and his appointment to fill Cromwell's place as Lord Privy Seal gave the King personal satisfaction, for they had been friends since childhood. After leaving Wolsey's service he had spent his whole life at court, except when called to fight in the Channel or in France; he had been wounded in action off Brest in 1513 and was to die fighting the Scots in 1542. Utterly reliable, Fitzwilliam had no malice in him, he kept clear from factions and had no inordinate striving for riches, for all along his sole ambition had been to render service to his King. He stood in marked contrast to his eventual successor to the earldom of Southampton – for he had no heir – Thomas Wriothesley.

Wriothesley, who had played a leading part in the divorce from Anne of Cleves and had ferreted out so many of the unsavoury details about Catherine Howard, had always been cocksure and self-assertive, using anyone whom he thought might further his career. His father, with an eye to social climbing, had changed the family name from 'Writh' to Wriothesley, though some of their relations persisted in spelling it phonetically as 'Risley'. At Cambridge Thomas had sat at the feet of the young Stephen Gardiner to learn civil and canon law, but he left the university early to chance his ambitions at court, soon marrying Jane Cheney, a woman of means who was related to Gardiner. Cromwell had singled him out among the clerks of the Signet as a man of great potential, so that he was active during the Dissolution of the Monasteries, and he did rather well for himself in acquiring the possessions of Quarr Abbey in the Isle of Wight and of Titchfield and Beaulieu Abbeys in Hampshire. Titchfield he developed as his principal house, being fine enough for a King 'and for any baron to keep his hospitality in'. During the Pilgrimage of Grace he had gone with Henry to Windsor, to act as Secretary while the crisis lasted. Diplomatic missions followed and then, in 1540, he became with Ralph Sadler principal Secretary of State, and was easily the more forceful partner. In due course he would succeed Audley as Chancellor. Wriothesley would come to terms with whichever faction achieved power and would profit thereby. A courtier thought him 'an earnest follower of whatsoever he took in hand and did very seldom miss, where either wit or travail were able to bring his purpose to pass.'

The fall of the Howards was mitigated by the King's affection for Norfolk's eldest son, Henry Howard, Earl of Surrey, who, though no more than twenty-five when Catherine was executed, had already earned distinction as both poet and soldier. The King admired the many facets of Surrey as a Renaissance man and regarded him as a great ornament to his court, for in his qualities and bearing he closely resembled Henry himself as a youth. Holbein's series of portraits show Surrey's lordly arrogance: one, where he is wearing a scarlet cap worn at a jaunty angle, might even have been a portrait of the King in the year of Howard's birth; in another painting the scholar, who had just found a post in his household for the great Hadrianus Julius, holds a book; in a third the soldier has his hand on the pommel of his sword. There was another affinity between King and Earl, for Henry regarded Surrey much as the twin of his natural son,

Sir Thomas Wriothesley,
later Earl of Southampton;
principal Secretary of
State, 1540, and Lord
Chancellor, 1544; from a
miniature by Holbein.

Richmond, because the boys had spent two impressionable years together at
Windsor Castle, 1530–2, and Richmond had married the Earl's sister Mary.

Within a year of Richmond's early death Surrey was back at Windsor under
close confinement, for he had struck a courtier in Hampton Park who had
repeated a rumour that he was sympathetic towards those who had risen
with Robert Aske. Striking a man at court, as we shall see, was nearly as
serious an offence as being a sympathiser of rebels, and it was only Surrey's
youth and his friendship with the King that saved him from much more
severe punishment. During his summer's confinement he wrote much verse,
the most poignant being his poem about Windsor and his memories of the
happier times there with Henry Fitzroy, now tinged with melancholy:

> In greater feast than Priam's sons of Troy
> Where each sweet place returns a taste full sour.
> The large green courts where we were wont to hove
> With eyes cast up unto the maiden's tower
> And easy sighs such as folk drew in love.

He recalled the dancing, the tennis and the tilting, the hours on horseback
riding in the forest with hounds after a stag and, above all, the depth of
their companionship:

The secret thought imparted with such trust
The wanton talk, the divers change of play
The friendship sworn, and promise kept so just
Wherewith we passed the winter nights away.

It was at Princess Mary's household at Hunsdon that Surrey first met Lady Elizabeth Fitzgerald, the orphan of Kildare, when she was little more than ten years old. He developed a platonic relationship with her that spurred him on to write his finest love lyrics, in conscious imitation of Petrarch's love for Laura. 'Fair Geraldine' came to court to serve Catherine Howard and stayed on, to Surrey's delight. A year or so later, when Geraldine was still only fifteen, to the Earl's dismay she married an aged widower, Sir Anthony Browne, by now master of the Horse and King's standard bearer, who had risen to prominence in Henry's service with his half-brother, William Fitzwilliam, Earl of Southampton. The Irish beauty now spent her days at Battle Abbey, living in what had been the prior's lodging.

Sir Thomas Wyatt the Elder, poet and diplomat.

At jousts Surrey was still the apple of the King's eye and the idol of the ladies, yet when crossed he was the most quick-tempered of men. A quarrel with a man from Stockwell led to Surrey challenging him to a duel, and when the authorities found out he was put in the Fleet Prison for a fortnight. He wrote from the Fleet apologising to the council, blaming 'the fury of restless youth', yet half excusing himself in a rather grand third person, appropriate he thought for the youngest knight of the Garter: 'He is not the first young man to have enterprised matters that he afterwards regretted.' He was released on his own surety to keep the peace in the incredible sum of 10,000 marks (or £6,666 in the currency of the day).

The death of Sir Thomas Wyatt (1542) affected Surrey deeply. Wyatt, fifteen years his senior, had escaped from the odium of friendship with Anne Boleyn to serve Henry in further diplomatic missions to the Emperor and to the French King, always longing to be back in the Garden of England. Towards the end of his short life, when his travels to foreign courts were over and he became an MP for Kent, Wyatt wrote satires about the court for his friends John Poyntz (d 1544) and Sir Francis Bryan (d 1550), who like himself were devotees of the Muse but became so caught up in diplomacy and the royal service that their literary output dwindled to a trickle. The satire to Poyntz, *Of the Courtier's Life*, tells how Wyatt has fled the press of courts for freedom to walk in his native Kent and read and rhyme for pleasure. The satire dedicated to Bryan, *How to use the Court and himself therein*, mocks declining moral standards, the greed for gold and the restless activity of those in the sovereign's service, wearing themselves out:

And therewithal this gift I shall thee give;
In this world now, little prosperity
And coin to keep, as water in a sieve.

Wyatt's greatest contribution was to adapt the sonnet from the Italian model to English literature, with its canons of rhyme and precise length, that was to become a vehicle for some of the greatest lyric verse in English. One of his last sonnets on a favourite theme was *The Lover laments the death of his Love*:

224

The pillar perish'd is whereto I leant;
The strongest stay of mine unquiet mind:
The like of it, no man again can find,
From east to west still seeking though he went.

To mine unhap; for hap away hath rent
Of all my joy the very bark and rind;
And I, alas! by chance am thus assign'd
Dearly to mourn, till death do it relent.

But since that thus it is by destiny,
What can I more but have a useful heart;
My pen in plaint, my voice in woeful cry,
My mind in woe, my body full of smart,
And I myself, myself always to hate,
Till dreadful death do ease my doleful state.

In the summer of 1542 at Henry's request Wyatt reluctantly left home to journey to Falmouth, where the Emperor's ambassador had landed, to conduct him to court, but the heat and the exertion of the long ride were too much for him; he developed a fever and died at Sherborne.

With Wyatt's death Surrey lost his mentor and with much feeling wrote several epitaphs on Sir Thomas:

A tongue that serv'd in foreign realms his King,
Whose courteous talk to virtue did influence
Each noble heart; a worthy guide to bring
Our English youth by travail unto fame.

John Poyntz, a loyal servant of the Privy Chamber.

Wyatt's mantle fell on Surrey, who was bent on proving himself a scholar of distinction in the Renaissance tradition. His awareness of classical and Italian literature moulded him into an English Petrarch and in contrast to contemporaries, who stuck to theological controversy, his religious writings went no further than verse paraphrases of the Book of Ecclesiastes and of various psalms; he was far happier searching for a suitable metre for a translation of the *Aeneid* than becoming involved in metaphysical discussion.

After a season fighting with the army against the Scots Surrey returned in glory to celebrate noisily in court and capital. He became the leader of a group of high-spirited young men including Thomas Wyatt, the poet's son, who would one day inspire the men of Kent to rise, and William Pickering, who in years to come would be reckoned 'the perfect courtier' and, despite the difference in age, was considered by some an admirable consort for the young Queen Elizabeth. They went about smashing the windows of churches and aldermen's houses and surprising night-walkers with 'stone-bows'. One night they rowed on the river, and 'shot at the queans on the Bankside' with pellets. The identity of the ringleader of these escapades soon became known and the fact that he held his court at Mistress Arundel's cookhouse in St Lawrence Lane, where she kept him and his fellows well supplied with meat, even in Lent. A butcher then reported what he had discovered and Millicent Arundel was examined by the Lord Chamberlain. It was revealed that she had told her kitchen-maids how furious Surrey had been about the purchase of some cloth and had burst out 'I will marvel they will thus mock a prince.' 'Why', asked one of the girls, 'is he a prince?' 'Yea, mercy he is', answered Mistress Arundel, 'and if ought should come at the King but good, his father [Norfolk] should stand for King', for the Earl had told her as such. No one in 1543 thought such pretensions to the Crown more than women's gossip. Surrey, Wyatt and Pickering were called before the council at St James's, as a result of a formal complaint by the Lord Mayor and Recorder of London, though the Duke of Norfolk thoughtfully kept away. Pickering at first denied all, but the evidence of Surrey's servant, Thomas Clere, was conclusive. The Earl claimed he had a special licence for eating meat during fasts, but admitted he had broken the peace by smashing windows and shooting at prostitutes. It had grieved him, he said with as straight a face as he could, to see the licentious manners of Londoners, 'which resembled the manners of Papal Rome in her corrupted state.' So he was sent a second time to the Fleet and spent his imprisonment writing *A Satire Against the Citizens of London.*

> London! hast thou accused me
>   Of breach of laws? the root of strife!
> Within whose breach did burn to see,
>   So fervent hot, thy dissolute life . . .

These quirks of behaviour were not much different from the hooliganism of the young bucks of the Chamber a generation back and Henry's affection for Surrey remained, even though he was 'the most foolish proud boy that is in England'.

The harsh laws for keeping the peace within the royal household and the fearsome ceremonial followed in their administration come across in the case of Sir Edmund Knyvett, a Norfolk knight who had long held the post of serjeant porter. There had been an affray in the tennis court at Greenwich in which Knyvett struck one of Surrey's servants, the same Thomas Clere involved with Pickering's case, and drew blood in February 1541. Both were bound over in recognisances of five hundred marks to keep the peace and attend before the council when summoned. It was nearly two months before they were formally charged and placed under arrest in the custody of the Knight Marshal to await trial in the Court of the Verge in which the controller, cofferer and other palace officials sat as judges. Many reckoned that the blame would fall on Clere, since Knyvett could count on the Duke of Norfolk's influence, but at the trial in Greenwich Great Hall Surrey spoke up for his man and the jury found Knyvett guilty. The judges pronounced the sentence which the law laid down as appropriate for striking a man and drawing blood in the hallowed area of the royal court: Knyvett was to be imprisoned during the King's pleasure, to forfeit his lands and goods and to lose his right hand.

With awful pomp officials attended on the appointed day to execute the barbaric sentence of amputation. First came the serjeant surgeon with his instruments, then the serjeant of the woodyard carrying the mallet and the block on which Knyvett was to rest his hand; the King's master cook bore the knife, which the serjeant of the larder was to place on the joint; the

Above Sir Thomas Wyatt the Younger, Surrey's companion, and son of the poet. He was to be executed by Mary Tudor, for his rebellion against her.

Right Henry Howard, Earl of Surrey, poet and soldier, painted by Guillim Scrots, 1546

Below Drawing by Holbein of an astronomical clock.

ANNO·DNI·1546·ÆTATIS·SVE·29

serjeant farrier brought searing irons, the yeoman of the chandlery dressings, the yeoman of the scullery a pan of fire to heat the irons and a chafer of water to cool them, and the yeoman of the ewery a basin, ewer and towels. Following a curious piece of ritual the serjeant of the poultry brought a live cock 'which shall have his head smitten off upon the same block and with the same knife', as used for the prisoner. Officials from at least ten of the household departments took part in such sentences to impress on the rank and file throughout their establishments of the heinous crime of disturbing the King's Peace, while others gathered to watch the gruesome business and were served wine, ale and beer by the serjeant of the cellar. When all was ready the Knight Marshal was summoned to bring in the prisoner. Granted permission to speak, Knyvett confessed his guilt and threw himself on the King's mercy. At that late hour he begged that a message might be taken to His Majesty imploring him to alter the sentence so that he could lose his left hand instead of his right, for 'if my right hand be spared I may hereafter do much good service to his Grace as shall please him to appoint.' The judges held up the proceedings while the King was informed and Henry was so impressed by the man's loyalty that he immediately pardoned him from his entire sentence. Knyvett lived on at court as serjeant porter for another five years and significantly no further case of an affray came before the Court of the Verge during Henry's reign. Thomas Clere henceforward accompanied Surrey wherever he went and when the Earl was wounded at the siege of Montreuil saved his life, but only at the cost of his own; his bravery is commemorated in one of Surrey's most moving sonnets.

The familiar faces at court were growing fewer and this made Henry feel his age. Wyatt and Holbein died within a few days of each other in the autumn of 1542. Holbein's last paintings included exquisite miniatures, the picture of *Solomon and the Queen of Sheba*, now at Windsor, in which Henry served as the model for the ancient king and, in a very different vein, the scene of Henry presenting a charter to the Company of Barber Surgeons of London – a piece of historical documentation commissioned by the livery company (see page 217) which remained unfinished at the artist's death. Had Holbein survived he would undoubtedly have become serjeant painter to the King in succession to the workaday Andrew Wright, who had come to Henry's notice through decorating ships, carriages and trumpet banners. Instead, however, the post went to Antonio Toto del Nunziata, the first artist proper to serve in the office. Toto had originally left Florence to work for Wolsey and found subsequent employment with the King at Whitehall and Hampton Court, painting decorated panels and shields. Not until 1538 did he decide to become an English subject, and then courted patronage by offering Henry New Year's gifts, such as *The Story of King Alexander*. Before the end of the reign two other artists of distinction, both from the Netherlands, had settled in England – Hans Eworth of Antwerp and Guillim Scrots, for some years chief painter to Mary of Hungary, Regent of the Netherlands. Henry enticed Scrots to his service by offering him an exceptionally generous stipend. His painting of Surrey set a new fashion in English portraiture; for here statues, cherubs, masks and arms in true Renaissance style flank an arch, under which the Earl stands in gorgeous Italianate costume, a courtier to his fingertips.

Princess Elizabeth, about the age of twelve; portrait by an unknown artist, c. 1545.

Henry's astrolabe.

7 Whispering gallery

Above Thomas, Lord Seymour of Sudeley (1508–49), brother of Jane and the Earl of Hertford, who married Catherine Parr after Henry's death.

Left Queen Catherine Parr, whom Henry married in 1543; portrait by an unknown artist.

'In this confusion of wives, so many noblemen and great personages were beheaded, so much church plunder committed and so many acts of disobedience perpetrated that it may be said that all that ensued and is still going on, is the penalty of that first sin.'

Daniel Barbaro to the Venetian Senate (1551)

'The Court is closed to all but the Privy Council and some gentlemen of the Chamber.'

Van der Delft to Mary of Hungary (Dec. 1546)

After the bitter experience of Catherine Howard, Henry seemed likely to remain a widower. That unhappy chapter, coupled with increasing pain from his leg, had prematurely aged him; he was now 'very stout and daily growing heavier' from lack of exercise and seemed rather to resemble his maternal grandfather, Edward IV 'in loving rest and fleeing trouble'. He remained very moody and depressed, but when he made the effort to join the ladies at court he enjoyed their company 'as a man nurtured among them'. The victories over the Scots in the winter of 1542 cheered him and in celebration he summoned Princess Mary to court for Christmas and planned banquets for the ladies. Next summer, eighteen months after Catherine Howard's execution, Henry surprised everyone by making his sixth marriage.

Catherine Parr, the new Queen, had already buried two aged husbands, Sir Edward Burrough in 1529, when she was only seventeen, and John Neville, Lord Latymer, in March 1543. She had served as a gentlewoman of the Chamber to Catherine Howard, and on her fall returned to Snape Hall in Yorkshire to supervise the upbringing of her three step-children. Lord Latymer had left her well provided for and a rich widow of thirty-one was unlikely to be short of proposals. Her mother, Maud Parr, had consistently turned down offers of marriage when widowed at twenty-two in order to devote herself to the education of her three children, but Catherine in 1543 had no children of her own. Sir Thomas Seymour, the Earl of Hertford's brother, had just returned home after a two-year embassy in Vienna and with an eye to the main chance offered marriage. Catherine, a devout as well as highly educated woman, was fascinated by this unprincipled rake and would have accepted him but, as she put it, was 'over-

Above left William Parr, brother of Catherine, who was created Earl of Essex in 1543, and later, Marquess of Northampton.

Above right Sir Anthony Denny, privy councillor and patron of learning; he was close to Henry in his final months.

ruled by a higher power'. Under very different circumstances a few years later Seymour was to become her fourth husband, but for the moment he discreetly left court to undertake first an embassy and then a military command in the Netherlands.

Henry, lonely and sick, had singled out Catherine as a companion of intellectual ability who would make an ideal step-mother for his children, as she had for Lord Latymer's. If her matronly qualities as nurse, step-mother and blue-stocking made her the antithesis of everything that Catherine Howard had been, she was still young enough to be capable of bearing children. Chapuys was amazed at Henry's choice and passed on to Charles V the rumour that Princess Anne of Cleves 'would like to be in her shirt (so to speak) with her mother' as she was so upset by the marriage, for Catherine 'is not nearly so beautiful as she; besides there is no hope of issue, seeing she had none with her two former husbands.'

The marriage was solemnised at Hampton Court Chapel by Bishop Gardiner and then, as with Catherine Howard, Henry took his bride to Oatlands on the start of a long honeymoon progress through the southern shires and Home Counties, accompanied by Princess Mary. Catherine wrote from Oatlands in Latin to her brother William to tell him it had pleased God to incline the King to take her as his wife, which was 'the greatest joy and comfort that could happen to her', and with a sisterly touch she asked him to write and visit her 'as frequently as if she had not been called to this honour'. Among her first appointments were those of her uncle Lord Parr of Horton as Lord Chamberlain, her sister Mistress Herbert (soon to be Countess of Pembroke) as a lady of the Bedchamber and her step-daughter Margaret Neville as a maid of honour.

Catherine's education in the liberal, Renaissance tradition had led her to question many of the accepted facets of the old Catholic tradition, though she was never an innovator overturning fundamentals but one who saw study as an essential exercise for the increase of faith. Even though Lord Latymer had ridden under the banner of the Five Wounds of Christ during the Pilgrimage of Grace, his wife kept up her scholarly connexions with Reformists and after his death her house became a second home for Miles Coverdale and Hugh Latimer. Throughout it was Erasmus, not Luther, who was her spiritual mentor and her own writings reveal a pietism that had nothing in common with mid-sixteenth-century Protestantism. In the *Lamentation of a Sinner* King Henry is the heroic Moses who has led the English people out of the Egypt of papalism, and hot-gospelling Anabaptists were as repugnant to her as Romanists. In outlook, perhaps, she was nearer to Cranmer in 1543 than to anyone else. But Catherine's open-minded tolerance, where a theologian had a real grasp of scholarship, made her household a haven for some who had moved to a more extreme position. Her learning was always the handmaiden of piety and as Nicholas Udall, headmaster of Eton whom she called in to help Princess Mary with her Erasmian paraphrases, expressed it, queens and high-born ladies, instead of spending their days in courtly dalliance 'embrace virtuous exercises, reading and writing and with most earnest study, early and late, apply themselves to extending knowledge.' Under her, as Erasmus had once so profoundly hoped, the English court became a university. A Mr Goldsmith, who had been a successful suitor for a humble place in her household, thanked the Queen that 'her rare goodness has made every day a Sunday, a thing hitherto unheard of, especially in a royal palace.'

Sir John Cheke, Cambridge humanist, who became tutor to Prince Edward in 1544.

Sir Anthony Denny, a councillor close to Henry throughout his last three years, had like Leland been a pupil of Lily's at St Paul's before distinguishing himself at St John's College, Cambridge. Drawn to the court, he found himself well-placed to further the careers of his humanist friends, John Cheke and Roger Ascham, who delighted Catherine Parr with their learning. Ascham had written a remarkable treatise, *Toxophilus*, which, while at one level it was a tract urging improvements in the art and science of archery, also surveyed the state of the realm, skilfully eschewing religious controversy, and made an effective plea for the literary use of the English language. In it Ascham showed his supreme command, of 'the speech of the common people' and displayed how suitable it was for sustained intellectual argument where other humanist authors would automatically use the vehicle of Latin prose. He took the title role of 'Toxophilus' himself in this dialogue and introduced Cheke in the guise of 'Philologus'. Ascham had written it with the aim of attracting court favour, nor was he disappointed even though, through Henry's absence at Boulogne, it was not until the summer of 1545 that he could obtain an audience to present his handiwork to him in the gallery of Greenwich Palace. The King 'did so well like and allow it' that he gave Ascham a pension of £10 a year on the spot, ensuring that henceforth the author would have ready access to the court and further patronage.

In May 1544 Thomas Berthelet, the King's printer, produced copies of the 'Psalm Prayers, gorgeously bound and gilt on the leather', which the Queen had selected and paraphrased, and these were used straightway by George Day, Sampson's successor as Bishop of Chichester whom Catherine had appointed her almoner. (Day, a moderate conservative in outlook, who would be deprived of his see in the next reign, was permitted to retain the provostship of King's College, Cambridge). That same year William Harper, the clerk of the Closet, paid for the illuminations of a manuscript primer with the Epistles and Gospels in Latin and English and for a French New Testament for Catherine. In 1545 Berthelet printed her *Prayers stirring the mind unto heavenly meditations*, which was immediately reprinted because of the demand in London for copies, and within a few months she had followed this with a much more extensive collection of *Prayers and Meditations* that became the most popular pietistic work of the decade. While still a Queen, Catherine completed most of the work on her principal literary project, *The Lamentation of a Sinner*, an account in the Erasmian spirit of a deeply religious experience, which emphasises more strongly than Henry would have approved the necessity of faith in a Lutheran sense.

Roger Ascham, Cambridge scholar, whose *Toxophilus* earned him a royal pension.

Catherine had her own consort of viols, consisting of Albert and Vincent, both from Venice, and Alexander and Ambrose, both from Milan, and she paid them each 8d. a day. She also employed the artist John Bettes, who had earlier undertaken heraldic paintings at Whitehall, to limn royal portraits engraved in stone and to make miniatures.

Compared with Anne Boleyn and, indeed, with all her predecessors, Catherine's purchases of clothes for herself were extremely frugal, though she was generous with her gifts to her ladies and to the royal children. With no child of her own, she took a keen interest in Prince Edward's wardrobe and at Christmas 1544 ordered his tailor, William Holte, to make him an outfit of crimson velvet, richly embroidered and lined with satin, that cost £18. There were gilt buttons and gold braid on the coat, brocade on the doublet and a feather in the velvet cap. The whole of that year she bought for herself no more than some Lucca velvet for a French hood, satin lining for it, some Venice sleeves, a length of Italian cloth of silver for a 'French gown' and finally a piece of black damask for a nightgown, for black was then regarded as representing modesty. In her wardrobe at Baynards Castle were all the jewelled dresses and other fineries that had belonged to Catherine Howard and it was in part, perhaps, because she inherited so lavish a collection, many items of which could be altered, that she needed to spend so little on herself. She certainly had no wish to be cheeseparing where court expenses were concerned and she insisted on having spangles sewn on her footmen's coats to make the show that was expected of her. The Queen's one apparent personal extravagance was shoes, for in one year she bought for her own use forty-seven pairs. Some were court shoes in crimson, white, blue and black, all trimmed with gold, at 14s. a pair, and in black velvet at 13s. Much cheaper were the six pairs of 'corked shoes lined with red' and the dozens of 'quarter shoes', costing 5s. a pair, that were discarded after very few wearings. The shoes Catherine gave away to poor women at the Maundy ceremony cost 7d. a pair.

Watches of the 1540s, known as 'Nuremberg eggs'.

Of all Henry's wives Catherine was the one most interested in flowers, and there were daily sums for floral decorations in her apartments as well as purchases of 'perfume for the chamber', especially juniper and civet. Her favourite dogs were greyhounds which were regularly given milk to lap.

It would be wrong to think of Catherine Parr as being tied to Whitehall nursing a sick husband throughout their marriage. Until the last autumn of his life Henry always roused himself from his sick-bed as soon as he was able, eager to be on the move, however much it hurt him. The pace of a royal progress had not slackened and in his Queen's accounts the constant journeyings come across, and the suggestion of living out of chests – the costs of shoeing horses and providing them with fodder, of sending six men and a boy two days ahead of the main entourage to make ready the Queen's chambers whenever she changed residences, of transporting the royal bed by easy stages from Oatlands to Woodstock and the provision of a new barge, constructed by a Lambeth shipwright, which was the pride of her bargemaster, Robert Kyrton.

As early as March 1538 Edward had been assigned a separate establishment, costing £6,500 in the first year, with Sir William Sidney, a man bred in Henry's Privy Chamber, as Chamberlain and Sir John Cornwallis as Steward, though the two people most intimately concerned with the Prince's care were Sibyl Penne, his dry nurse, and Lady Bryan, the lady mistress of the household. Mrs Penne was Sidney's sister-in-law and in recognition of her service 'in the nurture and education' of the prince, she and her husband were granted ex-monastic properties in Little Missenden and Penn, Buckinghamshire. Lady Bryan was a sister of Lord Berners and a cousin of Anne Boleyn and had served the King successively in the nurseries of Mary and Elizabeth. Her son, Sir Francis Bryan, the gentleman of the Chamber who had earned Cromwell's nickname of 'vicar of hell' for his part in Anne's downfall, and received Wyatt's praise for his sonnets, still contrived to stay in post whoever was Queen; he had now struck up a friendship with Catherine Parr's brother to whom he was to dedicate his graceful translation of Antonio de Guevara's *A dispraise of the life of the Courtier*, a theme which denounced most of his career. Edward was moved from Hampton Court to Havering in Essex when he was a year old and then, in 1539, his household was settled in Hunsdon House in Hertfordshire, from which he later transferred to Ashridge, near Berkhamsted, twenty-five miles away.

Henry was always torn between on the one hand having Edward at court to lavish his affection on him and show him off, and on the other to rest assured that the boy was breathing country air, safe from the plague and unwholesome influences. The fact that he contracted a fever on a visit to Hampton Court in 1541 made his father all the more certain that the child for whom he and his people had hungered so long should spend his days in Hertfordshire, where no precautions for his safety should be too great. He ordered that no one was to have any more servants of his own in Edward's household than was allowed by a list approved and signed by himself to prevent undue influence. At Royston, where the infant was brought to the royal hunting lodge so his father could romp with him on progress, Henry dallied with him 'in his arms a long space' and held him in a window so the townsfolk could see their prince. Privy councillors were invited to Hunsdon

to note his physical development and Lord Chancellor Audley loyally said he had never seen so goodly a child for his age, as he 'shooteth out in length and waxeth firm and stiff and can steadfastly stand'; he could perhaps already walk, but his nurse restrained him for fear of injuring his legs. Henry delighted to hear in due course from Lady Bryan that when the minstrels struck up a tune the two-year-old 'danced and played so wantonly that he could not stand still and was as full of pretty toys as ever I saw a child in my life.' Edward's own recollections of his father before he had married Catherine Parr were non-existent; as he wrote himself in his chronicle, he was brought up until six 'among the women'.

Catherine convinced Henry that it would now be in the boy's best interests to bring him to court for longer periods, partly because it was natural for him to see more of his father, and partly because his whole education was being developed to help him in his future responsibilities; a future King should know the ways of courts. It was good for Edward to be given tasks, such as welcoming the Admiral of France on an embassy and, as he was anxious to do what was required of him, the boy asked Catherine Parr whether the Frenchman was a good classical scholar, for if she thought him an expert he would spend more time perfecting his Latin lines. From her first days as his step-mother she had sent him tokens of her affection and she took a specialised interest in the education of this precocious child with a real zest for books. To contemporaries it was a commonplace that 'to be masters of princes on earth is to have the office of gods that be in heaven . . . For certain, he that hath a charge of a prince is the governor of the ship, the standard of an army . . . because they have, among their hands him that afterwards ought to govern all the world.' On Catherine's recommendation in 1544 Richard Cox, a Cambridge scholar of distinction who was already the Prince's tutor, became his almoner and was given formal charge of his education, while John Cheke, professor of Greek and the most brilliant of all Cambridge humanists, was brought in to bear the brunt of the boy's instruction. Cheke had just dedicated to Henry two homilies of St John Chrysostom, with Greek and Latin texts, that astonished the King by their breadth of scholarship. Just before Cheke took up his post Dr Cox wrote from Ashridge that his six-year-old pupil 'understandeth and can frame well his three concords of grammar and hath made already forty or fifty pretty Latins and . . . is now ready to enter into Cato and to some proper and profitable fables of Aesop, and other wholesome and godly lessons that shall be devised for him'.

It would be easy, in the knowledge of what happened after 1547, to label Cox, Cheke and their circle 'Protestants' and declare that Prince Edward was being indoctrinated in the last three years of his father's reign with the views that would be epitomised in the First, if not the Second, Edwardian Prayer Books. Those chosen to guide the boy's studies were in fact men in the Erasmian tradition, humanists concerned with scholarship, not ministers preaching a gospel. They may have been regarded by Catherine and her Reformist friends as 'Christ's special advocates', but there was no taint of what Henry would have called 'heresy' in their outlook. Cox had assisted in writing *The King's Book*, a conservative doctrinal statement, and if by 1544 he had radically changed his views he kept them quite to himself. Similarly John Cheke was chosen for his academic brilliance and that alone.

It was the pronunciation of Greek that he set out to reform, not the doctrine of the Church, and in these difficult waters he once said he could 'be merry on the bank's side without dangering himself on the sea', so Cheke was quite clearly not a man burning with zeal for a religious revival. A little later Jean Belmaine, a Calvinist by profession in France, was engaged to teach Edward and Elizabeth French, yet with memories of the fate of Dr Barnes and the moves against the Windsor heretics, he knew he would be endangering his life if he attempted anything so foolish as making the royal children translate phrases from Calvin's works. Whatever the unconscious assimilation of challenging ideas to the Catholic faith, Edward heard mass daily in his household with his tutors, for 'every day in the mass time he readeth a portion of Solomon's proverbs', learning from them 'to fear God, to fear God's commandments, to beware of strange and wanton women, to be obedient to father and mother and to be thankful to him that telleth him of his faults.' 'God's Imp' was indeed schooled in conscientious duty, to prepare himself 'in part to satisfy the good expectation of the King's Majesty, my father', he himself admitted – in part only, for by reason of Original Sin he could never succeed in being wholly satisfactory to his father or to God, and God must have seemed in his eyes to be very much in the image of his earthly father.

The unbending curriculum through which Edward's mind was moulded comprised, in his own words, 'learning of tongues, of the Scripture, of philosophy and all liberal sciences.' So at home did the boy find himself in this world of paradigms and particles, so easily did he master the rules of Latin composition and New Testament Greek, that it comes as something of a relief to remember that he had spirit enough to protest at having to master Biblical proverbs, and once received corporal punishment from Dr Cox. As a change from the schoolroom, he practised riding and archery and also music; to Henry's satisfaction Edward was taught the lute by Philip van Wilder, a Fleming. Little Jane Dormer, daughter of Catherine of Aragon's favourite lady-in-waiting, would come to Ashridge to play, but soon Catherine Parr had established a royal school with other boys from noble families joining Edward's household for lessons. These included Henry Brandon, Duke of Suffolk, Lord Thomas Howard, Lord Lumley and Lord Mountjoy, Barnaby Fitzpatrick, the son of an Irish peer, and perhaps Lord Hastings. Of them all Barnaby Fitzpatrick was the Prince's closest friend.

None welcomed Henry's sixth marriage more warmly than Princess Mary. Though she still spent part of the year at royal manors at Enfield, Tittenhanger, Hunsdon and Hertford, she was more frequently at court than at any time since 1532. Catherine regarded her more as a sister than a stepdaughter, saw that she was present for the wedding and let her join the progress to Woodstock, Grafton, Dunstable and beyond, which served as the honeymoon. Unostentatiously Catherine showed Mary many kindnesses, giving her jewels and money – of which she had always been short – sending her own litter for her when she was poorly, and treating her as a princess even before she was put back in the succession after her brother. Once, when Mary was in Hertfordshire, Catherine sent her a token which she asked one of her musicians to carry, and wrote in the letter that the messenger 'will be welcome for the sake of his music', for she knew how much Mary missed music-making when away from court. When Eustace Chapuys, who had been Charles v's ambassador in London since before Wolsey's fall, came to take his leave of Catherine 'in the garden facing the Queen's lodgings' at Whitehall in May 1545 before returning to the Continent, the Queen made a point of letting the old man have the chance of a private farewell with Mary who for so many years, as the Emperor's cousin, had been at the centre of Hapsburg policy towards England.

Catherine Parr's pietism, even if different in kind from Catherine of Aragon's, was a link between the two women that was strengthened by Mary's own scholarly abilities. It was Catherine who suggested she should undertake a translation of Erasmus's paraphrases on the New Testament; the task well begun had to be abandoned through illness, when Nicholas Udall saw the work to completion. Mary's health was, indeed, a constant concern for Catherine and at this time she was taking a great many pills of mastick and of Elsham ginger. She became very depressed through her fear of remaining a spinster, for she longed for a husband and children of her own, and experience of so many negotiations and enquiries for her hand had left her bitterly disillusioned. When suitors came, she said, 'there was nothing to be got but fine words, and while my father lives I shall be only the Lady Mary, the most unhappy lady in Christendom'. As a distraction from these broodings there were the antics of Jane the Fool and Lucretia the Tumbler, that so amused little Elizabeth, and Mary's treasurer, Richard Wilbraham, had always managed to find their wages, however straitened the finances of her household. Latterly Mary had developed a passion for gambling and would give small sums to Elizabeth, then try to win them back at dice – once she forfeited her breakfast in a wager at bowls, but hunger persuaded her to redeem it for 10s. In her wardrobe purple and black had always predominated rather sadly, until her return to court in 1543 required some fineries of cloth of silver. Because of her small allowance she had for years had to make do and mend, and even when through Catherine's generosity there was more money for new clothes, Mary continued her ingrained habit of 'translating' one garment into another, as she put it.

Elizabeth, seventeen years younger than Mary, and nearly ten when Henry married Catherine, was delighted to have a step-mother who took an interest in her and could be the chief mediator with her father, whom she worshipped. Edward's birth had meant that she had been degraded and put out of the succession; but of much more concern to her, she lost the presence of Lady Bryan, who had cared for her almost from birth. Catherine Champernowne, who now became her governess, quickly gained the girl's confidence and laid the foundations of the superb grasp of languages and classical scholarship which the Princess was to acquire from Cheke and Ascham. 'Kat' Champernowne was to marry John Ashley, close friend of Ascham's, and husband and wife were to remain in Elizabeth's service until their death. When she was six years old, Wriothesley came to test her progress and remarked she would still be an honour to her sex if her formal education ceased straightaway, for the girl talked to him with as much assurance as a woman of forty. 'If she be no more educated than she now appeareth to me, she will prove of no less honour and womanhood than shall be seen her father's daughter.' Four years later she at last had quarters

Thomas Tallis, the 'Father of English music' (1510–85), who entered the Chapel Royal in 1541.

at court next to the Queen. Her earliest surviving letter, written in Italian in a beautiful italic script, was a touching request for Catherine to intercede with her father, then at the wars in France, to end some piece of misunderstanding. By Christmas she had finished a translation of Queen Margaret of Navarre's devotional work, which she presented to Catherine as a New Year's gift – '*The Mirror or Glass of the Sinful Soul*, out of French rhyme into English prose, joining the sentences together as well as the capacity of my simple wit and small learning could extend themselves.' Although carefully penned, with the binding splendidly embroidered, Elizabeth knew the work could not be perfect, yet she hoped her stepmother would 'rub out, polish and mend the words . . . which I know in many places to be rude.' Next year her present was a translation in Latin, French and Italian of Queen Catherine's own prayers and meditations and this manuscript is a superb example of the Renaissance in miniature, needing this time no apologia about imperfections. It was to these blue-stocking years that the portrait of Elizabeth at Windsor belongs, in which she is holding a small book, while at her side on a reading-desk is a large volume. Books were her life-blood, and Catherine Parr guided her reading wholeheartedly, and sensibly took a lenient view of her sewing – that she had herself disliked so much as a child in Kendal.

There was a new luminary in the Chapel Royal, whose compositions were to outshine the motets of Richard Fayrefax and elevate English sacred music to an unrivalled pitch. Thomas Tallis had been organist and master of the choristers at Waltham Abbey in its last days and the singing of the choir had impressed Henry on his visits to the monastery. At the Dissolution Tallis was more fortunate than many, for he secured a post as lay clerk in the re-organised foundation of Canterbury Cathedral. Before long, however, Henry had persuaded him to take a place in his own chapel and in 1542 he appears half-way down the list of thirty-two gentlemen of the Chapel Royal, then under Richard Brown's direction. He was to remain here, at the heart of English music-making, throughout the religious changes of the next forty-three years, developing his skill as a master of counterpoint to become 'the Father of English music'. Although his compositions were not to be published until 1575, Tallis' four-part mass and his motet *Miserere Nostri* belong to these early years in the Chapel Royal; in all likelihood Henry VIII also heard the magisterial weaving of sound in his intricate Latin motet for forty voices, and more than any other listener appreciated its architectonic character, for this motet (like the 'Art of Fugue' and the last Beethoven string quartets) is essentially musicians' music.

Changes in the liturgy that were to lead to the First Prayer Book of Edward VI were already in hand during the last years of Henry's life, with Cranmer's experiments in a service book in English. In particular the litany gave Tallis the first opportunity of attempting a musical setting of vernacular words for public worship for the Chapel Royal and from this early exercise, still in the repertoire of cathedral and collegiate choirs today, followed a great body of distinctively Anglican church music. Litanies were sung as in turn Henry, Edward and Mary were *in extremis* and archbishops, like sovereigns, came and went. Of all the principal figures of the English

Reformation, it was only Thomas Tallis, the court musician, who spanned the full half-century linking the old Latin rites of Waltham to the use of the Chapel Royal in Queen Elizabeth's heyday.

The royal collections at Windsor and Whitehall were in the care of John Leland (1506–52), who had been appointed keeper of the King's books about 1530. At St Paul's School Leland had received an excellent grounding in classical scholarship from William Lily, which he pursued in earnest first at Christ's, Cambridge, and then at All Souls, Oxford, before leaving for Paris, by now the home of humanist studies, where he came under the influence of Guillaume Budé, philologist and lawyer. On his return to England Norfolk engaged him as a tutor for his younger son, Lord Thomas Howard, and from this it was but a short step to obtain royal patronage. Leland was busy setting in order the books and manuscripts of Henry, his first Queen and his mother, Elizabeth of York, for the new library at Whitehall, but almost at once found himself launched in a great enterprise in a new post as King's Antiquary.

Detail from the screen of King's College Chapel, showing the initials 'H' and 'A' for the King and Anne Boleyn.

Leland was commissioned by Henry 'to peruse and diligently to search all the libraries' belonging to cathedrals, colleges and monasteries and make a survey of their treasures before it was too late. He left court for a series of prolonged travels (1535–43) and as he moved about England he made voluminous notes, not only of books and manuscripts in collections of all kinds in the very years in which the religious houses were closing, but also memoranda on the shape of the countryside, the nature of its towns, local customs and legend and local worthies, that made him the pioneer of those topographical studies where history and geography meet. The detail he amassed was a prodigious feat, even if he had a few blind spots as, for some reason, not considering that Stonehenge was worthy of mention. Leland never fully succeeded in putting his notes in order and it was not until the early eighteenth century that his *Collectanea*, embodying his reports on the libraries, and his *Itinerary*, describing his travels, were both published. He was in fact too much the grand collector of information to weave 'the thing of threads and patches' into a literary composition, though in 1545 he did present to Henry a summary of his twelve years' labour in *A New Year's Gift*. Leland had already been rewarded with a canonry at Christ Church, a prebendary at Salisbury Cathedral and a country rectory, but he lived mostly in London, frequenting the court, a repository of a vast knowledge of England's past. At length – grim warning to all historians – 'his antiquarian studies overloaded his brain and he became irremediably insane' a few months after Henry VIII's death. Yet Leland's efforts preserved the memory of things about to disappear and from his enthusiasm stems the work of Camden, Stow and the Elizabethan antiquaries.

Right at the end of his life Henry made amends for his long neglect of higher education by his foundations of Christ Church, Oxford and Trinity College, Cambridge. At the beginning of his reign there had been notable benefactions at both universities, stemming from the influence of his grandmother, the Lady Margaret, who had refounded Christ's and founded St John's at Cambridge. Her protégé William Smyth, who became Dean of the Chapel Royal and Bishop of Lincoln, founded Brasenose College, Oxford with Richard Sutton, a lawyer, as co-adjutor, and in 1512 this was

King's College Chapel, Cambridge, the rood screen and organ loft, completed in 1533 with the help of a royal gift.

incorporated by royal charter as 'the King's Hall and College of Brase Nose'. The statutes enjoined the young men to study sophistry, logic and philosophy as a training for holy orders and despite the modernity of the buildings the college was essentially medieval in outlook and constitution. Bishop Foxe's foundation of Corpus Christi in 1517 was a very different institution. Originally he had contemplated endowing a house where the monks of St Swithin's of Winchester could be trained, but when he resigned the Privy Seal and devoted himself to his diocese of Winchester he decided the real need was for a college where secular clergy could be taught humanist studies. So Corpus developed as 'Foxe's bee-hive' of industrious scholars, working in the rooms built by William Vertue in the shadow of Merton, and here Greek became for the first time at Oxford an integral part of the curriculum. Erasmus termed it 'one of the chief glories' of England and ventured that it would draw more men to Oxford than had ever been attracted to the colleges in Rome. Before he died Foxe also made notable benefactions at Magdalen, Oxford and Pembroke, Cambridge.

The young Henry did not live up to the promise which Erasmus had found in him and for long the universities were merely allies to which he turned for support in his divorce proceedings from Catherine of Aragon. While Henry VII had given £10,000 towards the completion of King's College Chapel, it was not until his son had reigned for twenty-three years that he provided money for the chapel to enable the rood-screen or organ loft and the stalls beneath it to be carved (incorporating his and Anne Boleyn's devices) and, according to John Caius, helped the college with the doors, paving and the last of the great windows. Cromwell's visitors played havoc with both universities, securing the confiscation of the friaries and the

Windows of King's College Chapel, Cambridge – the work of Galyon Hone, Henry's glazier.

Tom Quad of Christ Church, Oxford. The cloisters and the second storey of the quadrangle were never completed after Wolsey's fall; it was not until 1681 that Wren built Tom Tower.

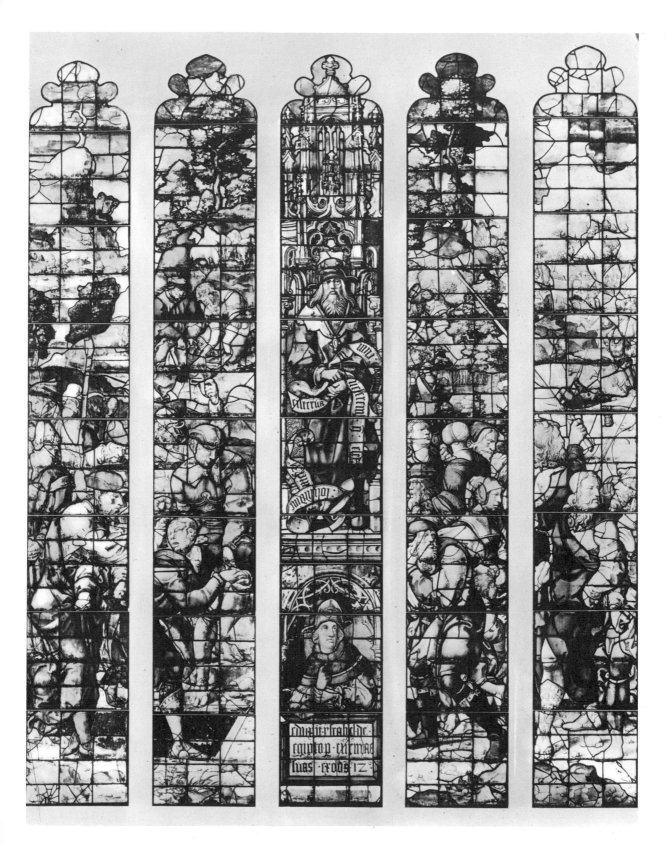

243

demise of the halls, as cells of great monasteries like Canterbury, while with the Dissolution impoverished courtiers 'gaped after' the endowments of the colleges. Henry had defended them: 'I tell you, sirs, that I judge no land in England better bestowed than that which is given to our universities, for by their maintenance our realm shall be well governed when we be dead and rotten' – yet the fate of Cardinal College, Oxford, so richly endowed by Wolsey in 1525, with an annual income of 3,000 ducats from suppressed religious houses to provide a magnificent establishment of 177 persons, had been dispiriting. By the end of 1526 the lodgings on the west court were finished so far as the battlements and were roofed in lead, and at the south end the tower gateway rose in splendour while the kitchens were completed in time 'to give the dean and canons their Christmas victuals'. The great hall, designed by John Lesbons and Henry Redman, both of them architects in the King's service, took longer but was ready, unlike Wolsey's cloister (now Tom Quad), by the Cardinal's fall. His grandiose scheme was abandoned and many of the lands were 'begged away to hungry courtiers'. The rump of Wolsey's foundation was, however, saved, for when a deputation came to the King pleading for its survival, Henry told them: 'Surely we purpose to have an honourable college there, but not so great and of such magnificence as my Lord Cardinal intended to have.' He took the college into his own hands and reformed it as an exclusively ecclesiastical institution, divorced from university teaching and, indeed, from any authority but his own.

At last in 1546 he kept his word by refounding the college as Christ Church, that was to be both a royal college and a cathedral for the recently founded see of Oxford; the 'cathedral' of the diocese was removed from Osney and the bell known as Great Tom was moved with the bishop's throne. Such was 'Ecclesia Christi Cathedralis Oxon., on the foundation of King Henry VIII'. Once he had decided on a royal foundation nothing was to be done by halves. Besides the lands of St Frideswide's and of Osney Abbey, the site was extended by the old halls of residence of the Cistercians (St Bernard's) and of Canterbury College and the buildings of Peckwater Inn. Richard Cox, the first dean, ruled over a body of eight canons, three professors of Hebrew, Greek and Theology, one hundred students with censors and readers to teach them and a full establishment of chaplains, lay clerks and choristers, to sing the services in the cathedral with its fine 'presbytery' vaulting that was at the same time the college chapel. The House became the largest and wealthiest of all collegiate bodies, and boasted the sovereign as its Visitor.

The previous year the Act for the Dissolution of Chantries had produced panic in Cambridge, even though Henry had told Parliament that he would never allow learning to decay. None doubted his power to seize King's College or St John's, even as he had seized Glastonbury and the Charterhouse. Matthew Parker was certain that men at court were 'importunately suing to him to have the lands and possessions of both universities surveyed' and Henry had to admit that he could not remain deaf to the demands of courtiers for grants of lands in reward for 'doing the service for the realm in wars and other affairs'; the ravening wolves were ready to pounce. The university was saved by the influence of Cheke, professor of Greek and Prince Edward's tutor, and even more of Thomas Smith, the thirty-year-

The gate of Trinity College Cambridge, with a statue of Henry VIII, the college's founder.

old vice-chancellor. Smith, destined to become provost of Eton and Secretary of State in turn to Edward VI and Elizabeth I, was now the first holder of the Regius professorship of Civil Law, one of the five chairs which Henry had established at Cambridge in 1540. Ten years back he had been singled out by William Butts, Henry's physician and a fellow of Gonville Hall, for royal bounty as a King's scholar and now, despite his youth, was already reckoned 'the flower of the university', even though Cheke, Ascham, Redman and Ponet were in residence. Thomas Smith had a many-sided brilliance and was to be a prolific author. He constructed globes of the world, regarded himself as just as great an authority as Cheke on the thorny topic of Greek pronunciation, and devised a new English alphabet consisting of nineteen Roman, four Greek and six English letters, including ten vowels, with long and short accents. He was anxious to make Cambridge a centre for the study of civil law, now that the breach with Rome had closed the schools of Bologna and Padua to English civilians, and the King appreciated that there was no better training for the public service than the study of civil law. Smith's humble petition to Queen Catherine was in fact preaching to the converted. She replied that she was well aware that, as at Athens long ago, all kinds of learning flourished, and hoped that the study of Christian doctrine would receive its proper attention so that Cambridge would develop as a centre for divine philosophy. She assured the doctors and masters that she had already 'attempted my lord the King's Majesty' and that he 'being such a patron to good learning doth tender you so much that he will rather advance learning and erect new occasion thereof, than to confound those godly institutions.' Her words with her husband, based on the pleas of Cheke and Smith, saved the day and although the college lands were surveyed, the commissioners in charge were Cambridge worthies, headed by Matthew Parker and John Redman, not agents of the Court of Augmentations. Except for the new foundation of Magdalene, so recently endowed by Lord Chancellor Audley, all the colleges were found to be in financial difficulties, for only two had an income of over £500, and when the King perused the commissioners' report he declared that he 'thought he had not in his realm so many persons so honestly maintained in living by so little land and rent.' He would force the university no further in satisfying the greed of his own servants who coveted their property, and kept his promise to Catherine about erecting a new house of learning. Within a few days of establishing Christ Church, Oxford on a new footing he granted a charter for the foundation of Trinity College, Cambridge out of Michaelhouse, King's Hall and the Physwick Hostel, then in the possession of Gonville Hall. (It was Fuller who said Henry's foundation was so called not only on account of its dedication, but also because he made 'one of three colleges'.) To this very considerable site was added the church, cloisters and other buildings of the Franciscan friars and almost at once the master and fellows began negotiations with the town for other adjoining lands. John Redman, the last warden of King's Hall, became the first master of Trinity and soon there were fifty fellows and sixty scholars and Bible clerks in residence. As with Christ Church, once Henry had finally reached a decision on founding a college, he implemented it with customary grandeur and munificence, so that 'no Cambridge foundation and probably no academic institution in Europe furnishes so striking an example as does Trinity College of the change from the medieval to the modern conception of education and learning.' (J. B. Mullinger, *The University of Cambridge*, vol. ii.)

Just as Henry was planning to cross to France with his army in the spring of 1544 his ulcerous leg flared up again, for he had to stay in bed for a week and to keep to his room for rather longer. It was then that Catherine threw palace convention to the winds by moving her bed to a small room leading off her husband's bedchamber, so she could be near him in his illness. But though his 'chronic disease and great obesity' was considered by his ally Charles v to be a liability in the campaign, he insisted on taking the field in person when he had sufficiently recovered and left Catherine for three months as Regent. It was with relief that she heard from Hertford, who was with him at Boulogne, that Henry was in as good health as he had known him for seven years. His old friend and physician, William Butts, died that winter, and he felt his loss, fretting about his health, insisting that he had been ten times fitter on a horse in France than he was stumping about Whitehall since his return.

The accounts of Queen Catherine's apothecary include many items which she purchased for Henry's maladies – preservative lozenges, cinnamon comfits, liquorice pastilles, suppositories made from olive oil ointment, 'the King's lozenge cordial', plasters for the spleen and sponges for fomentation,

Brown calf binding for a presentation copy to Henry of a narrative of the campaigns of the Emperor Charles v in 1544. The royal initials are flanked by medallions of Plato and Dido.

Prince Edward, the heir to the throne, at the age of six; the pet animal he is holding is perhaps one of Will Somers' monkeys.

for dressing his leg. At this time Henry acquired reading-glasses in gilt frames, perhaps on Catherine's advice.

Spring was becoming a dangerous season for the King. In March 1545 he had, as he put it, 'a burning fever for several consecutive days and subsequently the malady had attacked the leg', and he took care that his subjects, who were convinced he had a robust constitution, should not know that he had been ill. A year later he was laid up for rather longer, but on recovering bravely gave out that he was determined to visit the distant parts of the realm; he was poorly in July and then was seriously ill at Windsor and had to abandon the progress. Wriothesley attempted to deny to foreign envoys there was the slightest cause for alarm, though in fact there had been little hope of his recovery. He was well enough to do a little hunting and then, in mid-November, returned to Whitehall to take 'preparative medicine for certain baths which he usually has at this season'. Those about him knew that the future was fraught with uncertainties.

In 1546, or possibly the year before, Henry began using a special chair or 'tram' with shafts back and front, something akin to the later sedan chair, in which he was carried from room to room when his legs were weak. There was nothing elaborate about it and an ambassador who mentioned seeing the King 'while passing in his chair' at Whitehall did not think the conveyance needed special comment. An inventory of furniture in the palace records 'two chairs called trams for the King's Majesty to sit in, to be carried to and fro in his galleries and chambers, covered with tawny velvet, all over quilted . . .'. With its royal cargo it must have been an extremely heavy affair and those who had not seen it let their imaginations wander. The rumour went abroad that because Henry was so huge and feeble on his legs 'he could not go up and down the stairs and was let up and down by a device'. But there is nothing to suggest a lift or other piece of machinery, nor was there any call for one, since all the King's private apartments were on the first floor at all his residences, even his chapel pew, and unless he needed to go out of doors he could remain on one level.

Stephen Gardiner and the conservatives had all long considered that Cromwell's greatest blunder had been to require copies of the English Bible to be placed in every church and, after his fall, they had preyed on Henry's fears that the Great Bible was not an impartial translation but a specifically Protestant text. When Cranmer had been forced to ask Convocation whether the English Bible could be retained without 'scandal, error and open offence to Christ's faithful people', a majority of the bishops replied that it could not, so the Archbishop apportioned the text for detailed examination by various committees, while an independent appraisal was to be made by the two universities. But Gardiner stole a march by persuading the King in 1543 to give his assent to an Act of Parliament seriously curtailing the study of the Scriptures in English, which was euphemistically termed the 'Act for the advancement of true religion'. Because of so many 'crafty, false and untrue' translations, including Tyndale's, Bible reading was to be a privilege of the educated few – the upper and middle classes. Noblemen and gentlemen could read translations aloud to their families, while merchants of substance and gentlewomen were to be allowed to read to themselves alone, but the common people were to be denied any personal acquaintance with the Scriptures. Later Henry was to complain to Parliament that

Henry in 1544, drawn by Cornelius Matsis.

the 'most precious jewel, the Word of God, is disputed, rhymed, sung and jangled in every alehouse and tavern', for it was in such places that Bible readings for the illiterate chiefly took place.

Because of the concentration of peers, gentlemen and their families in the royal household, the court was legally immune from the operation of the Bible study act, just as it was immune from the sumptuary laws about dress. But the operation of the Act of Six Articles of 1539, particularly those against heresy, was another matter and it was here that the humanists and Protestant sympathisers who had gathered round Catherine Parr were truly vulnerable. Even before her marriage to Henry there had been a witch-hunt at Windsor.

Dr John London, warden of New College, had been active as one of Cromwell's visitors during the Dissolution, but adapting himself to the times he had more recently made his college and university aware of his intense distate for Protestantism, and through Gardiner's influence became appointed a canon of Windsor in 1542. When he moved to St George's he soon busied himself tracking down a veritable 'nest of heresy' in the cloisters. His first victims included a priest, a lay clerk in the chapel choir and a tailor, but he had less success in his proceedings against the organist, John Marbeck, when he sent him to be examined by Gardiner, who lodged him in the Marshalsea Prison in irons, 'for seditious opinions and other mis-behaviours'. Marbeck's offence lay in compiling what was the earliest Con-cordance of the English Bible ever attempted, and for this work he had translated various letters of Calvin's, which made him immediately suspect, though the real danger lay in his daring to translate the Latin terms of the Vulgate and the medieval Church into the common tongue. *Hoc est corpus meum* decently obscured doctrinal difficulties which an English gloss could not escape, and Marbeck was too dedicated and courageous a theologian not to face them squarely. If, said Bishop Gardiner, such a book as the Concordance 'should go forth in English, it would destroy the Latin tongue' and, he might have added, Catholic dogma. Dr London could not believe that a musician was capable of embarking unaided on a work of such immense labour and detailed study, and he was convinced that behind Marbeck lay an important mentor and patron at court. Accordingly he was closely questioned on five occasions and the Bishop urged Mrs Marbeck, who had come with their baby to see him in prison, to persuade her husband to reveal the identity of these 'naughty fellows', telling her how much he admired his musicianship 'wherein he has pleased me as well as any man'. Yet John Marbeck steadfastly denied he knew any whom he could accuse. When he was tried at Windsor, the jury at first could not agree and then they found him guilty of infringing the Act of Six Articles; only Gardiner's personal intervention saved him from being burnt at the stake as a heretic.

Although Marbeck had revealed no names, Dr London subsequently thought he had found bigger fish to fry and was preparing a case against no fewer than eleven members of the royal household. The draft indict-ments for heresy he had drawn up were intercepted however, thanks to the initiative of Master Fulk, a servant of the Queen, and some of those impli-cated gained Henry's ear. At this very time the King was supporting Cranmer against Gardiner's personal attack and the methods of Dr London's proceedings annoyed him, for he always resented cases against members of

Sir Philip Hoby (1505–58), drawn by Holbein. He served Henry as a gentleman of the Privy Chamber and as a soldier. Later, as a diplomat, he became a friend of Titian.

his household. A few enquiries satisfied him that London should be arrested, while those suspected of heresy were given a free pardon. Those involved included two gentlemen of the Privy Chamber, Sir Philip Hoby, a diplomat and step-brother of Sir Thomas, the translator of Castiglione's *The Courtier*, and Sir Thomas Calverden of Bletchingley, and their wives; Thomas Sternhold, groom of the Robes, who was already working on his metrical version of the psalms, and a radical priest, Anthony Peerson. London had over-reached himself in his whispering campaign against courtiers and the privy council found him guilty of perjury. The 'stout and filthy prebendary', who had earlier in his career been twice convicted of adultery, was sentenced to ride backwards on horseback through Windsor, Newbury and Reading, to stand in the pillory in each town and then return to imprisonment in the Fleet, where he died later in 1544.

Marbeck had escaped the flames, yet his huge manuscript had been confiscated and on being pardoned he returned to Windsor to begin all over again. When he had finished, the new text was so voluminous that no printer would risk money in bringing it out, so Marbeck undertook an extensive revision to reduce it to some nine hundred folios of three volumes. This was finally published in 1550, dedicated to King Edward VI, and the same year appeared Marbeck's other great work, his musical settings of the services for congregational singing known as *The Book of Common Prayer Noted*. In all humility in the preface to the Concordance he denied any pretensions to literary elegance as he had 'never tasted the sweetness of learned letters but altogether brought up in your Highness' College at Windsor in the study of music and playing on organs, wherein I consumed vainly the greatest part of my life.' His was a remarkable dual achievement, the kind of versatility that Henry VIII so admired in a man. In due course his son became a physician to Queen Elizabeth and, as provost of Oriel College, made a very different head of a house from his father's enemy, Dr London.

The danger to Reformist sympathisers at court had not ended with London's disgrace, for in the closing years of the reign, with schemes being laid for obtaining power on Prince Edward's accession, Gardiner and Wriothesley led a much more intensive campaign to discover and punish crypto-Protestants in high places. Five of Catherine's ladies were to be in danger of their lives – her sister, Mistress Herbert, Ladies Denny, Tyrwhit and Hertford, and young Lady Jane Grey – and the fact that Catherine and her friends had such influence on the education of the heir to the throne made their positions all the more dangerous. On the King's side, apart from the husbands of Catherine's married ladies, there were Lord Thomas Howard, the black sheep of the family who was found to dispute of 'Scripture matters more largely and indiscreetly than good order did permit', Sir George Blage of the Privy Chamber, who admired the preaching of the troublesome Dr Edward Crome, and Henry's physician Dr Butts. Among the men of lesser rank who feared the Bishop of Winchester's threats more than the King's wrath were Master Wourley, a page, who had made 'unseemly reasoning' from Scriptures, John Lassels, now a sewer, whose statement to Cranmer in 1541 had led to Catherine Howard's downfall, and William Morice, who so nearly followed Lassels to Smithfield. Henry was fond of Sir George Blage, whom he nick-named his 'pig', and when he heard of his condemnation for heresy he sent for Lord Chancellor

Wriothesley, swearing at him 'for coming so near him, even to his Privy Chamber', and ordering a pardon to be made out. The next time the King saw Blage he greeted him 'Ah, my pig! Are you safe again?' 'Yes, Sire', he replied, 'and if Your Majesty had not been better than your bishops, your pig had been roasted ere this time.'

A further heresy hunt was launched by the council in the early summer of 1546, following Gardiner's return from an embassy with Charles V. Dr Edward Crome, a popular preacher who had declaimed against purgatory and masses for the dead, made a mockery of the recantation he was required to make at Paul's Cross and, while he was subsequently in custody at Greenwich Palace, was prevailed upon by Wriothesley to accuse of heresy 'divers persons as well of the court as of the city', thus providing Bishop Gardiner with invaluable clues. Among those the council summoned for examination were Latimer and Shaxton, who had resigned their sees with the passing of the Act of Six Articles in 1539; the former now maintained his doctrinal position and was imprisoned, while the latter publicly recanted his unorthodox views on the sacrament and went free.

Another suspect was Anne Askewe, daughter of a Lincolnshire knight who had been married off as a child bride, though after she had embraced the Protestant faith her husband had put her out of his home. She came to London, where for over a year she had caused a stir as the most militant of reformers – and a woman at that. Gardiner, presiding at the council table, asked her for her own interpretation of the sacrament and when she was evasive he warned her not to speak in parables. Next day he tried again to persuade her to renounce her errors to be safe from the stake, and Lord Parr, the Queen's brother, who was present with John Dudley, Lord Lisle, urged her to confess that the Sacrament was the 'flesh, blood and bone' of Christ. She would not be shifted and with great conviction and entrenched obstinacy told the councillors 'it was a great shame for them to counsel contrary to their knowledge.' Anne Askewe was duly tried at the Guildhall and condemned to death as a heretic, but while in prison was interrogated by Bishop Bonner of London and others about the ladies of the court who were suspected of supporting her with gifts, because they shared her beliefs. At first she impudently answered that her money came from collections her maids had taken among the London apprentices, but at last she admitted receiving gifts from Lady Hertford and Lady Denny. On the strength of this Wriothesley and Sir Richard Rich, the Solicitor General, determined to rack her in the Tower to extract further names of well-wishers at court, particularly hoping to implicate the Queen. These two lawyers, with total disregard for the law, racked the condemned woman with their own hands until all her joints were distorted, and so alarmed was the Lieutenant of the Tower at their proceedings that he hurried to the King for a pardon to absolve himself of any responsibility in the racking. Anne revealed nothing further. Even on the day of her burning at Smithfield Wriothesley sent her a promise of pardon if she would only recant, but with great self-possession she answered she had not come hither 'to deny her Master'. Her death was the climax of the policy of reaction and overnight she became the heroine of English Protestantism, the proto-martyr of a new martyrology, serving to strengthen convinced Protestants in their stand against Catholic theology.

It is probably to the days following Anne Askewe's brutal torture and

Woodcut of the burning of Anne Askewe as a heretic at Smithfield, 1546.

death that we should assign the attempt to secure a condemnation for heresy against Catherine Parr. This makes such a purple passage in John Foxe's *Book of Martyrs*, with its invented dialogue and curious outcome, though other evidence for the incident is lacking. Catherine's Lenten readings of the Scriptures with her ladies were well known and these were often followed by sermons or led to discussions that ranged widely over theology and Church affairs; nor did she hesitate to talk to Henry about the points that had emerged. Gardiner and Wriothesley had for some time felt that the Queen's influence on her husband was dangerous, but they now sought to exploit her vulnerability and expose her heretical leanings once and for all. The King's temper and suspicious nature inevitably increased with his sickness and 'the sharpness of the disease had sharpened the King's accustomed patience.' It was not surprising that Catherine's theological arguments began to irritate him and he showed 'tokens of misliking'; perhaps Catherine had even intervened with him to spare Anne Askewe. Gardiner risked much in raising the question of the Queen's orthodoxy with Henry and apparently told him that 'the religion by the Queen so stiffly maintained did not only disallow and dissolve the policy and politic government of princes, but also taught the people that all things ought to be in common' – a concern for public order that Henry readily endorsed.

It may be, as Foxe states, that the books in the Queen's closet were now closely examined and that Henry chided her with the sarcastic words, 'A good hearing it is when women become such clerks; and nothing much to my comfort in mine old days to be taught by my wife.' It is just possible, too, that Henry's anger at her outbursts of independent opinions and his suspicion that he had been cherishing an heretical serpent within his own orthodox bosom was so great that he signed bills of articles against her, and the ladies closest to her, that would have brought them to trial. At any rate an incriminating document was allowed to fall from a councillor's pocket and, learning from it of the danger she was in, Catherine was taken with violent hysterics. Henry heard the crying and sent Dr Wendy, who acted as mediator, and next morning a complete reconciliation was effected. Catherine fully confessed that she was unfit to hold personal views on religion and made it clear that the wisdom of her spouse, Supreme Head of the Church, was her sole anchor under God. 'Not so, by St Mary', he answered. 'You have become a doctor, Kate, to instruct us, as we take it, and not to be instructed or directed by us.' This she firmly denied, telling him she had only argued to distract him from his great pain and to learn from his lips what true doctrine was. 'And is it even so, sweetheart, and tended your arguments to no worse end?' replied the King. 'Then perfect friends we are now again as ever at any time before.' When Wriothesley with a detachment of guards came that afternoon to arrest the Queen and her ladies while in the gardens at Whitehall, the King made sure he was present and swore at the Lord Chancellor as an 'arrant knave, beast and fool', for Wriothesley had been too preoccupied to hear the latest whispers and he was sent packing. Whatever the details of these incidents, embroidered by Foxe, the main outline of the attempted attack on Catherine rings true. Now she was out of danger and persecution effectively ceased so long as Henry breathed. Daily he came to be more and more dependent on her as his nurse, while the fall of the Howards and the King's quarrel with Gardiner made the Seymours dominant at court and in council.

The renewal of the wars with Scotland and France had given Norfolk and his son further opportunities of service which might make them more acceptable at court. The Duke, a veteran of Flodden, now claimed credit for the rout of Solway Moss. Two years later, though over seventy, he was appointed lieutenant-general of the army in France and nearly lost Boulogne after its surrender, through tactics that provoked one of the King's severest rebukes. Norfolk, he wrote, had acted 'so clean discrepant from our commandment . . . We cannot but marvel that men of such experience as we know you to be' should take such risks, and ordered him 'to seek no more indirect excuses to cloak your ill-favoured retreat, but rather study, and be as to seek our honour, herein somewhat touched, redubbed.' Subsequently Surrey succeeded his father at Boulogne and distinguished himself, leading raids into enemy country, proud when the King reproved him for needlessly exposing himself to danger. But in January 1546 came his first reverse when he was defeated at St Etienne and the casualties were unnecessarily heavy. As a result he was supplanted by Edward Seymour, Earl of Hertford, who returned to England with the laurels of war, while Surrey and his father licked their wounds at Kenninghall.

The Seymours had always been in Howard eyes an upstart family, bent on ousting the older nobility from their traditional places about the King, and with Henry's health deteriorating there was intense jockeying for position at court. Edward Seymour, as victor of the French campaign and uncle of Prince Edward, was ideally placed. Allied to him was a relative newcomer to the council, John Dudley, now Lord Admiral, who had recently been created Lord Lisle. As with Hertford, the war had helped him to establish himself and when Henry was recovering from a fever he spent the days playing cards with Lisle; it was incongruous that at the end he should be losing money to the son of Edmund Dudley, whom he had beheaded for financial malpractices at the outset of his reign. During that

Sir Richard Southwell (1504–64), who had served under Thomas Cromwell, remained a firm enemy of the Howards.

Sir Gawen Carew, soldier and courtier.

summer while Anne Askewe was being examined, Norfolk saw that he must attempt a *rapprochement* with Hertford, distasteful though it was, and he even asked the King to help him arrange a match between his daughter of Richmond and Hertford's brother, Sir Thomas Seymour – who had already failed to win Catherine Parr. Such a marriage would, he hoped, be the first of a whole series of alliances between the Howards and the Seymours. The scheme was still-born, yet Surrey contrived to press his sister to favour that great womaniser, Thomas Seymour, and when she proved unhelpful, suggested she might become her royal father-in-law's mistress.

With the King growing weaker, those nearest to him at last began to doubt if he could ever recover sufficiently to rule. On every hand there was scheming and speculation in this whispering gallery of politics concerning the regency for governing England on Edward's accession. There were frequent quarrels in council and once Lisle so far forgot himself as to strike Gardiner and had to retire from court, though within the month he was back at the council table, as confident as ever. He and Hertford spoke such 'violent and injurious words' to the Bishop and to Wriothesley that an informed observer doubted whether there was any who could dare oppose the Seymour-Dudley alliance. Seeing the way the wind was blowing, Wriothesley and Paget, the Secretary, deserted Gardiner for Hertford, and any remaining hopes the Bishop nurtured about overturning his opponents were dashed by the dramatic downfall of his chief allies, the Howards.

Early in December 1546 Sir Richard Southwell, a Norfolk MP, who had served Cromwell zealously in the Dissolution of the abbeys, informed the council that he had evidence about Surrey 'that touched his fidelity to the King'. When the Earl heard of this he declared he would fight Southwell 'in his shirt', but for the moment both men were detained in Wriothesley's house. Norfolk was summoned from the country and on arrival in London was taken by barge to the Tower. Twelve years back he had said shrewdly to Sir Thomas More, 'By the mass, Master More, it is perilous striving with princes', and now his own fate made its wry comment. The wildest rumours were afoot as Surrey joined his father. Some said the Howards had planned to murder all the council, others that they aimed at the custody of Prince Edward.

When Southwell and others went down to Kenninghall they found hearsay evidence enough from the Duke's household to make a case against Surrey. Mary, Duchess of Richmond admitted her brother was a 'rash man' and had repeatedly said the Seymours and 'these new men loved no nobility, and if God called away the King they should smart for it.' She remembered, too, that Surrey had made an alteration in his arms and had replaced his coronet with a crown, and underneath the arms was a cypher 'H.R.' Elizabeth Holland, Norfolk's mistress, anxious to save herself and her possessions, related various remarks of the Duke's about his unpopularity in the council; none of them loved him 'because they were no noblemen born themselves', and he had told her that the King 'was much grown of his body and that he could not go up and down stairs . . . and that his Majesty was sickly and could not long endure.' Others recalled very dark sayings from Surrey about who should govern on Henry's death – Sir Gawen Carew enlarged on the Earl's intrigues to interest the King in his sister:

she should dissemble the matter and he [Surrey] would find the means that the King's Majesty should speak with her himself; she should in no wise utterly make refusal of him, but leave the matter so diffusely that the King should take occasion to speak with her again, and thus by length of time it were possible that the King should take such a fantasy to you that ye shall be able to govern like unto Madame D'Estampes [the mistress of Francis I].

Sir Edmund Knyvett, who never forgot Surrey's part against him that had almost cost him his right arm, deposed that when he had charged the Earl with malice towards him he had replied, 'No, no, cousin Knyvett, I malice not so low; my malice is higher . . . These new erected men would by their wills leave no noble man on life.' Another Norfolk knight, Sir Edward Warner, told of Surrey's 'pride and vain glory' and in particular of his bearing the arms of Edward the Confessor.

When Garter King of Arms was questioned he said that some while back Richmond Herald had asked him to speak with the Earl about his arms, and in the gallery at Howard House, Lambeth, Surrey had shown Garter 'an escutcheon of the arms of Brotherton and St Edward [the Confessor], and Anjou and Mowbray quartered. I asked him by what title and he said that Thomas of Brotherton' – the eldest child of Edward I by his second queen, who became Earl of Norfolk – 'bare it so, and I showed him it was not in his pedigree.' Clearly, Garter had been reluctant to take up the matter with Norfolk, as Earl Marshal. Evidence then came to light that Surrey ordered a Norwich glazier to put the Confessor's arms into a window at Mount Surrey, his Norwich mansion, that he purchased a stamp with the same arms for engraving his plate and had them painted in his chambers at Kenninghall.

In the end it was for the heraldic offences that Surrey was to be tried – not before the Court of Chivalry, but for high treason with Hertford and his other enemies sitting as special commissioners. It was Surrey's foolhardiness at the very time when all the Court were speculating on the succession of a child to the throne, that he should boast of his own Plantaganet blood and proclaim his right to the throne heraldically; this was the more serious since, as eldest son of the Earl Marshal, he should have known better.

Ill though Henry was, he took the greatest interest in the case, so closely touching his regality. Though he could hardly hold a pen, he corrected the memoranda drafted for him in his own hand. 'If a man compassing himself to govern the realm do actually go about to rule the King and should for that purpose advise his daughter or his sister to become his harlot . . . What this importeth?' At the trial, though the verdict was a forgone conclusion, the Earl fought fiercely with his accusers. He lashed out at Paget, whose father had been a constable: 'Thou Catchpole; what had thou to do with it? Thou hadst better hold thy tongue, for the kingdom has never been well since the King put new creatures like thee in the government.' When the sentence was given he made a final outburst: 'I know that the King wants to get rid of the noble blood round him and employ none but low people.' Surrey, whom Henry had once loved like a son, was executed on 19 January 1547.

Compromised by the Earl's indiscretion, Norfolk was at the mercy of his enemies, yet he persisted in maintaining his loyalty. 'I have had great

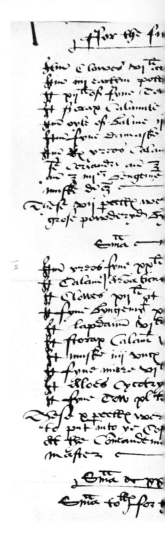

Account of Thomas Alsopp, royal apothecary, for materials supplied for Henry's funeral, 1547; the items include spices for embalming 'delivered severally' to put into the coffin of lead with the corpse.

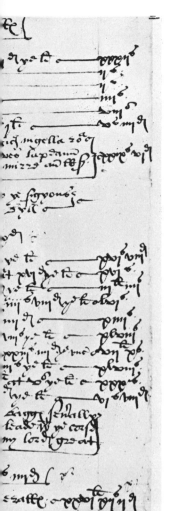

enemies', he reminded the council, alluding to Buckingham, Wolsey and Cromwell, and even his own kin. 'The malice borne me by both my nieces whom it pleased the King to marry, is not unknown to such as kept them.' The day before Surrey's trial he drew up a confession about his own faults in concealing his son's treason in illegally using the Confessor's arms and even admitted that he had himself been in error in bearing for twenty-two years in the principal quarter of his arms 'the arms of England, with a difference of three labels of silver, which are the arms of my lord the Prince.' This, the Earl Marshal now acknowledged, was high treason and he begged for mercy. Following this confession and Surrey's execution, a Bill of Attainder was brought into Parliament against them both, to secure their extensive lands for the Crown. Norfolk's execution seemed certain; it was only to be Henry's death that saved the Duke's life. The Howards had fallen largely because their house had been divided against itself – husband against wife, brother against sister, the prolific cousinage taking sides, – and family quarrels had been exploited by astute opponents who feared Norfolk and his kin for being too close to the throne in blood, and had brought Henry to share their fear. Their fall, so sudden and complete, astounded the courts of Europe when accounts were sent abroad. Ambassador Wotton in France reckoned their actions 'the most execrable and most abominable intent and enterprise', while Bishop Thirlby, then with the Emperor, pondered the fate of 'those two ungracious *non homines*, the Duke of Norfolk and his son . . . Before God, I am so amazed.' The crows were ready to swoop. Detailed inventories were made of their jewellery, plate, cutlery and the rest of the family heirlooms worth a million pounds, and most of the loot went in time to Hertford. Courtiers in 1540 had been delighted at the windfall of items from Cromwell's wardrobe, but this was nothing to the finery of Norfolk and Surrey now ready for distribution; there was irony even in the saying 'waiting for dead men's shoes'. Hertford pilfered Surrey's Parliament cap, his spurs and even two pairs of stockings, while his brother seized his shirts and shoes.

Gardiner had no ally left. Indeed, the topics of Norfolk's interrogations included the Bishop's attitude to the Papacy, for in negotiations at Ratisbon five years earlier he had hinted at some *modus vivendi* between Pope and King. No one forgot that Germayne Gardiner, the nephew who served as his secretary, had been executed for upholding the Pope's authority, and the Bishop having kept his nerve through those anxious days, did not see the danger of his position at the end of 1546. To tidy an awkward corner of the royal estate the King wanted to exchange various lands with Winchester, but Gardiner, feeling he was as secure as ever, declined to make an agreement which he thought was disadvantageous to himself. Henry was furious. Gardiner suspected that Hertford and Lisle had misrepresented him, magnified the incident out of all proportion and that it was they who were responsible for him being denied entry to the Privy Chamber. He asked Secretary Paget to ensure that the King read his letter humbly setting down his utter loyalty, craving mercy and seeking the chance of coming to court to explain himself, 'because I have no access to your Majesty'. This letter did more harm than good for Henry replied that he would not deny him an audience 'at any meet time', making plain that the present was most inopportune. We are told that Gardiner hovered about the outer chamber at Whitehall, at the best hoping for a summons and, if not, making a point of leaving the palace with the councillors closest to the King, to give the outside world the impression that he was still powerful and favoured.

A lawyer by training and the author of the most substantial tract justifying the royal supremacy, Gardiner found himself caught in the snares of his own brilliance. The Conservative theological position he held was too much at variance with the views his legal mind had so forcibly expressed for him to compromise himself. As the reign drew to a close he was looked on as the architect of the Six Articles and the man who in the name of rigid orthodoxy had hounded Dr Barnes, silenced Latimer and Coverdale, sent Anne Askewe to the stake and aimed his deadliest arrows at Archbishop Cranmer and Queen Catherine. Allowing for the unremitting vituperation of the Reformers, there is more truth than malice in the sketch of Gardiner drawn by John Ponet, his successor as Bishop of Winchester. Stephen Gardiner, he wrote, was of a swart colour, with a hanging look, frowning brows, deep-set eyes, a nose hooked like a buzzard, great paws (like the devil), an outward monster with a 'vengeable' wit; yet so long as Henry lived he felt safe.

Hertford and his henchman Lisle had been careful to play down their Protestant sympathies so that observers could note that they leaned 'neither on the one side, nor on the other.' Even before the Howards had fallen and Henry had quarrelled with Gardiner about his lands, Hertford could reckon himself the principal councillor. When Henry had been leaving for France in July 1544 he had appointed him lieutenant of the kingdom, subject only to the Queen's powers as Regent. Now, with Catherine sent away to keep Christmas at Greenwich, and the court at Whitehall effectively closed, it was Hertford, the successful soldier and the Prince's uncle, who seemed the obvious choice as guardian of the realm during a minority. Henry did not see it quite in this way, for he found safety in numbers. When, thinking the end was near, he summoned to his room Hertford, Lisle, Paget and Denny on the night of 26 December, he asked for the will, drawn up thirty months before, to be read out to him and there and then revised the list of those named as councillors of Regency for his son. There was surprise when he left out Gardiner's name, but he said 'he was a wilful man and not meet to be about his son', nor was Thirlby, Bishop of Westminster, to be in the list as he had been schooled by Gardiner. Paget and, we are told, the others implored the King to reconsider this decision, but he was adamant. A few days later Sir Anthony Denny, kneeling by the King's bed, suggested the Bishop of Winchester's name had been left off by mistake and that Henry would want to reinstate him. From the great bed the matter was settled beyond doubt.

Hold your peace. I remembered him well enough and of good purpose have left him out; for surely, if he were in my testament, and one of you, he would cumber you all and you would never rule him, he is so troublesome a nature. Marry, I myself could use him and rule him to all manner of purposes as seemed good unto me; but so shall you never do.

In the interest of unity the Bishop, who stood for so much that the King himself professed, was cast aside. The revised will was ready for his signa-

The opening of Henry's will, signed at the head with his wooden stamp, since the King was too weak to make a holograph signature, 30 December 1546. This document provided for a council of Regency for Edward, and settled the succession to the Crown, after Edward and his heirs, in turn to Mary and Elizabeth.

Mercy

In the name of god and of the glorious and blessed
virgin our Lady Saint Mary and of all the holy
company of Heaven We Henry by the grace
of god king of England France and Ireland
defender of the faith and in erth ymmediatly
under god the Supreme hed of the churche of
England and Ireland of that name theight
callyng to our remembraunce the great gyftes and
benefites of Almighty god gyven unto us in this
transitory life gyven unto him our moost lowly
and humble thanke knowlegyng our sellf insufficient
in any part to deserve or recompence the same
But fere that we have not worthely received
the same And consydering further also to our sellf
that we be as all mankind is mortall and born
in synne beleving neverthelesse and hopyng that every
christen creature lyvyng here in this transitory and
wretched woorld under god dying in stedfast
and perfaict faith endevoring and exercising himsellf
to execute in his lief tyme if he have leasor suche
good dedes and charitable workes as scripture commaundeth
and as may be to the honour and pleasir of god

ture on 30 December and he handed it to Hertford, in whom he had complete trust. To her surprise Catherine was not appointed a councillor of Regency – perhaps Henry thought such an appointment an unfair imposition for a woman – yet his will paid tribute to her virtues: 'for the great love, obedience, chastity of life and wisdom being in our . . . wife and Queen', she was to receive £3000 in plate, jewels and household goods, £1000 in money and the sum for her dower already settled by statute.

As 1547 opened the court had become a whispering gallery of rumours that the King was already dead. In the middle of the month he made a tremendous effort to receive both the French and the Imperial ambassadors, juggling with international affairs as of old, but after they had taken their leave only a handful of councillors and personal servants were allowed to see him. The Queen, the Prince and his sisters were all deliberately kept from Whitehall, the musicians ceased to play, the busy routine was stilled and the world without waited. On 27 January Norfolk's attainder received the royal assent by commission in the House of Lords since, as Wriothesley unnecessarily explained, the King was too ill to come to the House in person. That evening Denny realised Henry was dying and summoned up the courage to tell him so. He would only see Cranmer, who was sent for from Croydon to be with his sovereign, now speechless, as he died in the early hours of 28 January. As a personal sign of mourning for his master, the Archbishop vowed never to shave again. Yet it was to be Gardiner, not Cranmer, who preached the funeral sermon and celebrated the chief requiem mass at St George's Chapel, Windsor, when Henry's great coffin was laid to rest next month in Jane Seymour's grave. The splendid tomb, taken over from Wolsey, had never been completed, but centuries afterwards a noble use was found for the empty sarcophagus, for it served as Nelson's tomb in the crypt of St Paul's Cathedral.

When the solemn dirges were sung, a new court with a different ethos was already in being, dominated by Hertford as Lord Protector, who was advanced to the dukedom of Somerset, and Henry VIII's reputation was already at the mercy of posterity. When the dust had settled Henry was seen securely in a central position in England's development, yet no character has aroused more controversy over the years. His qualities and achievements can be traced in various ways, but in this book he has been portrayed for the first time as the miracle-maker who turned the water of medieval kingship into the heady wine of a personal, national monarchy, with the court as its chosen vessel.

A candlestick cast for Henry's great tomb at Windsor, which was planned but never executed. The candlestick is now in the cathedral of St Bavon in Ghent.

Further reading

1 BIBLIOGRAPHIES

A great many books and articles in periodicals relating to Henry VIII and his reign are listed and appraised in M. Levine, *Bibliography of Tudor England, 1485–1603*, 1968, which replaces the 2nd edition of the *Bibliography of British History: Tudor Period* by Conyers Read, 1959. The fact that such a revision was produced within a decade indicates the considerable spate of publications. Most of the books listed in sections 4–14 below contain select bibliographies and, in some cases, notes about source material.

2 RECORD SOURCES

More abstracts of the official correspondence of the period have been published than for any other reign, beginning with the 11 vols of *State Papers of the Reign of Henry VIII* printed by the State Paper Commission (1830–52), which contain full transcripts of letters. *The Calendar of Letters & Papers, Foreign & Domestic, Henry VIII*, extending to 37 vols (1864–1932), was a grandiose scheme for placing abstracts of the State Papers alongside other select public records, materials in the British Museum and transcripts from foreign archives. This *Calendar* is a monument to the industrious scholarship of the Victorian age, and though the abstracts printed in it cannot serve as a substitute for the original documents (as the editors intended) they are a marvellous guide to them. Supplementing the *Letters & Papers* are the Calendars of despatches of the Spanish, Imperial and Venetian ambassadors, culled from Vienna, Brussels, Simancas and Venice. *The Calendar of State Papers, Spain* for Henry's reign comprises 14 vols (1866–1947), and *the Calendar of State Papers, Venice* 4 vols (1867–73). Many select historical documents with commentaries are printed in *English Historical Documents* vol. v, ed. C. H. Williams, 1967 and in G. R. Elton, *The Tudor Constitution*, 1964.

3 CONTEMPORARY CHRONICLES

Edward Hall, *The Union of the Two Noble and Illustre Famelies York and Lancaster* (ed H. Ellis, 1809; also ed C. Whibley, 1934); Charles Wriothesley, *A Chronicle of England, 1485–1559* (ed. W. D. Hamilton, Camden Society, new series vols 11 and 20, 1875–7); and Polydore Vergil. *Anglica Historia* (ed D. Hay, Camden Society 4th series vol. 74, 1950).

4 GENERAL ACCOUNTS OF THE REIGN

J. A. Froude, *History of England from the Fall of Wolsey to the defeat of the Spanish Armada* vols 1–4 (1856–8); also available in Everyman's Library; H. A. L. Fisher, *The Political History of England from the Accession of Henry VII to the Death of Henry VIII*, 1912; K. Pickthorn, *Early Tudor Government: Henry VIII*, 1934; S. T. Bindoff, *Tudor England*, 1950; J. D. Mackie, *The Early Tudors, 1485–1558*, 1952; and G. R. Elton, *England under the Tudors*, 1955. The introductions by J. S. Brewer and J. Gairdner in the *Letters and Papers* (2 above) are full of insight.

5 THE KING

Shakespeare's *Henry VIII*, though not one of his greatest plays, brings out facets of the Tudor court, of which half a century later he had first-hand knowledge. Lord Herbert of Cherbury's *The life and raigne of King Henry the Eighth*, 1672, has drawn on certain documents now lost, and is written in splendid prose. A. F. Pollard's magisterial life of the King, 1905, still holds the field, though J. J. Scarisbrick's biography, 1968, corrects and supplements it, notably in foreign affairs and the divorce. Muriel St Clare Byrne, *The Letters of Henry VIII*, 1936, skilfully translates letters not in English. Lady Mary Trefusis, *Ballads and Instrumental Pieces Composed by Henry VIII etc.*, 1912, is not readily accessible as it is a Roxburghe Club volume. Henry's health is fully discussed in F. Chamberlain, *The Private Character of Henry VIII*, 1932, and in A. S. McNalty, *Henry VIII; a difficult patient*, 1952.

6 THE QUEENS AND THE CHILDREN

G. Mattingly, *Catherine of Aragon*, 1950; P. Friedmann, *Anne Boleyn, a Chapter in English History, 1527–36*, 1884; and Lacy Baldwin Smith, *A Tudor Tragedy: the life & times of Catherine Howard*, 1961. There are lives of all six queens in Agnes Strickland, *Lives of the Queens of England* vol. 2, 1866. For the royal children see the earliest chapters of H. F. M. Prescott, *Spanish Tudor; the life of Bloody Mary*, 1940, N. Williams, *Elizabeth I, Queen of England*, 1967, and W. K. Jordan, *Edward VI: the Young King*, 1968.

7 THE ROYAL HOUSEHOLD

Much information about the household will be found in *Collections of Ordinances & Regulations for the Government of the Royal Household* (Society of Antiquaries, 1790); S. Giustinian, *Four Years at the Court of Henry VIII* (trans. Rawdon Brown, 1854); S. Anglo, *Spectacle, Pageantry & Early Tudor Policy*, 1969; C. G. Cruickshank, *Army Royal; An Account of Henry VIII's Invasion of France, 1513*, 1969; F. C. Dietz, *English Public Finance*, 1920; G. R. Elton, *The Tudor Revolution in Government*, 1953 and *Star Chamber Stories*, 1958; David Mathew, *The Courtiers of Henry VIII*, 1970; W. C. Richardson, *Tudor Chamber Administration, 1485–1547*, 1952; Joycelyne G. Russell, *The Field of Cloth of Gold*, 1969; and Lawrence Stone, *The Crisis of the Aristocracy*, 1965.

8 LIVES

There are two outstanding contemporary biographies, George Cavendish, *The Life & Death of Cardinal Wolsey* (ed Sylvester for the Early English Text Society, 1959) and William Roper, *The Lyfe of Sir Thomas Moore, Knight* (ed Hitchcock for the same Society, 1935). There are readable lives of *Thomas Cranmer* by Jasper Ridley, 1962; *Thomas Cromwell* by R. B. Merriman, 1902; *John Fisher* by E. E. Reynolds, 1955; *Stephen Gardiner* by J. A. Muller, 1926; *Thomas More* by R. W. Chambers, 1935; *Richard Pace* by Jervis Wegg, 1932; *Cuthbert Tunstall* by C. Sturge, 1938; and, the finest of all, A. F. Pollard's *Wolsey*, 1929.

9 THE REFORMATION

For the Breach with Rome and religion see A.G. Dickens, *The English Reformation*, 1964, the most outstanding work in this difficult field; Philip Hughes, *The Reformation in England; vol. 1 The King's Proceedings*, 1954, an account by a Roman Catholic; H. Maynard Smith, *Henry VIII & the Reformation*, 1948, and T.M. Parker, *The English Reformation to 1558*, 1950, both of them Anglicans; G. de C. Parmiter, *The King's Great Matter*, 1967; F.M. Powicke, *The Reformation in England*, 1941, an essay by a medievalist who was a Free churchman, and E.G. Rupp, *Studies in the Making of the English Protestant Tradition*, 1949, an historian who is also a Nonconformist minister.

For the Dissolution of the Monasteries see A. Savine, *English Monasteries on the Eve of the Dissolution*, 1909; M.D. Knowles, *The Religious Orders in England* vol. 3, 1959; G. Baskerville, *English Monks & the Suppression of the Monasteries*, 1937; and M.H. & R. Dodds, *The Pilgrimage of Grace and the Exeter Conspiracy*, 1915.

10 HUMANISM AND POLITICAL THOUGHT

J.W. Allen, *A History of Political Thought in the Sixteenth Century*, 1928; F. le van Baumer, *The Early Tudor Theory of Kingship*, 1940; W.E. Campbell, *Erasmus, Tyndale & More*, 1949; F. Caspari, *Humanism & the Social Order in Tudor England*, 1954; Whitney R.D. Jones, *The Tudor Commonwealth, 1529–59*, 1920; J.K. McConica, *English Humanists & Reformation Politics under Henry VIII & Edward VI*, 1965; Thomas More, *English Works* (ed W.E. Campbell & A.W. Reed, 1931) and *Utopia* (trans. P. Turner, 1965), for which J.H. Hexter, *More's Utopia: the Biography of an Idea*, 1952, is a valuable guide; C. Morris, *Political Thought in England, from Tyndale to Hooker*, 1953; J.E. Paul, *Catherine of Aragon & her Friends*, 1966; L.V. Ryan, *Roger Ascham*, 1964; and W.G. Zeeveld, *Foundations of Tudor Policy*, 1948.

11 LITERATURE

E. Casady, *Henry Howard, Earl of Surrey*, 1938; J.V. Cunningham, *The Renaissance in England*, 1946; C.S. Lewis, *English Literature in the Sixteenth Century, Excluding Drama*, 1954; G.F. Nott, *Works of Henry Howard & Sir Thomas Wyatt*, 1815; E.M. Nugent, *The Thought & Culture of the English Renaissance: an Anthology of Tudor Prose, 1481–1555*, 1956; P. Thomson, *Sir Thomas Wyatt & his Background*, 1964.

12 ARCHITECTURE

The opening chapters of John Summerson, *Architecture in Britain, 1530–1830*; J. Dent, *The Quest for Nonsuch*, 1962; T. Garner & A. Stratton, *The Domestic Architecture of England during the Tudor Period*, 1929.

13 ART, SCULPTURE AND THE FINE ARTS

Erna Auerbach, *Tudor Artists*, 1956; J. Lees-Milne, *Tudor Renaissance*, 1951; Roy Strong, *Holbein & Henry VIII*, 1967; and the earliest chapters of E. Waterhouse, *Painting in Britain, 1530–1830* (revised edn, 1963); and of Margaret D. Whinney, *Sculpture in Britain, 1530–1830*, 1964.

14 MUSIC

A. Hughes & F. Abraham, *Ars Nova & the Renaissance*, 1960; J. Stevens, *Music & Poetry in the Early Tudor Court*, 1941; W.L. Woodfill, *Musicians in English Society*, 1953; Ernest Walker, *A History of Music in England* (3rd edn, revised by J.A. Westrup, 1952); and the opening chapters of John S. Bumpus, *A History of English Cathedral Music* vol. 1, 1906, and of Edmund H. Fellowes, *English Cathedral Music*, 1941.

Genealogical Tables

RED ROSE DYNASTY

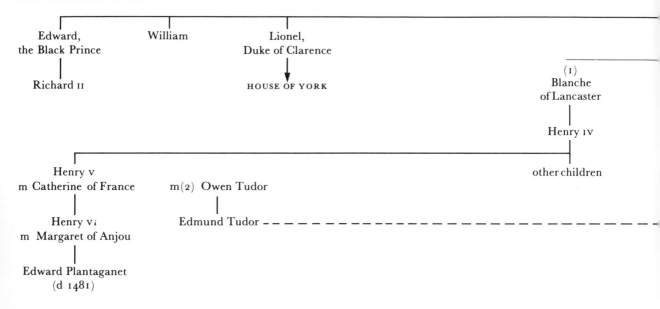

Edward,
the Black Prince — William — Lionel,
Duke of Clarence

Richard II

HOUSE OF YORK

(1)
Blanche
of Lancaster

Henry IV

Henry V
m Catherine of France   m(2) Owen Tudor

other children

Henry VI
m Margaret of Anjou   Edmund Tudor -----

Edward Plantaganet
(d 1481)

WHITE ROSE DYNASTY

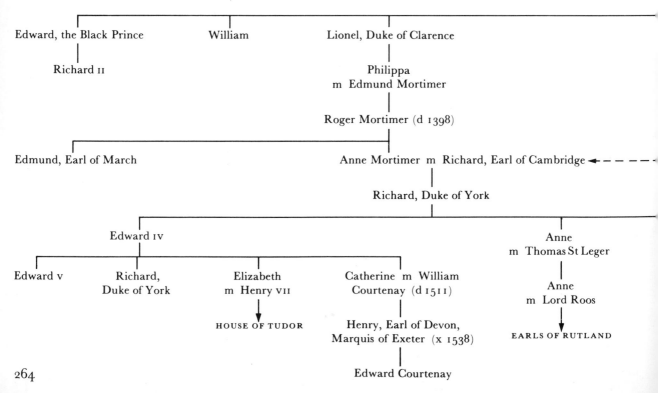

Edward, the Black Prince   William   Lionel, Duke of Clarence

Richard II

Philippa
m Edmund Mortimer

Roger Mortimer (d 1398)

Edmund, Earl of March   Anne Mortimer m Richard, Earl of Cambridge ◄-----

Richard, Duke of York

Edward IV

Anne
m Thomas St Leger

Edward V   Richard,
Duke of York   Elizabeth
m Henry VII   Catherine m William
Courtenay (d 1511)   Anne
m Lord Roos

HOUSE OF TUDOR

Henry, Earl of Devon,
Marquis of Exeter (x 1538)   EARLS OF RUTLAND

Edward Courtenay

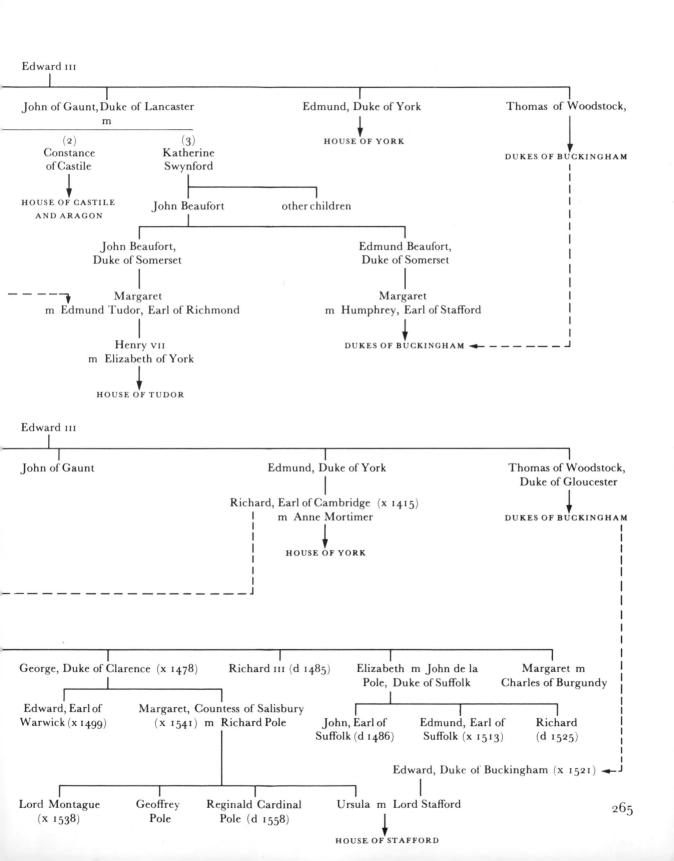

Edward III

John of Gaunt, Duke of Lancaster
m

Edmund, Duke of York

→ HOUSE OF YORK

Thomas of Woodstock,

↓ DUKES OF BUCKINGHAM

(2)
Constance
of Castile

(3)
Katherine
Swynford

↓ HOUSE OF CASTILE
AND ARAGON

John Beaufort   other children

John Beaufort,
Duke of Somerset

Edmund Beaufort,
Duke of Somerset

Margaret
m Edmund Tudor, Earl of Richmond

Margaret
m Humphrey, Earl of Stafford

DUKES OF BUCKINGHAM ← – – –

Henry VII
m Elizabeth of York

↓ HOUSE OF TUDOR

Edward III

John of Gaunt

Edmund, Duke of York

Richard, Earl of Cambridge (x 1415)
m Anne Mortimer

↓ HOUSE OF YORK

Thomas of Woodstock,
Duke of Gloucester

↓ DUKES OF BUCKINGHAM

George, Duke of Clarence (x 1478)   Richard III (d 1485)   Elizabeth m John de la
Pole, Duke of Suffolk

Margaret m
Charles of Burgundy

Edward, Earl of
Warwick (x 1499)

Margaret, Countess of Salisbury
(x 1541) m Richard Pole

John, Earl of
Suffolk (d 1486)

Edmund, Earl of
Suffolk (x 1513)

Richard
(d 1525)

Edward, Duke of Buckingham (x 1521) ←

Lord Montague
(x 1538)

Geoffrey
Pole

Reginald Cardinal
Pole (d 1558)

Ursula m Lord Stafford

↓ HOUSE OF STAFFORD

265

HOUSE OF TUDOR

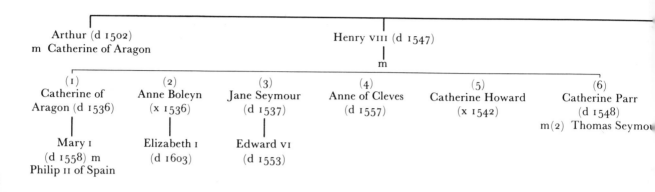

Arthur (d 1502)
m Catherine of Aragon

Henry VIII (d 1547)
m

(1)	(2)	(3)	(4)	(5)	(6)
Catherine of Aragon (d 1536)	Anne Boleyn (x 1536)	Jane Seymour (d 1537)	Anne of Cleves (d 1557)	Catherine Howard (x 1542)	Catherine Parr (d 1548) m(2) Thomas Seymou
Mary I (d 1558) m Philip II of Spain	Elizabeth I (d 1603)	Edward VI (d 1553)			

HOUSE OF HOWARD

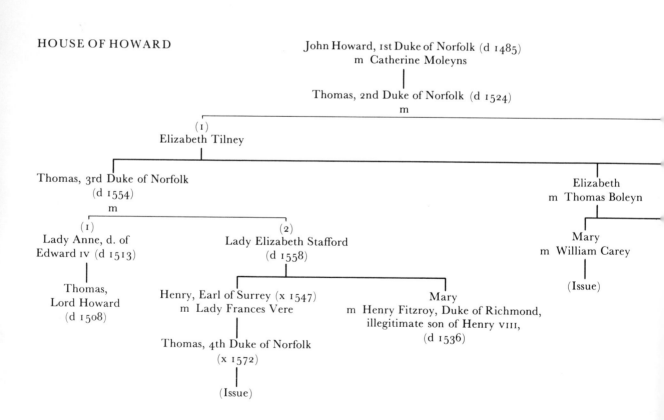

John Howard, 1st Duke of Norfolk (d 1485)
m Catherine Moleyns

Thomas, 2nd Duke of Norfolk (d 1524)
m

(1)
Elizabeth Tilney

Thomas, 3rd Duke of Norfolk
(d 1554)
m

Elizabeth
m Thomas Boleyn

Mary
m William Carey

(Issue)

(1)
Lady Anne, d. of
Edward IV (d 1513)

(2)
Lady Elizabeth Stafford
(d 1558)

Thomas,
Lord Howard
(d 1508)

Henry, Earl of Surrey (x 1547)
m Lady Frances Vere

Mary
m Henry Fitzroy, Duke of Richmond,
illegitimate son of Henry VIII,
(d 1536)

Thomas, 4th Duke of Norfolk
(x 1572)

(Issue)

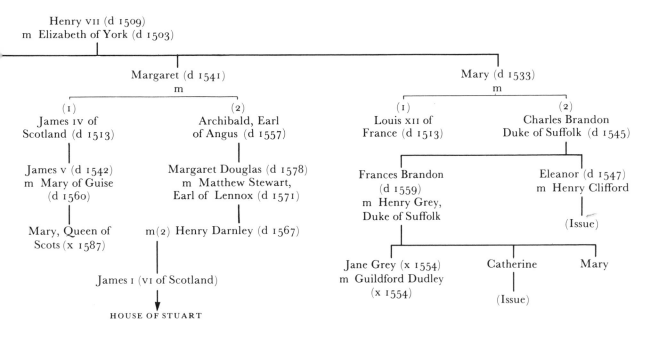

Henry VII (d 1509)
m Elizabeth of York (d 1503)

Margaret (d 1541)
m

(1)
James IV of
Scotland (d 1513)

James V (d 1542)
m Mary of Guise
(d 1560)

Mary, Queen of
Scots (x 1587)

(2)
Archibald, Earl
of Angus (d 1557)

Margaret Douglas (d 1578)
m Matthew Stewart,
Earl of Lennox (d 1571)

m(2) Henry Darnley (d 1567)

James I (VI of Scotland)

HOUSE OF STUART

Mary (d 1533)
m

(1)
Louis XII of
France (d 1513)

(2)
Charles Brandon
Duke of Suffolk (d 1545)

Frances Brandon
(d 1559)
m Henry Grey,
Duke of Suffolk

Eleanor (d 1547)
m Henry Clifford

(Issue)

Jane Grey (x 1554)
m Guildford Dudley
(x 1554)

Catherine

(Issue)

Mary

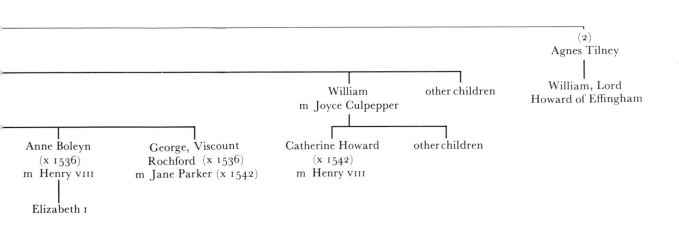

(2)
Agnes Tilney

William
m Joyce Culpepper

other children

William, Lord
Howard of Effingham

Anne Boleyn
(x 1536)
m Henry VIII

Elizabeth I

George, Viscount
Rochford (x 1536)
m Jane Parker (x 1542)

Catherine Howard
(x 1542)
m Henry VIII

other children

Index

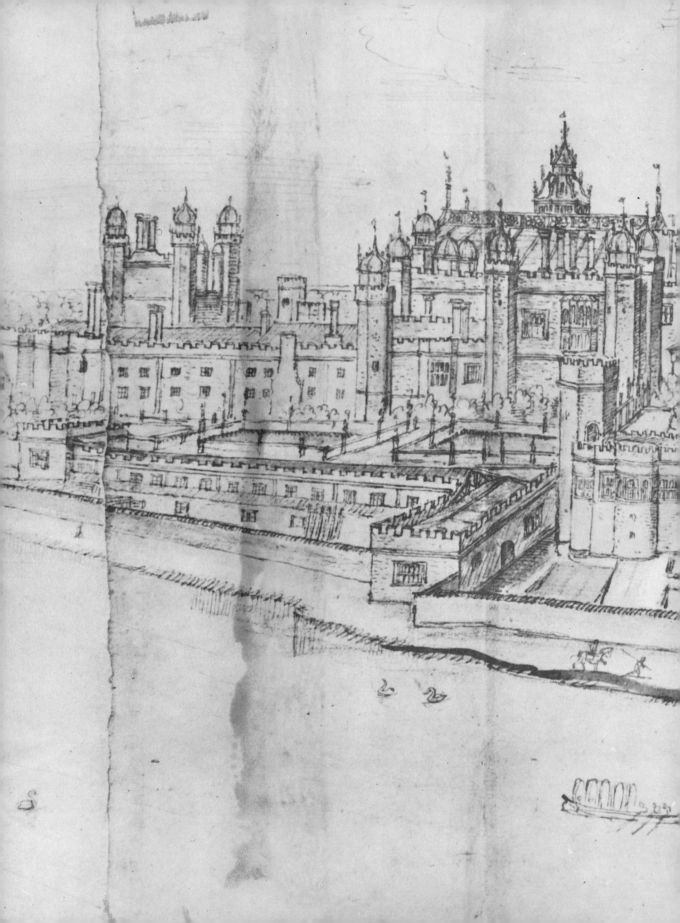